How I Lost 10 Pounds in 53 Years

....

A Memoir

KAYE BALLARD

WITH JIM HESSELMAN

BACK STAGE BOOKS

Senior Editor: Mark Glubke
Project Editor: Stephen Brewer
Interior Design: Barbara Balch
Production Manager: Katherine Happ

First published in 2006 by Back Stage Books,
an imprint of Watson-Guptill Publications,
a division of VNU Business Media, Inc.
770 Broadway, New York, NY 10003
www.watsonguptill.com

Library of Congress Control Number: 2006929111
ISBN-13: 978-0-8230-8478-4
ISBN-10: 0-8230-8478-7

Manufactured in the United States of America

First printing 2006

1 2 3 4 5 6 7 8 9 / 11 10 09 08 07 06

THIS BOOK IS DEDICATED with great love and appreciation to Mr. Beau James, Myvanwy Jenn, my sister Jean, and my beloved Nana. . . they've always been there for me . . . no matter what. And in celebration of my naïveté over the years . . .

Lucky's back In town!

Contents

Foreword
by Jerry Stiller

T hink of Kaye's memoir as a ship's voyage. Kaye is the captain, and I happen to be a cabin boy on board for one of many trips.

The time was 1954, and the show was *The Golden Apple*, which opened at the Phoenix Theatre on Second Avenue, won the New York Drama Critics Circle Award, and moved to the Alvin Theatre on Broadway, then to the Carter Barron Amphitheatre in Washington, D.C., playing to 8,000 people a night. Kaye Ballard was one of the stars. The musical was based on the *Iliad* and the *Odyssey*, the story of Ulysses, and Kaye played Helen of Troy.

I was Mayor Juniper. No lines. My big moment was roller-skating across the stage on one skate, which paid me the munificent sum of fifty-five bucks a week, the same money Kaye and everyone else in the cast received.

Here's what might be called a "you had to be there" moment and why I'll never forget Kaye Ballard's artistry. On opening night something went wrong as the curtain went up. Kaye was onstage, sitting in a rocker fanning herself, as the grips scurried madly, the orchestra vamped, and the screw-ups continued. Kaye, very much in character, turned and watched this unscheduled mayhem, and kept rocking and fanning herself and smiling at the audience. She then started swatting imaginary flies with her fan. The audience, by now sensing this was not part of the show, was totally engrossed by her comic antics and began applauding. The chaos ended, and the orchestra, under the direction of Hugh Ross, finally started "Lazy Afternoon," the John LaTouche and Jerome Moross ballad that Kaye Ballard sang and turned into a mega-hit (and that got her on the cover of *Life* magazine).

During the play's run Kaye always took time to encourage me in my comic pursuits and suggested I do an act with my wife, Anne Meara. When Anne and I did start performing together Kaye was often in the audience, rooting us on. She pushed buttons with nightclub owners who booked a husband and wife comedy team whose name no one could pronounce.

Later Kaye and I worked together in England, when she played my sister in Terrence McNally's screen version of *The Ritz*. On off days we visited Windsor Castle, had lunch with Tommy Steele, met Albert Finney after seeing him in *Hamlet*, and visited flea markets, where she bought me a grandfather clock and a scarf that I still hold dear. She treated me like her brother.

In her memoir Kaye recounts the wonderful journey of a gifted actress, comedienne, and musician, and she shares her stories of all the stars who've touched on her life. Some wag once put it this way: No memoir is worth reading unless the author is willing to reveal mistakes, screw-ups, and missed opportunities. This, then, is a book you won't want to put down. I'm sure Jane Fonda will love this book, because Kaye Ballard has a big mouth. Kaye admits her mouth has gotten her into trouble, so we're stuck with these wonderfully written and honestly spoken memories about a period when nightclubs, television, and theater were creating the legacy of what we now consider to be the golden years of entertainment.

It's the story of a time when women were not supposed to be funny. It was okay to be a star like Doris Day or Peggy Lee, because they sang and were also gorgeous. Kaye could sing, and she was beautiful, funny, and foxy. She could also play the flute. (Where did that come from?) When you played the Strand Theatre, six shows a day with Spike Jones, and you were a kid just out of high school and were from Cleveland, where did you go with your gift of making people laugh? Well, that's the story of Kaye Ballard.

Don't let the title fool you. This book is not about weight. It's about Kaye's willingness to let her life explode on the printed page. Wow, did I wanna hear all of what I read? Yes, because the truth is what rings the bell with an audience, and Kaye is a truth monger. What she's written comes from the soul of one of the country's great comediennes in the tradition of Fanny Brice, Martha Raye, Beatrice Lillie, and Lucille Ball. Add Kaye Ballard to this illustrious list.

Kaye tells of memorable moments that include Marlon Brando,

Doris Day, Lenny Bruce, Phil Silvers, Carol Burnett, Liz Smith, Mabel Mercer, and Dorothy Parker, to name a few. She played Mr. Kelly's, the Bon Soir, and the Hungry i. What stories. The whole megillah. Imagine you, the reader, sitting in the audience and listening to Kaye on stage doing a one-woman show just for you.

So, if you want yesterday to feel like it's happening now, read on.

How I Lost 10 Pounds in 53 Years

....

A Memoir

Introduction

You may wonder what finally gave me the nerve to write a book about my life. I mean, let's face it, there are a lot of actresses more famous, much richer, and a hell of a lot *thinner* than I am!

But how many of them can say they played the tuba in The Spike Jones Orchestra, sipped Sanka with Mother Teresa at six a.m. in the Bronx, did a New Year's Eve show at San Quentin, played the Tooth Fairy on *Captain Kangaroo*, and had knives thrown at her and been stabbed with an ice pick on *The Mike Douglas Show*! (To think, I might have *died* for *scale*!)

Joyce Geritay, a friend of my sister Jean, was the first to mention that I should write this book. I thought, "Yes, well, maybe some day," but never did anything about it. I began this journey at the urging of an Episcopal minister, Eric Law. He convinced me that my stories might actually be of interest to more than just my closest friends.

Then I met a soul mate. In the fall of 2003 I was offered the chance to reprise my role as Reverend Mother in the twentieth-anniversary all-star tour of Dan Goggin's musical comedy phenomenon *Nunsense*. Jim Hesselman, the assistant stage manager on our tour, quickly became a good friend. I knew he was a winner from our first day of rehearsal. What I didn't know was that he was also an actor, director, and play-wright who took the job in order to further his dream of having his own theater some day.

Jim and I began talking about what I had written. We taped what became dialogue sessions that started to bring the events of my life into focus. It's strange how people sometimes seem to fall into your path at just the right moment.

It's difficult for me to remember each event in my life in the precise chronological order in which it occurred. I have tried to record the facts and circumstances correctly, but sometimes memories get taken out of order. One event relates to another that happened years before or years after. People have come in and out of my life in ways that sometimes seem to have no connection to what I was doing at the time. Then again, I have met so many remarkable people throughout my lifetime that it seems almost impossible to relate some of them to a specific date or event. In order to compensate for this fault and still do justice to the individuals concerned, I have sandwiched in short passages that I call Interludes, about people whom I might mention at other times in the book but to whom I want to give a little extra time. Please forgive any confusion this incongruity may cause and think of these pages as little "palate cleansers" between chapters.

As I look back I can't believe that I have been in show business for almost sixty-five years. I've learned two things doing comedy: Always tell 'em the truth, and the joke's not funny if the audience doesn't identify with it. So I promise you the truth, and hope like hell that you'll identify with it. Who knows, maybe those of you not old enough to remember me may even learn a few things that will make your journey through life a little easier.

This memoir is really two different books. On one hand, it is a sort of history of twentieth-century show business, before the make-'em-a-star-overnight mentality of *Star Search* and *American Idol* took over. Don't get me wrong. Many marvelous singers, dancers, and actors out there today work very hard at what they do. But just as handcrafted furniture has been replaced by stamped-out, plastic, veneer-coated junk, performers who have worked their whole lives in this business seem to have been shoved aside and forgotten. Who could ever have imagined that a mere generation after people like Jimmy Durante, Jack Benny, Martha Raye, and Maurice Chevalier died, a lot of people wouldn't know, or care, that they had ever lived. Even worse, a lot of people wouldn't know why they were important! Well, I'll remind you why they were important because I knew them, worked with them, and loved them.

At the same time, this book is about my struggle through life as an Italian Catholic woman born into a world where she never seemed to fit. I would hazard to guess that everyday life changed more, and faster, in the eighty years I have been around than at any other point in history.

They throw the term "survivor" around a lot these days. Like the word "star," the meaning of survival has been reduced to thirteen weeks on a TV show. But I've got news for you. The secret is in the long haul. Surviving is the day-to-day, week-by-week task of working at life with as much honesty, integrity, and love as you can manage. It's damn difficult. And, as some of you who are included in the following pages might agree, I certainly haven't always been as successful at that task as I'd have liked to be. But, I'm eighty years old, and I'm proud to say that not only have I survived, I'm still working at it!

WHERE TO BEGIN . . .

I dealt with two dilemmas as I got into this book. The first concerned the subject matter. After talking to various publishers, I found that they believe the general public would not be interested in the story of my life unless I include a lot of sordid, X-rated type material having to do with things like how I lost my virginity. Okay then, here it is: I lost my virginity riding my brother's bicycle. The whole experience was quick and painful. (And that's about all the juicy sex stuff about me you're going to get.)

The other dilemma was the title. How do you capture eighty years in a few words? Since you have made it to this page, you already know which title I eventually chose, but here are some of the others I considered:

> I Just Happened to Be There
> The Truth Hurts
> Buy This Book or I'll Kill You
> Is the World Trying to Drive Me Crazy?
> I'll Never Do *That* Again
> Surviving Success
> Over the Rainbow, Not Over the Hill
> That's Interesting, Isn't It?
> As I Was Saying . . .
> Kaye Ballard: An Open Book
> Let's Do It All Again
> Red Carpet My Ass (borrowed from Alice Faye)
> The Show Goes On
> Just One More Cannoli

Chapter One

Mia Familia

Sitting in the third row at the RKO back in Cleveland
Sitting there in wonder gazing at the screen
I remember thinking at the RKO back in Cleveland
I've so far to go, I've so far to go . . . but one thing I know . . .
Up there, that's where I want to be
Up there, for all the world to see
Let that MGM lion lovingly roar in my ear
I wanna be up there . . . not here!

From my one woman show, *"Hey, Ma!"*
by Jerry Goldberg, Leslie Eberhard, and David Levy

On January 2004, Larry King devoted an entire show to remembering Jack Paar. That evening Phyllis Diller included me in a rather prestigious list of funny people—Jack Paar, herself, Bob Hope, Drew Carey, Teri Garr, Tim Conway, Tom Poston, Richard Lewis, Arsenio Hall, Jack Weston, Jamie Farr, Jonathan Winters, and several others. It turns out that we were all comedians who had grown up in Ohio. I always thought it was just Cleveland I wanted to get away from, but perhaps there's something about the Midwest in general that inspires certain personalities to develop their humor in order to make a break for it. Don't get me wrong. I'm very grateful to have been brought up in Ohio (even with the cold weather). I would not trade my midwestern values for anything.

I was born Catherine Gloria Balotta on November 20, 1926. . . . Okay, hold it right here for a second. That's my birth date according to all the official biographies. Why? Because that is the date I began to use all those years ago. Here is the first big revelation of this book: I am really a year older than I've always said I am. I feel that until a woman reaches seventy, taking a year off is the equivalent of adding an extra little touch of makeup and is certainly her right. But now, off comes the rouge! I'm taking that year back because I've *earned* it! All right, you may continue. . . .

I was born Catherine Gloria Balotta on November 20, 1925, to a first-generation Italian-American family in Cleveland, Ohio. As in so many immigrant families in the early 1900s, the children were taught to work hard and start families. Formal education beyond what was necessary to get along in this new country was not a priority. My mother, Lena (maiden name Nacarato), left school after the fourth grade, and my father, Vincenzo, never went at all. My parents were extremely traditional Italians whose marriage had been arranged. Even so, the union lasted nearly six decades, until my mother and father passed away just a couple of years apart in the early 1980s.

My father was an incredibly kind man. I never knew him to do anything but work, come home, have dinner, sleep, and get up early the next morning for work again. He was a cement finisher who put down sidewalks. He used to take me all over Cleveland showing me his work. He'd say, "I put dis sidewalk-a-here in-a nineteen tirty-tree" or "Nineteen-a-forty-six we didn't have much cement but we put dis down over here." He was so proud. Especially of having fought in World War I, when he lost an eye for his new country. (My father had a glass eye that he would take out and leave in a cup overnight. Believe me, I let out a shriek more than one morning while looking for a drinking cup!)

During the hard years of the Depression, Papa made sure there was meat on the table at least twice a week. We lost our house during this time because he refused to borrow the $175 due on the mortgage. Papa taught me how to box, and he used to say to me, "Catherina, you don't have to get-a-married. You can support yourself." Looking back now, I see what a radical concept that was for an Italian Catholic father. His words gave me the courage to follow my dreams.

I never knew my father's parents, but my mother's father, Dominick, was the first in his family to come to the United States. Once he established himself, he sent for his wife, Gabriella (my Nana), who booked passage for herself and four children on a cattle boat. They had three girls and one boy, just like my parents did. It was not an easy way to cross the ocean, and Nana lost one of her daughters to diphtheria on the twenty-eight-day trip. That child was never discussed.

My brother, Orlando, was two years old when I was born, and my sisters, Jean and Rosalie, followed soon after me. We were brought up in an upper-lower-middle-class Italian neighborhood until I was in high school. Then we moved up to the middle-middle class. A nice, clean, comfortable house in a nice, clean, comfortable neighborhood.

It was difficult being a girl in such an Old World Italian family. One of the traditional concepts my grandparents imported to America was that daughters were somewhat less important than sons. Men were the wage earners, and women were expected to stay home and care for the house and their families. My mother catered to my brother far more than she did to my sisters and me.

On the weekends, Mama would cook breakfast and we girls would have to wait to be served until after the men of the family got their food. During the week, she slept late and we were left to fend for ourselves. (To this day, I am very impatient when it comes to ordering in a restaurant. If you're going to eat with me, you'd better know what you want even before you sit down.)

My mother's view of women carried over into everything. I wanted to swim and ride a bike like my brother, Orlando, did, but according to Mama, girls did not participate in those kinds of activities. It simply was not done. Instead, we girls were told, "Learn how to do the dishes. Learn how to cook." The Balotta household was like *Fiddler on the Roof* Italiano style. From food to guilt and back to food again, the cultural similarities between Jewish and Italian families have always amazed me. Maybe that's why I've always been so comfortable playing Jewish mothers!

Mama must have known I was not going to be an easy daughter to raise when, at the age of about seven, I took my Papa's straw hat and hammed it up doing imitations of Maurice Chevalier for family, neighbors, and anyone who would listen. I would dance across the kitchen floor, and with my best version of a French accent, I'd sing "Mimi, you funny little good for nothing, Mimi!" at the top of my lungs. Years later, Monsieur Chevalier himself paid me the greatest compliment when he told me I was the American Beatrice Lillie. Bea was one of my idols. Little did I know that like so many other people I grew up admiring, I'd actually meet and get to know her!

Well, to my mother's horror, I wanted to be in show business. This notion was contrary to every conventional belief she possessed. Mama did her best to dislodge this foreign idea from my head. "You're too ugly, you can't be in show business the way you look!" she'd say. "Have a cannoli."

Mama told me this so often that I guess part of it stuck. I have never considered myself to be pretty, and I still don't quite know what to say when I am paid a compliment. Inside me there is still a little girl with embarrassing dark circles under her eyes (just something I was born with) who thinks that when people praise her they are only being nice.

I've also had a lifelong battle with my weight.

My Nana didn't help things in that department. She fed me spaghetti sandwiches for lunch. At the time, tuberculosis was rampant. Nana was scared to death that I'd catch it and believed that as long as I was a little chubbette I was healthy. She would tell me, "If you no eat, you gonna get the TB. Honest, it look to me like you gotta the TB!" By the time I was nine years old I weighed a hundred and forty pounds! To this day I could live on bread and pasta for three meals a day and be happy. (A little red sauce on the side.)

No matter how hard Mama tried, the one thing that she couldn't drive out of me was my determination to become an entertainer. The elementary school I attended would take a group of us children to concerts at Cleveland's Severance Hall on Saturday mornings. Those symphonies always made me cry. The beauty of the music (especially the violins) was overwhelming. I was too young to know why the music had such a profound effect on me, but I was just so excited being there. I suddenly knew I wanted to be able to make people feel the way those musicians made me feel. For the first time in my life I was in awe—star-struck.

I have always been very independent. When I was ten years old I decided that the city bus was not for me. I skipped lunches so I could use the money for cab rides. Boy, I must have been a sight, standing out there in front of the school yard in my short skirt with knee-high stockings, waving frantically (and I'm sure dramatically) for a cab. I had delusions of grandeur, even as a child. It was also at about this age that I lost the hearing in my right ear. My family had gone to visit relatives who lived on a farm. Being a city kid, I knew nothing about cows and chickens and pigs. A rooster began to chase me, so I climbed a tree to get away. As I reached for one of the higher branches, I fell and landed hard on the ground. I was taken to a small-town doctor, but he failed to drain the damaged ear and the fluid built up inside, damaging the nerves. This condition has always affected my balance a bit, but I have been extremely fortunate to be able to perform for all these years in spite of near total deafness in my right ear.

I may have set my sights on show business, but I did not neglect my education. I remember being afraid that I would not be able to read, probably because my parents couldn't. I enjoyed learning and was a fairly good student, especially when it came to history and art. Except for the time when I was fourteen and snuck out after second period to see *The Wizard of Oz*, I had a perfect attendance record.

You know, good teachers can make such a difference in a child's life. Quality educators with a real passion for teaching have never been appreciated enough in this country, and they certainly have never earned the kind of wages they deserve. Some classes in school came very easily to me, and I found that I had a natural aptitude for visual arts. I had a wonderful art teacher in high school named Paul Vincent Ulen. I would always do imitations of people during class and vow that someday I'd be on Broadway! Well, Mr. Ulen didn't approve of my comedy. He said my imitations were corny and horrible and that I should stick with my proven artistic talent. As a punishment he'd send me to the greenhouse to draw a cactus. In fact, this became such a regular occurrence that I acquired the nickname "Cactus Kate."

I must have been born with the ability to draw, and as a consequence I really didn't have to put forth too much effort. But Mr. Ulen would not let me slide. He taught me that I could go after anything I wanted as long as I wanted it badly enough to finish what I started. He'd say, "Quit daydreaming, Balotta, quit daydreaming! You're a fake! Now go out there and *do* it." How right he was. Nothing worthwhile in life is ever just handed to you. I'll always be grateful to him for never letting me do things halfway.

In high school I learned another skill that would facilitate my entrance into show business a few years later. I just had to be in the band, and I wanted to play the clarinet. For some reason they gave me a flute instead, and a flute has been part of my act my entire career. We hated our band uniforms, because they were dark blue with red piping on the sides. Every time we wore them home people thought we were with the Salvation Army! We held fundraiser after fundraiser, and the year after I graduated, the band finally got new uniforms—my timing has always been just a smidgeon off!

Day-to-day life in the Balotta household was not very different from life at the Vanuccis' next door, or the Lancalottas' down the street. And though the performer inside of me was bursting to break out, I conformed to normality as best I could. In some ways I think I actually frightened my parents as I grew older because they couldn't understand me. My siblings were constantly being supervised or disciplined, but not me. I don't know if this was because my mother and father trusted me or because they had no idea what to do with me. At some point they must have accepted the fact that little Catherine was marching to the beat of a different drummer and decided to give up any attempt at parental control.

My first job was working at Bert's, a record store. I was only twelve years old. They believed me when I lied about my age because of the huge dark circles under my eyes. (I had found at least one advantage to my appearance.) The owner must have thought I was either forty years old or that I suffered from an acute kidney condition. Every week, I gave my mother five dollars from the money I earned. In my mind this bought my independence. I'd come home from work and announce that I was going out for a while and that I'd be back about nine o'clock. I didn't ask my parents, I *told* them. I'm sure once the door slammed behind me, Mama and Papa looked at each other wondering where this little freak of a daughter had come from.

I've always loved giving gifts, and one Christmas I gave all my friends records. I don't know whether I thought I was buying friendship or whether I just liked the feeling I got from giving them. Whatever the reason, and I hate to admit this, I had stolen them from Bert's. I thought I was pretty clever until Christmas Eve, when everyone else at the store got a blue check and I got a pink slip. Being fired from my first job served to straighten me out but good!

Saturday mornings I would go to the RKO Palace Theatre with my best friend, Carolyn Vanucci. We'd sit in the dark theater for hours completely mesmerized by the people up on the screen. Even today my favorite activity in the world (aside from the occasional spin at a slot machine) is to sit in a dark theater and watch a movie. I would imagine what it must be like to be Irene Dunne or Gene Tierney. My entire life was built around those magical afternoons at the movies. If I saw a Lionel Barrymore picture, I would become his granddaughter when I left the theater. I loved the musicals, especially the ones in which Eleanor Powell danced—she was so classy. Once I saw *The Wizard of Oz* I knew I wanted to be Judy Garland. But then I looked in the mirror and thought, "Well, okay, let's set our sights a little lower. I could maybe be a clown like Bert Lahr." I lived whatever parts happened to be playing that week. At fourteen I got a job ushering, and I was in heaven. I wasn't very good at the actual ushering part (I kept singing and dancing in the aisles), but I could see movies seven days a week!

I became the number one fan of everyone in show business. I learned to do impressions by watching vaudeville performers like Arthur Blake and Lena Romi impersonate the top stars of the day. Whenever stars came to town, I would wait outside the theater door in the pouring rain for autographs. I met Bobby Jordan and Huntz Hall, both of whom were Dead End Kids, the singer Kenny Baker, and the great comedian Willie

Howard. Through my persistence (or obnoxiousness), these performers got to know me and my aspirations. They were actually very protective of the young girl with the blue knees and the dark eyes. I remember how they would lecture me, telling me that if I wanted to get into show business I had to finish high school first. Looking back all these years later, I realize that those people certainly didn't have to put up with an obnoxious teenager with stars in her eyes, and I am so grateful for their kindness and encouragement.

When I was fifteen, I met Martha Raye through a friend of mine, Betty Hope. Betty's family was from Chicago and quite wealthy. She took me to Chez Paris, where Martha's husband, Nick Condos, was performing. I got to sit next to Martha, who was eight months pregnant with her daughter Melodye. Through the entire show I kept thinking, "Oh, my God, I am sitting here next to one of my idols!" I was beside myself with joy. By the way, years later Martha would tell people that we were the same age. Amazing how other people in show business manage to get younger while I keep getting older!

When I graduated from Cleveland's West Tech High School I was offered a scholarship to Cleveland Art College. I decided not to take it because a little voice inside me told me that even though I had a little artistic talent, I would never be the best. But the same voice whispered quietly that I might, just might, be able to be the best (well, one of the best) in show business. Obviously nothing had changed since the days of my Maurice Chevalier impersonations. The day I finally got up the nerve to tell my parents of my decision not to take the scholarship and to try my hand at show business instead, my father gave me a silver dollar and said, "Keep this with you, Catherina, and you'll never be broke." All my sweet, darling Papa wanted was for me to be happy. From him, "I wish you luck" always meant "I love you." It was just his way of saying it.

My mother was a different story. Upon hearing the news she looked at me calmly and said, "Are you crazy? The way you look?"

"But, Ma," I complained.

"You're not too old to hit, you know," she interrupted.

"But, Ma, I want to take singing lessons." She slapped me.

"I want to take dancing lessons." She slapped me again and said, "Learn to do the dishes. I'll give you show business!"

"But, Ma," I pleaded, "I want to make people laugh!"

"Cook dinner tonight, they'll laugh. Movie stars are pretty. They're tramps, but they're pretty. Go and look in the mirror!"

It's funny, my mother never said "hello" to me. She'd shout, "Hello!" as if warding off the devil. She was extremely emotional and could be quite dramatic. If Mama ever found herself on the losing side of an argument she would start to yell very loudly. If that didn't work, she would end the debate by passing out. What's ironic is that I think my mother would have enjoyed being a performer. Yes, I think I must have gotten it from her. We were always somewhat combative with each other. When I was a teenager and invited a boyfriend home, my mother would compete with me for his attention. She'd bring him food and listen to his every word. She would even tell jokes. What really made me angry was the fact that Mama told them better than I did.

If my mother ever felt maternal pride in any of my achievements, she never shared those feelings with me. In fact, in the early years of my career, no member of my family ever came to one of my performances. My mother always gave the tickets I'd given her to the butcher or a neighbor. I don't think she wasn't proud of me. In her own strange way, giving those tickets away was probably her way of showing her pride. Crazy, huh? Years later, after all the competition was over, I grew to feel sorry for Mama. She never had the life she'd wanted. She simply did the best she knew how to do, with what was given to her.

My biggest support at home came from my grandmother. When I was young and did something wrong, my parents went straight for my neck. I used to go hide behind Nana and she'd say, "Non u toucha this kid. That's-a good-a kid!" I always had Nana to turn to. If I ever gave Nana a dirty look she'd say, "Don-a you look on me cockeye. I no like." She was the most important person in my life. When I told Nana that I wanted to be in show business, she said, "Go on, go. But, I no wan-a you to smoke and you no show your legs." I kept my word, and to this day, no audience has ever seen my legs. (By the way, I made my little sister Jean take dance lessons, and that's why she has such nice legs today!)

My grandmother never adjusted to the elevator, the escalator, or the telephone. She was terrified of all three—especially the telephone, which she was convinced was a gadget that would never catch on. Nana would be cleaning house and I'd call her on the phone. She would answer, "Hello," but then there would be silence. "Nana, are you there?" I'd ask. "I no can-a talk for you now," she'd say. "The house is upside and down." Click.

When my grandfather Dominick died in 1954, I was in rehearsal for *The Golden Apple* on Broadway. Nana was so convinced that now she, too, would pass away that she sold her house, gave everyone in the family a thousand dollars, and prepared for the worst. Well, she lived! She ended up moving into my parents' house and from then on my father had to pay all the bills! But Nana helped out, too. She worked as a cleaning woman at the May Company in Cleveland until she was well into her seventies. I can still see her at her retirement party, sitting there with all the other cleaning women gathered around her. After she retired, Nana decided she wanted to finally get her citizenship papers. So at the age of seventy-five, after I taught her the names of the members of the cabinet, she did. Nana stood before the judge and proudly, with her thick Italian accent, said, "Hello, your honor. Sec-a-tary War, Sec-a-tary Labor, Sec-a-tary Commerce, Sec-a-tary Interior, Sec-a-tary Agrakoochy." The judge looked startled and asked, "What?"

"I'm sorry, your honor, no speak English too good," Nana apologized.

The judge smiled. "Don-a you worry," he told her with a thick accent of his own. "You gonna get your papers!"

On the day I left home for my first professional job, Nana stopped me and pleaded, "I no see you no more."

"Nana," I explained, "I'm only going to the Moose Club in Ashtabula. I'll be back home tonight."

"I no see you no more," she cried. Nana truly believed that each time I left the house to go to work it would be the last time she would ever see me. Her sobs of good-bye were so heartbreaking that I would start to cry, too. This went on for thirty years until my darling Nana passed away at the age of ninety-three. I miss her to this day. Jerry Goldberg, Leslie Eberhard, and David Levy wrote a song about my grandmother for my one-woman show, *"Hey, Ma!"*:

> *Nana, you taught my dreams how to fly.*
> *Nana, you made my eyes aware of all there is to see.*
> *Nana, there is so much of you in me.*
> *Nana, you taught me hope with ideal.*
> *Nana, you said believing made it real.*
> *Nana, you're with me everyday, we'll never be apart.*
> *Nana, you live within my heart.*
> *Nana.*

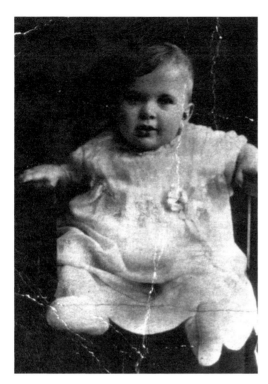

My baby picture. Time was I would have said this photo was taken in 1926, but since I've promised to reveal all, here's the truth: It was taken in 1925!

My brother Orlando and me. The only other time in my life I've been on a horse was with Eve Arden in an episode of The Mothers-in-Law.

Confirmation day with Orlando. Those dark circles under my eyes made me look older than I was and helped me land my first job—at Bert's record store, when I was just twelve years old.

My mother comes backstage in June 1946, when I was touring in Three to Make Ready.

My mother, father, Nana, and nieces and nephews.

My beloved Nana. She was the most important person in my life and lived to be ninety-three.

With Pa on a visit home.

With Orlando and my sister-in-law, Grace. A spat between these two inspired an episode of The Mothers-in-Law.

With co-author Jim Hesselman (whom I count as family) and Toots, the canine editor.

My first professional job, 1943. Note that I was then Kay Ballad, as in "love ballad." (Wasn't I clever?) Everyone called me "Ballard," so I went along with them.

Blitzes Spitalny Show

tra when it plays the New York mount for two weeks in July. 's another Cass Daley," the Cleveland maestro said, with her gusto and nerve, I Kay should go as far as Cass vaudeville."

To Jean,
a dear friend
You're tops!!!
As Ever,
Gloria Kaye

My first headshot, as "Gloria Kaye." I only used this name once, on a burlesque tour. An accompanying article said I might go as far in vaudeville as Cass Daly!

Chapter Two

From Chin's Chinese to Spike Jones

When I was in high school, the only theater group in town was the Cleveland Playhouse. So I went down to the Playhouse and interviewed for a job as a curtain puller (that was what they called the apprentice actors) and didn't get it. Then I entered an amateur talent contest doing impressions of Betty Hutton and Judy Garland. I killed the audience, but I was followed by a tenor who got up and sang "(There'll Be Bluebirds Over) The White Cliffs of Dover." He held the top note for about a day and a half and I came in second. Right then and there, I decided there would be no more contests for me. If I wanted to be professional, I'd have to take things into my own hands.

I heard about a Cleveland radio show called *Duke Lidyard's Show Boat*. Duke would host amateurs, so I went down and did my impressions. One day, as the show was wrapping up, Duke said, "Hey, there's still sixty seconds of airtime left! We need somebody! Somebody get out there and do something!" So I went out and did an impression of Lionel Barrymore's daughter and I was a smash. I thought to myself, "Hey, I like this." I don't think I realized it at the time, but between hanging around the vaudeville theaters and working at the USO, I was slowly coming up with an act of my own.

I went down to the Frank Sennes Theatrical Agency, the largest talent agency in Cleveland. (Can you believe there was more than one?) I marched into the office of Dick Jackson, one of the underlings, and boldly stated, "I am the most talented person in the world!" When Mr. Jackson had finished laughing, he replied, "I don't have a clue as to whether you have any talent, young lady, but you certainly have guts, and that's what it takes in this business." Dick booked me at Chin's Chinese Restaurant, where Jack Soo was starring as a romantic singer. Jack would later make quite a hit in New York in the original Broadway cast of Rodgers and Hammerstein's *Flower Drum Song*. He also did the movie version and appeared in *Thoroughly Modern Millie* with Julie Andrews and Mary Tyler Moore. But most people remember him as Detective Nick Yemana from the television series *Barney Miller*, with Hal Linden.

I opened at the Victory Room Cocktail Lounge at Chin's. They billed me as the "Sensational Comedienne Kay Ballad" (like a love ballad—I thought I was so clever). They might as well have added, "Direct from high school!" The all-star show consisted of Cholly Wayne ("Humor at the Piano"), Madelon ("The Believe It or Not Girl"), Juan Navarro's Good Neighbors, and Jimmy Foster and His Music. When the engagement was over, I added the "e" onto Kaye, and I soon found that everyone was calling me "Ballard," so I went along with them. I was very well received at Chin's, and they paid me $40 a week. Even though this was a lot of money to me then, by the time I paid 10 percent to the agency, took the streetcar across town, and stopped to buy gifts for everyone, most of my earnings were gone.

As I refined my act, I would perform at any little supper club or restaurant I could find. I got a job performing in Mansfield, Ohio. The best part about that job was the fact that it took me sixty miles closer to my dream of being in Hollywood! After Mansfield came a job at a club in Akron. There were obviously some illegal activities that I was not aware of going on there, because one night we were raided. I was sixteen, and Kay Pierce, a stripper, protected me. Kay stood directly in front of me and told the police, "This girl has nothing to do with this. You leave her alone." And they did!

Then, just after I graduated from high school, Dick Jackson booked me on my first tour, with a group of entertainers who did burlesque. We played all through the South and traveled on a bus called the *Blue Goose*. The cities flew by so fast it was difficult to keep up with where we were from day to day, but there was one place and date I will never forget. We were in Atlanta on April 12, 1945, the day President Roosevelt died. He'd been president for most of my life. I wasn't old enough to remember the stock market crash, so after Pearl Harbor, his death was the most momentous national event of my lifetime. Franklin Roosevelt had passed away at the Little White House in Warm Springs, Georgia, just thirty-five miles from where we were playing. Most people today cannot relate to the feelings that my generation and my parents' generation had for FDR. He was president for so long and under such extraordinary circumstances. The moment I heard that President Roosevelt had died my memory flashed to the day a few years back when I had joined the crowds in downtown Cleveland to see him pass by in his open-air touring car. There he was, the President of the United States, waving to me. I think everyone in the cheering crowd must have felt as special as I did that day. We felt safer and more secure knowing he was in Washington, as if we all had a father or an uncle there watching out for us, leading us. Even in this age of cynicism and corruption I believe that's what we still hunger for in our politicians—people we can trust and in whom we can put our faith to lead us.

For my part in the burlesque show I did my impressions of Judy Garland and Betty Hutton. By now I'd also added Martha Raye, Bette Davis, and several others. I have always been able to manipulate my voice and capture people's personalities. I'd dreamed of being like these women for so long that they wore off on me. They inspired me to give all the energy I had. I always went out onstage and tried to stop the show. This was the only way I knew how to perform.

After a while I was offered the chance to play sketches with some of the comics. I'd play the straight woman and set up all their punch lines. I remember one sketch that went like this:

> *Lights up.*
> **First comic** (*walking down the aisle, shouting*): "Peanuts! Popcorn! Rubber balloons! Peanuts! Popcorn! Rubber balloons!"
> **Straight man** (*onstage*): "And now, ladies and gentlemen, introducing Miss Personality of 1944!" I would walk out on the stage and promptly faint. Two more comics would run out to see what had happened.
> **Straight man:** "What do I do? What do I do?"
> **Second comic:** "Rub her cheeks!"
> **Third comic:** "Rub her forehead!"
> **First comic** (*from the aisle*): "Rubber balloons! Rubber *balloons!*
> *Blackout.*

Too often, burlesque gets a bum rap for being sleazy and dirty, but that was the extent of the vulgarity to be found in most burlesque shows. I found that the people working in burlesque had far better manners and morals than the people who performed in most musical comedy. The men of burlesque treated the ladies with dignity and respect.

In late 1945 my agent and I were delighted when comic Harvey Stone helped me get booked into the Bowery Room, a club in Detroit. This was my big opportunity to break into vaudeville, which was considered a step up from burlesque. The famous dancer Mitzi Mayfair was the star of the show. Mitzi had just reached what was to be the peak of her career, costarring in the film *Four Jills in a Jeep*, with Martha Raye, Kay Francis, and Phil Silvers. There were eighteen acts on the bill, and I was thrilled when I found out I was to open the show! Nobody bothered to tell me that most of the audience didn't arrive until the twelfth act.

I soon discovered that not only does it pay to be at the right place at the right time, but it also pays to say the right thing to the right person in the right place at the right time. When I met Frank Barbero, the owner of the Bowery Room, it was as if my guardian angel gave me a cue. "Mr. Barbero," I said without hesitation, "you look exactly like Leo Carillo!" (Leo Carillo was the great character actor best known for playing Pancho in the 1950s television series *The Cisco Kid*.) *"Bella, bella, comme si bella,"* he answered joyfully. It seems Mr. Barbero loved the fact that I thought he looked like the handsome actor he worshiped. I immediately went from opening the show to second from last on the bill, and will always be grateful to Leo Carillo. If it wasn't for him only about ten people a night would have seen my act. I was still doing my impressions of the famous stars I admired, but now people were beginning to take notice. (Even the stars themselves!)

Throughout my career I have always tried to help people with talent get started. I feel this is a way to pay back those people like Frank Barbero who helped me. Mr. Barbero really liked me and held me over for several weeks at the Bowery Room. He told a friend of his on the West Coast about me. Mr. Barbero said, "You gotta see this kid!" The friend was Spike Jones. Mr. Barbero let me speak to Spike on the phone in his office. "Kid," Spike told me, "if you ever get to Hollywood, I'll give you a job."

Spike Jones began as a drummer for Bing Crosby. Spike was not a very good-looking man, almost a caricature, with big ears and a wide grin. His personality contrasted starkly with the loud outfits he wore: Spike was as drab onstage as he was in real life. But he was a great businessman, and with the inspiration of the performers Red Engel and Carl Grayson, he put together the hit novelty songs "Cocktails for Two," "Yes! We Have No Bananas," and "Der Fuhrer's Face." These were the first of the satirical comedy numbers, with all the sound effects thrown in, for which Spike and his orchestra, The City Slickers, became famous. "Cocktails" was really Carl Grayson's idea, but Carl was always battling problems with the bottle, and things never seemed to work out for him until Spike took over as the brains of the operation.

Having the authority of innocence (not to be confused with intelligence), I quickly saved enough money and bought a one-way airplane ticket to Los Angeles so I could take Spike Jones up on his offer. Today I despise flying, but on that trip TWA flew through two storms and I was too naive to be afraid. I checked into the Biltmore Hotel with $75 in my pocket and immediately placed a call to Spike Jones. I was told that Spike was making a movie with his band over at Paramount Studios, so I left a message. Then I sat down in my room and crossed my fingers, hoping he would remember me. I ordered some food to be sent up and read the same newspaper and movie magazines over and over again so I wouldn't miss Spike when he called back (there was no television in the rooms then—hell, there was barely television). All the way back then I developed a fondness for room service that is still with me to this day.

Three long, lonely days later, Spike did call, thank goodness! I suppose I've always thought bigger than I should when it comes to living in comfort. The Biltmore was one of the finest hotels in town, and the meager amount of money I'd brought with me didn't come close to covering the bill, so Spike had to bail me out. But I got the job! After Spike paid my hotel bill, he hired me for $350 a week. I thought this was a fortune. Then I realized that my rent and all of my living expenses came out of that check, so after I sent money home, there wasn't a lot left over to save.

We did two shows a night, and I played the flute (thank you, West Tech High), doubled on the tuba, and had my own spot to sing. Spike's band was very popular, and we began the tour at the Trocadero Club in Hollywood. The Trocadero was located on Sunset Boulevard next to the Macombo. (Today both are part of the same parking lot.) Along with Ciro's, the Trocadero was one of the chicest places you could play on the West Coast. It was designed to look like a French café, with sidewalk tables and a huge awning out front. In 1939 the premiere party for *Gone with the Wind* was held at the Troc, and part of the original *A Star Is Born*, with Janet Gaynor and Frederic March, was filmed there. How much more Hollywood could I get? And Hollywood was there every night. Clark Gable, Joan Davis, Jimmy Stewart. I was in heaven. Eve Arden came backstage after a performance one evening and asked if she could use a piece of my material. Who could have possibly predicted that some twenty years later we'd find ourselves starring together on television in *The Mothers-in-Law*?

While we were playing the main room at the Trocadero, Nat King Cole was performing in the lounge. He was just as you saw him onstage, sweet and wonderful and warm. One night, Mel Tormé came in with Bob Wells. He called me over to the piano in the lounge and said, "Come here, Kaye. I want you to hear something we just wrote for Nat." I took a seat and listened to him sing the lyrics "Chestnuts roasting on an open fire." I was hearing "The Christmas Song" played for the first time anywhere. Nat instantly fell in love with the song, and when Mel got to the lyric "to kids from one to ninety-two," we were all so moved that we just knew it would be a huge hit, and, of course, it was.

Cleveland now seemed so far behind me. I may have looked and acted like I was about forty-five years old, but I was barely into my twenties, and I knew almost nothing about life. Even though I'd already lived on a tour bus, I was learning an awful lot from Spike and the boys, both professionally and personally. This was my time to really grow up emotionally, and I have to say, the guys in the band were very protective of me.

One evening during the tour, Keenan Wynn, son of legendary vaudeville and radio comic Ed Wynn, came to see the show. He gave me a great piece of advice. I was doing an imitation of Bette Davis, and at one point in the routine I would pretend to spit down my bra. Keenan came backstage and said, "You're not going to do that anymore." I was surprised, and probably a bit defensive, and told him, "I have to, that bit gets the biggest laugh." "It's the wrong kind of laugh," he continued. "I'm staying for your next show to make sure you don't keep that part in." I was apprehensive, but during the next show I followed his advice and left the bit out. The act was just fine, maybe even better. That night I learned the difference between getting a laugh of embarrassment and getting a laugh because you are funny. Keenan Wynn taught me about being tasteful. This probably wouldn't mean anything in the world of comedy today, but I was very grateful to him for taking the time to show me the way.

I got to meet so many wonderful people while I was performing with Spike. Besides Martha Raye and Judy Garland, I also got to know two other legends, Lena Horne and Bea Lillie. (I still have one of Bea's paintings and two of her hats!) It feels amazingly unreal to have your childhood heroes become your peers.

A couple of notes on Judy Garland:

Years later, I was performing at the Macambo, next door to the Trocadero on Sunset Boulevard. Judy Garland and Ethel Merman came in and sat in the first row! God, I was nervous. As I went through my songs I heard Judy shout, "Do me! Do me!" So there I was, onstage, doing an impression of Judy Garland *for* Judy Garland. This wonderfully talented lady whom I had watched at the RKO Palace in Cleveland, this person I had longed to be like, was watching me.

In the mid to late 1950s I was playing the New Frontier Hotel in Las Vegas, and Judy was also doing a show in town. By this time I had gotten to know Martha Raye quite well, but Judy and Martha had never met. I thought this was rather odd, since they had both been married to the bandleader David Rose. So I invited Judy and Martha to the Sahara to see Keely Smith perform. We got to the Sahara, and there I was, sitting with two of the ladies who had been such a great influence on my life and were such a big part of my act when I started out. Martha and Judy were very cordial, but something was bothering Judy. She appeared more and more nervous as we sat there, and she began to perspire a great deal. Then, even before the show began, she excused herself and said she couldn't stay. Judy was very overweight at the time, to the point that she had only one costume for her show. In fact, when my musical director, Arthur Siegel, and I went to see Judy perform and she came out onstage, Arthur said, "My God, she's become one of her own munchkins!" None of us guessed at the time that she was ill with hepatitis; in fact, she nearly died shortly after her Vegas engagement was finished. Judy was so talented and strong, but at the same time so vulnerable. Maybe that's the magic combination that made everyone fall in love with her. She was, and still is, the greatest star.

I found that I loved doing parody and satirical material, and I was developing quite a knack for it. Before joining Spike Jones, I had just been copying things I'd seen or heard in the movies and onstage. Performing with Spike's orchestra allowed me to stretch my wings and do a lot of funny new stuff. Spike taught me about writing and choosing comedy material, and through Spike I met Earl Brent, a songwriter at MGM, who introduced me to true satire. Earl later wrote a lot of special material for me. I remember I did a version of the song "All of a Sudden My Heart Sings," which went:

All of a sudden my heart sings
When I remember little things
Your finger stuck into my eye
That Mickey Finn
instead of rye . . .

My tour with Spike Jones crisscrossed the United States and Canada, and we played every vaudeville house in existence. After almost two years on the road with Spike, my dreams of being an actress were about to get a little closer to reality. The band finally landed in New York, where we played six shows a day at the Strand Theatre. Next door to the Strand was Joey Gold's Ticket Agency, and I became friendly with a guy who worked there, Jesse Burley. One afternoon Jesse said, "Here's a ticket. Go and see this lady playing down the street." I thanked him, hurried down to the Royale Theatre on West Forty-fifth Street, and saw the first legitimate play I'd ever seen. That lady Jesse referred to was Laurette Taylor, performing as Amanda Wingfield in Tennessee Williams's first play, *The Glass Menagerie*. At first, I wasn't all that impressed. She was so natural that you forgot she was acting. It was as if they had pulled some woman directly off the street and onto the stage. A screen test that Miss Taylor did for one of the major studios in Hollywood is included in Rick McKay's documentary *Broadway: The Golden Age* (2003). The performance is brilliant, but the studio turned her down because they didn't feel she was acting. Eventually, I came to realize the magnitude of Laurette Taylor's talent. Within a few years the acting techniques of a Russian named Konstantin Stanislavski would revolutionize Broadway and Hollywood, but Laurette Taylor had instinctively found the Method all on her own.

Jesse also got me a ticket to see my first musical, Irving Berlin's *Annie Get Your Gun*, starring Ethel Merman. *The Glass Menagerie* had really impressed me, but after seeing Ethel Merman I knew with absolute certainty what I wanted to do in show business: I wanted to perform in musical comedies.

Chapter Three

The Scarecrow, the Cowardly Lion, and Me!

L ike I said, the first time show business made a big impression on me was when I saw *The Wizard of Oz* back at the RKO in Cleveland. The idea that I would someday meet most of the major actors in that film never occurred to me, except as a fantasy. I was thirteen when I saw *The Wizard of Oz*. Eight years later, I was in a show with the man who played the Scarecrow. Four years after that, I was working with the man who played the Cowardly Lion. Unbelievable! Watching Ray Bolger and Bert Lahr from the wings as they performed in shows that I was part of, I felt like I was in Oz myself!

Just like Dorothy, I met the Scarecrow first. John Murray Anderson, the great theater impresario, had directed Billy Rose's huge *Aquacade* at the 1939 New York World's Fair Hippodrome and for years put together all of the Ringling Brothers circuses. In the spring of 1946, John Murray Anderson (he always used all three names) conceived and staged a Broadway revue called *Three to Make Ready*. I got into *Three to Make Ready* without having to audition. John Murray Anderson saw me when I was working with Spike Jones at the Strand Theatre in New York and hired me to join the last month of the Broadway run and then do ten months on the road.

John Murray Anderson was a funny, adorable genius. He christened me with the nickname "Kimmer." I soon discovered that I wasn't special; he gave nearly everyone a nickname. The dancer Harold Lang was "Beast of the Ballet," and the songwriter Hugh Martin was "Birdseed," because he was so fragile. My friends, and anyone he saw as related to me, became

"Big Kimmer," "Little Kimmer," or "Kimmer's other Kimmer" (that was Liz Smith). When he ran out of nicknames, he simply used John Murray Anderson. He was so beloved that at his funeral all the attendees signed the book with the names he had given them. As a result, nobody ever really knew who had attended! When I got into *Three to Make Ready*, I was twenty-one years old and very nervous about working with all these experienced performers. John Murray Anderson told me not to worry. "Imperfection is perfection," he said. If that was true, I thought, I should rise to the top in no time! I had been with Spike Jones for nearly two years, and I hated to leave. But even though *Three to Make Ready* was not a book show (a musical theater piece that includes substantial dialogue and a storyline, as opposed to a revue), it was still a musical! Just what I'd always wanted to do. *Three to Make Ready* was a wonderful experience, and I stayed with the show until the very end.

When I showed up for rehearsals I learned that I had a few bits and songs to do, and I was to understudy one of the principal women, Brenda Forbes. Well, I had no idea what an understudy did, and I didn't want to appear ignorant and ask. So it's a good thing I never had to go on, because I never did learn her part. Besides Ray Bolger, *Three to Make Ready* featured an incredible cast of young performers. Joining Ray was Carleton Carpenter (who later sang "Abba Dabba Honeymoon" with Debbie Reynolds), Arthur Godfrey, Harold Lang, Julie Wilson, and Gordon MacRae.

Gordon later became famous in films, playing Curly in *Oklahoma!* and Billy Bigelow in *Carousel*. During *Three to Make Ready*, all he seemed to care about was the racing form. The intro would start and Gordon would look up, sing his little bit in the song "Barnaby Beach," and go back to the form. He never missed a cue, but he also never took his head out of that paper!

Rehearsing for a stage musical was a bit different from being a member of the band. The guys on the road with Spike Jones had been so kind to me. It was naive of me, but I just assumed that everyone in show business was that way. I discovered that it paid to choose your friends very wisely. I started out lucky and chose very wisely indeed when I became friends with Harold Lang, the great dancing star. While we were still in New York, Harold introduced me to a world I never knew existed. He took me to see the great cabaret singer Mabel Mercer at Tony's on East Fifty-second Street. At first I found her voice and style to be a bit peculiar, but after the first couple of songs, I understood why Barbara Cook and

Frank Sinatra both copied her unique phrasing. I adored Mabel Mercer from then on. Harold also introduced me to Ruth Draper, the famous comedy monologist who did several characters at the same time. (The modern-day equivalents of Ruth Draper would probably be Lily Tomlin and Tracey Ullman.) Up to this point I had done imitations of people I admired and the broad comedy Spike Jones wrote for me. Mabel and Ruth helped shape my stage persona, and I began to develop a performing style of my own.

Back to Oz. Ray Bolger was an old hoofer from vaudeville. The star of *Three to Make Ready* and the definitive professional, he never failed to stop the show. I used to love watching him go into his song-and-dance routine in a number called "The Old Soft Shoe." I can still hear him singing "When me and my Alice was playin' the Palace in . . . twenty-five." He was a very kind man, and he taught me a lot about show business.

Ray's wife, Gwen, was a different story. She had to be banned from theaters on several occasions because she was so protective of Ray and would get in the way and start telling people what to do. Her role, that of a protector, is common in this business. A lot of great performers need an agent, a manager, a spouse, or even a parent to stick up for them so that they can concentrate on what they do best—performing. Sometimes this arrangement works out very well, as was the case with Mary Martin and her husband, Richard Halliday. The problem is that all too often these strong people are only out for themselves and tragic things happen to the performer's career.

Now, fast forward down the yellow brick road a couple of years, to the summer of 1951. My next experience with one of the Oz alumni would not be as pleasant. I auditioned for another revue-type show called *Two on the Aisle.* It was written in a satirical vaudeville format again, starring one of the best comedians ever to come out of burlesque, Bert Lahr. This was to be a first-class production with sketches and lyrics by Betty Comden and Adolph Green and music by Jule Styne. Comden and Green started out as part of a comedic song and dance act called The Revuers that also included the brilliant Judy Holliday. They went on to write the book and lyrics for such huge stage hits as *On the Town* and the motion picture *Singin' in the Rain.* Jule Styne wrote some of the best pop tunes of the day and such Broadway hits as *Gentlemen Prefer Blondes, Gypsy,* and *Funny Girl.* To top it off, the versatile Abe Burrows, who wrote and directed *Guys and Dolls,* directed the show. You just couldn't be surrounded by better people. The reason I find it necessary to name-drop so unashamedly here is to illustrate the circumstances surrounding the heartbreak of what was to come.

Dolores Gray was cast as the leading lady in *Two on the Aisle*. Dolores was a great singer with a terrific pair of legs. She had just done *Annie Get Your Gun* in London and was a big hit over there. She was certainly attractive but didn't really have the best complexion. (I'll tell you why I mention that in a minute.) Not that I was jealous. Here I was in a new Bert Lahr musical with a great song, "If (You Hadn't But You Did)," and some nice sketches. I was still very young and thrilled to be featured in a show bound for Broadway!

But beware of those protectors I mentioned, especially if you aren't the one they are protecting. Just as Ray Bolger had his wife, Dolores Gray had her mother. Dolores's mother, Barbara, did everything she could to build up her daughter's part. I guess she must have seen me as some kind of threat to Dolores, because, little by little, she convinced the producer and director to take away all my material. Barbara said, "Kaye, you're too fey." (Whatever that meant.) "Besides, it's not your turn now; it's Dolores's turn." By the time we reached New Haven, all I had left to do in the show were two little walk-ons. I remember in one of them I was dressed all in green, playing a Martian in a sketch with Mr. Lahr. My entire dialogue consisted of "Beep, beep, beep, beep." It was embarrassing. I was getting $550 a week (great money at the time) to play what had begun as a featured role, and I was taking my bow after the ballerina who had danced an entire number. I'd walk out and the audience would search their programs, wondering, "Who the hell is she?" I couldn't come into New York that way. I just couldn't. I figured if people saw me presented like that, my career would be over before it began. So I left the show before it came to New York. Was it the right decision? Who knows?

Mr. Lahr tried to make me feel better. Referring to Miss Gray, he'd say, "Forget about it, Kaye, forget about it. She's got a face like a golf course; thirty-six holes!" He sounded just like the farmhand telling Dorothy not to worry about Miss Gulch.

I loved Bert Lahr. He was such a tortured yet brilliant man. He used to tell me that he knew if MGM had renewed his contract if the guy at the gate said hello to him. He bit his fingernails down to the nubbins worrying about everything. Yet when he got out there on the stage he was the king, in total command of his adoring audience.

I was truly lucky. I learned so much from my Scarecrow and Cowardly Lion. Just watching them every night was an education for which I could never have paid. I learned what to do if the laughs didn't come, and how to play them when they did. I learned to respect those people out there in the dark who had paid for the privilege of seeing me perform. Because once you have respect for your audience, you can make them love you, and from then on you can do no wrong.

I also saw what it meant to be a professional. I learned never to be late, never to miss a performance, and how to treat the other actors and the rest of the company and crew. We all work together to create this precious thing called theater.

I am so proud to say that I was taught my profession by such marvelous, seasoned vaudevillians as Ray Bolger and Bert Lahr. I feel sorry for the kids today who have all the formal training in the world but no way to get experience. Even worse off are the ones who fall into what they think is stardom because of a TV talent show. In my book, finding a minute of fame and being a star are not the same. These kids will never get a chance to learn by doing, by watching and listening to the generation of performers who came before them, just as that generation did. Performing is a craft, and a craft must be taught. Bit by bit, we somehow seem to have lost a lot of our traditions in the theater. I hope they return someday soon.

P.S. When I see all the advances that have been made in the technical side of theater, from microphones to moving lights to special effects, I think that actors sometimes feel pressure to be as technically perfect as those machines. We are not machines, and if we become machines, live theater will most certainly die. I am reminded once again of what John Murray Anderson told me, "Imperfection is perfection." That statement takes on a new meaning in the fast-paced, computer-generated world of today.

Gypsy Rose Lee

Y ou'd think someone who has been in the theater as long as I have would find it difficult to choose a favorite role. Not me. My favorite role ever is the indomitable Mama Rose in perhaps the most perfectly written show in all of musical comedy history, *Gypsy*. What a thrill and what a workout! I've played Mama Rose twice, and both times I found her to be the most exhausting, most rewarding character I've ever come across in the theater.

The original production of *Gypsy* opened on Broadway in 1959. Jule Styne wrote the music, Stephen Sondheim wrote the lyrics, Jerome Robbins handled the musical staging, and Arthur Laurents adapted the brilliant book from Gypsy Rose Lee's memoirs. How could you go wrong with a stable of creative geniuses like that? (Oh, and add Ethel Merman in the lead role.)

Shortly after the Broadway run closed, Merman took *Gypsy* on the road with almost all the original Broadway cast. After touring for nine months, *Gypsy* finally closed in December 1961. The following summer, the Dallas State Fair Music Hall (which has evolved into the very successful and prestigious Dallas Summer Musicals) produced *Gypsy* with the same cast that Ethel had performed with, except I played Mama Rose and Jack Cassidy replaced Jack Klugman as Herbie. Though the run was short, I had a wonderful time, and I was delighted to win that year's Rosenthal Award for Best Actress. (Against some pretty serious competition, I might add; both Carol Burnett and Ginger Rogers were up for the award that year.)

Jack Cassidy was a terrific Herbie, even though he didn't play the role as an "everyman" character, as Jack Klugman had done on Broadway. Jack was a real matinee idol type, with a gorgeous smile and a John Barrymore profile. He had such presence and charisma that it was no wonder women fell in love with him on sight. Little did he know that the following season he would win a Tony Award for his role in the Broadway musical *She Loves Me*. Before every performance of *Gypsy* that summer, Jack would say, "Come on, old timer, let's go have some chili." And every time I'd tell him, "No, Jack, I don't want any chili." He kept it up until one night, going into our final performance, I relented and joined him. The script called for Herbie to hand me a note at the end of the first act that said, "Mama, I'm leaving." That night, the note read, "Mama, I'm leaving you because of your breath!" I had a hell of a difficult time launching into "Everything's Coming Up Roses" after reading what he'd written and realizing he'd been planning this little joke since the beginning of the run! I remember that in order to get through the song I imagined everybody I had ever known was dead!

Looking back, I see that I knew Jack just as he was getting to what would be the height of his career. Like me, he always felt that he was right on the brink of success and that he was never quite given the chance to realize his potential. Tragically, Jack died at the age of forty-nine in a fire. How ironic that Jack almost burned down my house when he was visiting. He called and said, "Old timer, I think I'd like to come and stay for a week or so in Palm Springs." He did, and one day he left the house with the coffeepot still on the stove and almost burned us to the ground! I'm sure Jack would be very pleased to know that his legacy continues through his three very talented sons, David, Shaun, and Patrick.

A little more than ten years after doing *Gypsy* with Jack, I got the chance to tackle Mama Rose one more time for a two-month run in San Diego. This time, Gavin MacLeod, fresh from his success as Murray Slaughter on *The Mary Tyler Moore Show*, played Herbie. Gavin and his wife, Patti, have been close, devoted friends over the years, but I also want to say a word about Gavin as a performer. Everyone knows him from his light, comic, good-natured roles on *The Mary Tyler Moore Show* and *The Love Boat*, but I once saw him play the older priest in a production of *Mass Appeal*, and I'm here to tell you that Gavin MacLeod is one hell of an actor!

One of the regrets that come with growing older in show business is saying good-bye to characters you'll never get to play again. Now, I was never considered an ingenue, so I didn't have to go through the trauma of realizing I was too old to play Laurie in *Oklahoma!* Hell, I would have been cast as Aunt Eller before I was thirty! But I do regret thinking that I'll probably never get to play Mama Rose again. I got my two shots at this spectacular, all-consuming character, and I miss her.

I never met the real Mama Rose (Rose Hovick), but I got to be very good friends with her daughter Rose Louise. Having known her, I can say for certain that the character of Rose was partly true and partially invented by straining real life through the incredible wit and imagination of Gypsy Rose Lee.

I don't remember exactly how Gypsy and I first met. It was at some point in the early 1960s while I was doing *Carnival*. You know, as I write about all the famous and infamous people I've met, I realize how unbelievable and fanciful it sounds. But once someone gains even a small amount of notoriety in show business, in New York or Los Angeles, his or her social life expands at a fascinating rate. Mine certainly did.

Gypsy Rose Lee was funny and wonderful, and I miss her dearly. Gypsy took the guts and determination her mother had given her and turned all the ugliness of her early life into a successful career as a performer and writer. The truth about the facts of her life never mattered to Gypsy as much as the *presentation* of those facts. Gypsy thought of herself as having no talent. She used to tell her son Erik, whose father was the famed director Otto Preminger, "Your mother cannot sing and she cannot dance, but never forget that she's a star." This witty, creative, savvy businesswoman was a marketing genius who could literally make nothing into something everyone wanted.

Gypsy the commodity was one of a kind, her own special creation. And no one knew better than Gypsy exactly how to sell it. Her mystery novel, *The G-String Murders*, became a best-seller, and then there was the Academy Award–nominated film *Lady of Burlesque*, starring Barbara Stanwyck.

Gypsy would often come to the dinners I gave at my place in Los Angeles. One time I was doing potluck, and everyone was supposed to bring something. Gypsy waltzed in with a tiny jar in her hand. I took her aside and reminded her that there were going to be eight people for dinner that night, and she said, "Kaye, this is ratatouille, a roasted appetizer. It is a delicacy, and everyone must have only a tiny taste."

When Gypsy gave a gift it was something you treasured. Having grown up in near poverty, she was not extravagant, and she often gave presents she made herself. Once she gave me a darling little doll, a man dressed in striped prison garb with large loopy earrings dangling from his ears. Gypsy Rose Lee was camp before camp was in.

If Gypsy ever regretted being thrown into show business and dragged around the country by Mama Rose, she never let it show. In fact, if anything, she took over right where Rose left off. Gypsy called me several times on the spur of the moment to invite me to go along with her on one of her trips. One time she said, "Kaye, I've just got an invitation to open a Hilton in Istanbul. Come with me, we can go for the weekend!" I've always hated flying, but Gypsy would toss a few things into a shopping bag and off she'd go.

Another time Gypsy was doing a television show and called me to say, "Kaye, I want you to come to San Francisco and do this show with me. You can stay at the Palace Hotel. I've found a five-hundred-pound ape who paints. I think you would be perfect with him!" When I asked what that was supposed to mean, Gypsy only laughed.

Rose Louise inherited her mother's common sense as a businesswoman. When her sister, June Havoc, was in the hospital after a thyroid operation, Gypsy paid her a quick visit. Poor June was so groggy after the surgery she was nearly comatose. Gypsy leaned over her bed and said, "June, can you hear me? I have a date in Indianapolis I cannot get out of, but I'm leaving a check for four thousand dollars in the nightstand by the bed in case you need something. You can pay me back at two-percent interest. And I don't think you'd do better with a bank!"

Erik Preminger, Gypsy's son, said about his mother after her death in 1970 that she always taught him not to care what other people thought. I think that's what came through in the way that Gypsy lived. I admired, and envied, the strength, confidence, tenacity, and joie de vivre of Gypsy Rose Lee. (I suppose many people who have come into contact with me over the years might think that the role of the domineering, controlling Mama Rose was easy for me to identify with. Not really. It's all an act. I can be very strong and opinionated on the outside, but on the inside I am constantly afraid of being found out for the coward I really am.)

I never knew how old Gypsy was. The fact is that while they were growing up, Louise and her little sister, June, lied about their ages so much, nobody ever knew how old they really were. I recently heard that June turned ninety-two! Gypsy also never dwelled on the disappointments in her life. She was truly one of the most optimistic people I've ever known. In fact, shortly after learning she had cancer, Gypsy had her face lifted. Now, that's a positive outlook!

P.S. Darling June Havoc has been a very welcome guest in my home several times, and I want to thank her for the fact that I even have a house. She always told me I must buy property, and I'm so glad I heeded her advice. June turned out to be a wonderful actress and an extremely talented director, and I love her every bit as much as I did her sister, Louise (maybe even a little bit more).

Chapter Four

My "Closet" Straight

Arthur Siegel was the kindest, funniest, most talented, and most devoted friend I have ever had. He was a major part of my life for more than forty-five years. During the times between my Broadway, movie, and television show appearances (and believe me, there were a lot of between times), Arthur and I would find work for our act. I met Arthur in 1947, when he played my audition for the first book musical I was ever in, *That's the Ticket.* We spent the next forty-seven years on and off the road doing the two things we enjoyed most, laughing and eating! (All right, in between meals we'd work a bit.)

Arthur may not have been the world's greatest piano player, but he was a wonderful accompanist (and that's an important distinction). He played for me in my act from coast to coast and overseas. We worked together so well that by the time Arthur passed away in 1994, it wasn't just my act anymore, it was *our* act. In fact, he sang so well and was so funny that I sometimes felt like I was the backup singer and *he* was the star. Arthur could have been a great club act in his own right.

Even though he had attended the American Academy of Dramatic Arts, I don't think Arthur ever intended to be a performer, nor did he ever see himself playing piano for someone else. When the young cabaret performer Michael Feinstein came along, he became Arthur's nemesis. Arthur would say, "Oh, sure, Michael Feinstein. A nice Jewish boy lounge singer who appreciates all the old standards. And just because he's young and cute he gets it all!" Arthur Siegel wasn't a good musical director and he couldn't really conduct. I remember one time the orchestra played a joke on him. The musicians were always frustrated because Arthur was such a soft-spoken, unassuming soul that at the end of a number instead of providing a nice, clean, decisive cut-off, he would sort of wave his hand across his face. Well, one night after just such a cut-off, the entire band laid down their instruments and waved back! I turned around and thought, "What the hell happened to the end of the song?"

Arthur considered himself to be, first and foremost, a songwriter. He was such a great composer—truly, truly great. He wrote most of the songs for *New Faces of 1952*, including "Love Is a Simple Thing." He also wrote most of *New Faces of 1956*, *New Faces of 1962*, and *New Faces of 1968*. All in all, he wrote more than two dozen off-Broadway musicals, revues, and cabaret shows, including *Corkscrews* in 1982, which lasted only fifteen performances, and a wonderful score for the 1983 Helen Gallagher musical *Tallulah*, which played forty-two performances. Arthur had an encyclopedic knowledge and great appreciation of American popular music, especially musical theater songs. I often thought that maybe he should have been a college professor instead of knocking around the world with me. There were no dishes in Arthur's kitchen cupboards, just stacks and stacks of sheet music. Every singer in show business would go to Arthur to find an obscure song. Barbra Streisand, Maureen McGovern, you name the singer—anyone I introduced him to would sooner or later call Arthur for material.

Ben Bagley, the renowned founder of the Painted Smiles recording label, built an entire repertoire out of Arthur's collection of sheet music. Ben's ambition was to preserve as many of the older, more obscure Broadway tunes as he could find. He's done a great service to the entertainment industry, and is so deeply admired for his work that many performers, including myself, recorded these songs free of charge.

When I say Arthur loved American popular music, I am talking about the music of the Gershwins, Johnny Mercer, Jerome Kern, Richard Rodgers, Sammy Cahn, Harry Warren, Jule Styne, and so many others who shaped and colored our lives throughout most of the twentieth century. Arthur was not a fan of the century's later years. He simply could not understand the changing music of the 1960s and 1970s, when rock and roll demolished crooners and melodies. Arthur detested the songs and lyrics he heard on television and on the radio. When Carole King sang her hit song with the lyrics, "It's too late, baby, now, it's too late," Arthur came rushing into the apartment, shouting at me, "What is this baby, 'now,' who is this *'baby, now'*? Oy!"

I think that every generation has probably had similar thoughts about the generation that followed, but what bothered Arthur is the same thing that bothers me. There is no wit anymore, no grace. There are a lot of smart young composers and performers out there with their computers and their telephones that do everything but the laundry. But, you know, once we got through the anger and love power and whatever else we were going through in the sixties and early seventies, we never went back to listening. Every product we invented was about being faster or cheaper. And the art world went right along with it. It is not a coincidence that Broadway musicals began to decline around this time. Once they did return, they were concentrating on sinking ships and flying helicopters instead of telling a story. The world started going so fast there was no time for the wit of a Noel Coward or a Lorenz Hart, no time for the grace of Lerner and Loewe.

Okay, off the soapbox. On the personal side, Arthur was one of the most unique people I've ever been lucky enough to meet. His quirks were fairly odd, but they only made him more endearing. For instance, Arthur would never go to the same barber twice, because he didn't want anyone talking while cutting his hair. I guess he thought if a barber got to know him, he'd be too tempted to strike up a conversation and not watch what he was doing. It didn't help. As a result of not having a barber who knew how to cut his hair properly, Arthur sported some of the most original haircuts in show business. To give you an idea of the origin of Arthur's neurosis, he once told me he had hemorrhoids because when he was about fifteen months old his mother left him on the toilet and forgot about him for three hours. God, how we laughed! And I don't know why, but he never showed anyone his toes; he'd wear shoes even when walking on the beach!

Arthur was not at all effeminate, but because of his demeanor, people always assumed he was gay. This wasn't true. Arthur was completely heterosexual. Could he help it that he happened to be born creative, funny, gentle, and sensitive? When he worked with Gypsy Rose Lee, she asked, "Arthur, have you ever been homosexual?" "No," Arthur answered, "I could never feel that way about a man." "Well, don't worry, dear," Gypsy told him, "you just haven't met the right man yet."

Whenever Arthur and I were performing for a distressingly small audience, I could always count on him to cheer me up. If we were bombing, all I'd have to do is turn and look at Arthur at the piano laughing himself silly, and the world was back in perspective. I told him one time, "Arthur, when Sophie Tucker died she left her accompanist twenty-five thousand dollars. Look around, Arthur. At the rate my career is going, all I'll be leaving you are my gowns." Arthur took a look around himself and answered, "At the rate my career is going, I'll take 'em!" When we were between jobs, we'd see each other on the street every once in a while, and our greeting was always the same: "Nobody wants you!"

In 1959, Arthur and I were booked in England. After the booking, we decided to take a short vacation through France and Italy. I wanted to see my native homeland, and Josephine Baker, whom I'd previously met in New York, was performing in Paris, so off we went. Our greatest pleasure was our unspoken search for the perfect restaurant. We found a place in Parma, Italy, that had a pasta we talked about for literally years to come (five cheeses!). I've often been tempted to go back and try to find the place again, but it just wouldn't be the same without Arthur.

Many women fell in love with Arthur. They soon discovered the way to his heart was through his sweet tooth. Arthur, of course, insisted on sharing the gifts of pies, cakes, cookies, and homemade fudge with yours truly. Just what I needed. If I haven't mentioned this before, I have absolutely no willpower when it comes to food, so I never protested too loudly. However, I did mention to Arthur that it was a pity I chose him as a partner instead of the Gabor sisters. They got minks, jewelry, or cold hard cash from their admirers. All we got were brownies.

Arthur became diabetic, and his doctor demanded that he give up sugar. I remember pleading with the doctor, "Please, can't Arthur have just one last piece of pie from Louise's Pantry in Palm Springs?" Our favorite place, it had the best pies in town. Just one more time I wanted to experience one of my favorite Arthur Siegel quirks. Whenever he had dessert, he had to have a cup of coffee along with it. He would take a bite of dessert, then a sip of coffee. He did this until they were both almost gone; bite, sip, bite, sip, bite, sip . . . the thing was, he couldn't finish one before the other. The dessert and the coffee had to finish at the same time! If he still had coffee left in his cup he would order another dessert. Needless to say, I never complained.

I love show business, but I'll never understand why one person can rise to the top when someone else with just as much or more talent never manages to make it big. Is it who you know? How you play the game? Or is it really simply the luck of being in the right place at the right time that gives you an edge? Arthur had that special quality of genius in his music and in his personality that should have made him rich and famous. But it never happened for him. What *did* happen was a wonderful career surrounded by people who truly loved and admired him. You couldn't help but love Arthur. The night he died I called him. I wasn't concerned when he didn't pick up the phone, because he always monitored his calls. I shouted into the receiver, "Arthur, you pick up this phone! Can you hear me?! Pick up this phone!!! Arthur, if you pick up the phone, I'll take you to a Broadway show!" They found him the next morning, dead of a heart attack caused by complications from diabetes.

Arthur and I always laughed at the headlines and the foibles of human nature, including our own. Every time I see that something ludicrous has happened in the news I wish Arthur was here to laugh with me. What an unlikely and perfect team we made. Coffee and Dessert. Only we didn't get to finish *together.* I miss you, Arthur.

Liz Smith

I met Mary Elizabeth Smith at a dinner party sometime around 1950. She impressed me immediately with her incomparable wit and intellect, and we've been friends ever since. Somehow I talked her into becoming my road manager, and we traveled together for three years. We became very close and even got to know each other's families. While we were doing a show in St. Louis, Liz's mother and niece came up from Texas to visit. Her niece, an adorable little girl named Rebecca, had a Texas drawl that wouldn't quit. It took her fifteen minutes to say anything! Instead of calling her aunt Mary Elizabeth, Rebecca would say "Mary Bibba," so I've called Liz "Bibba" ever since.

Bibba can read faster than anyone I've ever known. While we were traveling together, she was devouring four books a week, and that was long before anyone had ever heard of speed reading. It was a cinch that she would someday end up dealing in words for a living. She still teases me about the fact that it took me a full year to read *Kon-Tiki*. When its author, Thor Heyerdahl, passed away, Liz sent me a condolence card!

While I can't take any credit for Bibba's fabulous career, I did introduce her to Gloria Saphire, an agent who got Liz started writing pieces for a column by Cholly Knickerbocker. She eventually took over the entire column, and the rest is history.

I found an emotional connection with women like Liz that I could never find with a man. I don't know why or how it happened, but I do know that it has kept me single my entire life. And something about that makes me angry—not because I never got married. It makes me damn mad that my generation was never taught what to do if we didn't fit into a mold. Liz certainly didn't fit into any mold. She had to fight her way up to the top in a man's world that most of the time wasn't very welcoming (to say the least) to a strong woman. Halfway through the last century, women in business, any business, including show business, had to play an awful lot of games, especially if they didn't have men there protecting them. It was somehow wrong to be who you were. We were made to feel that we should be ashamed of ourselves for not being traditional females.

Ashamed of ourselves? I just realized what an awful thing that is to say. Shame of self. That kind of stigma stays with you an entire lifetime. And I think it destroys an awful lot of great people. Today, though, I see a glimmer of hope. I think the world is finally beginning to understand better the complexities of human relationships. Slowly, people are beginning to accept one another for who they were born to be. This was not the case throughout most of my life. I have seen a lot happen over the past seven decades—equality for women, for blacks, and for entire nations that were once ruled by tyrants. I wonder whether, had I been born thirty or forty years later and been able to equate religion with more than guilt, I might have been much more open, much more fulfilled.

Liz Smith seems to have been able to escape some of my demons. I'm very happy that after all these years she has found a life that not only fulfills her but makes her content. Liz is a great source of pride and joy to me. My Bibba went from earning $50 a week with Dell Publishing to more than a million a year as a widely read, highly respected syndicated columnist. (Boy, did I get a deal when I paid her $200 a week to manage me!) But the real source of pride is our friendship, and our mutual understanding. Billy DeWolfe once told me that you can count your true friends on your fingers. Well, Liz Smith is one of those fingers.

Chapter Five

TOUCH AND GO
in London

Before I get too far ahead of myself, I want to return for a second to the late 1940s and early 1950s—the years of my experiences with Ray Bolger and Bert Lahr. After the tour of *Three to Make Ready*, I returned to New York and worked the nightclub scene, waiting for my next opportunity to be cast in a musical comedy. I had never had any formal vocal training. I just went out there and did it. I learned by mimicking. Now that I knew I wanted a career in the legitimate theater, I had to figure out how to sustain my voice without the aid of a nightclub microphone.

In 1949 Harold Lang introduced me to Keith Davis, the renowned singing teacher. Keith was a remarkable man who, when he died at the age of eighty-five, still had the voice of a twenty-year-old. Many of the great Broadway performers studied with him. Keith taught voice production. He focused on technique and never tried to make his students sound a certain way. When Keith began teaching, performers couldn't rely on the sophisticated amplification systems theaters are equipped with today. Many actors who were accustomed to film or television could not sustain the volume and projection required for live theater. They would end up hurting themselves. Through the years, Keith helped Anthony Quinn, Lauren Bacall, Ruth Gordon, Barbara Harris, Tyne Daly, and many others when they were having problems with their voices.

Keith's technique was pure and simple: Produce sound by controlling the point of origin, the breath. There were no tricks, no strange vocal exercises. Today several of the vocal techniques, such as the Alexander Method, rely on the same principles of relaxation and support. The voice is a muscle like any other. If you take care of it, it will take care of you. Keith Davis helped me a great deal. I still use the worn-out warm-up tape we made together, and whenever I am in New York, I take lessons from one of his disciples, Judith Farris. By the way, one of Keith Davis's students was Doris Duke, one of the richest women in the world. Why she was taking voice lessons, none of us could figure out. Each Christmas, we students would give Mr. Davis a nice gift or bonus. Ms. Duke gave him a jar of homemade preserves. I guess she was proud of making something with her own hands!

It was the end of 1949, and I was off to audition! The theater was so much more personal back then. These days, kids need an agent to get seen by a casting director, who may or may not get them an audition with the producer and director. Not that it was easy to get a job back then, but you could actually get out there and pound the pavement and make the rounds of all the offices. The work of getting a job seemed much more cut and dried. I don't even remember using a resume. You just left your name and tried to get an appointment. One day in the late fall of 1949, I found out about an audition being held for a role in the Broadway show *Touch and Go*, which was to go on tour in England. I don't know why, but I have always had an affinity for England. Maybe it is the tradition of royalty and pageantry. Even today I am a sucker for an English accent! *Touch and Go* had sketches and lyrics by the husband-and-wife team of Jean and Walter Kerr. Jean went on to write the hit comedy *Mary, Mary,* and Walter became the much revered and respected drama critic for the *New York Herald Tribune* and later the *New York Times.* The score would be the last music ever written by Jay Gorney, the composer who wrote such popular songs as "Brother, Can You Spare a Dime?" and was responsible for several of the *Earl Carroll Vanities* revues in the 1920s and 1930s.

My heart sank when I walked into the audition and saw almost every other character actress I knew. We all tried out together in the same large room. The competition included Elaine Stritch, Pat Carroll, Bibi Osterwald, and Mary Wickes. Mary Wickes appeared in hundreds of movies as the spinster aunt or the maid, and she was a frequent guest on *The Lucy Show* in the 1960s. Besides being a terrific character actress, Mary was quite a character herself. That afternoon at the audition, she showed up looking tall, thin, and terrific. She announced in her wonderfully blunt manner, "I have a flower show to attend at Madison Square

Garden, so let's get this over with." We each took our turn and nervously sized up the others as they took theirs. After we finished, Mary got up and apologized for having to leave so abruptly. She went down the line saying, "Good-bye, Pat. Good-bye, Bibi. So long, Elaine." When she got to me she said, "Bon voyage, Kaye." Somehow she knew I was going to get the part!

The star of *Touch and Go* was Helen Gallagher. I have to hand it to Helen. She's another old broad like me, still out there working after all these years. In 1998 we appeared together again in a fabulous revival of *No, No, Nanette* at the Paper Mill Playhouse. She won the Tony Award for her role in the original Broadway production of *No, No, Nanette* with Ruby Keeler. Helen is well known to fans of the daytime soap *Ryan's Hope* and earned three Emmy Awards playing Maeve Ryan. Like myself (and come to think of it, like all the ladies at the audition that day back in 1949), Helen did very well in this business but never cracked through to that top layer of lasting fame. I guess you could consider all of us girls the workhorses of show business.

For the tour of *Touch and Go*, I replaced Nancy Andrews, who had played the part on Broadway. In the New York production, Nancy had done a song entitled "Miss Platt Selects Mate," which had stopped the show in New York. As the star, Helen Gallagher decided she would do that song in London, and I was allowed to replace it with a song of my own choosing. *Touch and Go* was a great success, but it turned out that the English audiences could not relate to "Miss Platt," a song about an American debutante, and the song flopped—a lucky break for me. For my spot, I tried out a couple of comic songs by my old friend Earl Brent. The first one, "I Called Him Al, 'Cause That's His Name" wasn't quite right, so I finally chose "I Looked Under a Log and He Was There." Good choice. To my utter delight, on opening night in London the people seated in the gallery screamed, "We want Ballard! We want Ballard!"

For those of you who don't know, the gallery is the highest balcony, and, of course, seats up there are a lot cheaper than those on the main floor. I had an Irish Cockney dresser, Patti, for that show. One day I gave Patti a ticket to see another show from the front row, and she refused to take it. In her thick Cockney accent, she said, "Ow, no, Miss Kaiye, 'at's not fo' the lawykes of me." She preferred to watch from her perch in the gallery—the Irish Eliza Doolittle!

That reminds me. I was in a pub one night listening to a woman singing "In the Still of the Night" in perfectly beautiful English. All of a sudden, she saw someone she knew come in at the back of the room and shouted, "Mite ya in the back 'a St. Georges's, luv!" and then continued singing as if she were a Park Avenue chanteuse! I love the English!

You know, I have to say, for all the infighting and backstabbing, show business is still like a large, albeit dysfunctional, family. Show people work very hard and learn to be open with each other in a very short amount of time. Our common struggle bonds us to all the other performers around the world whom we may never even meet.

In April 1950, very soon after the *Touch and Go* company got to England, the legendary ballet dancer Vaslav Nijinsky died. The dancers in our show, who called themselves The Debonaires, asked me to accompany them to Nijinsky's funeral. I hate to admit this, but at the time I had no idea who the hell Nijinsky was. We got to the service and I was stunned. It looked more like a Halloween costume party than a funeral. All the dancers came in full stage makeup, with eyes sparkling and lots of glitter everywhere. I thought, "What fun!"

Nijinsky's peers had turned an event I always thought of as somber and depressing into quite a production in and of itself. The great dance partners Anton Dolin and Alicia Markova came. In fact, it seemed like every dancer in the world was there. There was so much respect, admiration, and love for this great performer, and it was shown with such pageantry. I had never experienced this kind of theatrical ritual before. Here were all these bizarre, eccentric people staging a musical spectacle that was downright joyous, and very comforting to them. It had all the elements I had loved about the Catholic Church, without any of the guilt.

Touch and Go ran for ten months, so after a while I decided I needed to hire a cook. There was so little time between shows that I didn't want to waste it shopping for groceries and cooking. (We've already covered my affinity for domestic chores.) So I hired the son of the lady from whom I rented my apartment. His name was Clay. Clay Freud. Freud?! It couldn't be. But it was. When I rented the apartment, I had no idea that my landlady was Matilda Freud, one of Sigmund Freud's daughters! When I found out, I immediately asked her what her famous father was really like. She looked at me for a second, then took her forefinger and moved it in circles beside her forehead, the international sign for "He was nuts!" I thought that was hilarious, and yet it didn't stop me from spending a fortune on psychoanalysis in coming years!

By the way, Sigmund Freud's grandson was a great cook. World War II had been over for just five years, and food was still being rationed in England. Clay was very creative when it came to making excellent casseroles. (God only knows what was in them.)

We did two shows a day, seven days a week at the Prince of Wales Theatre. It was a very exhausting schedule. So exhausting that one evening I turned down a dinner invitation from Richard Burton. He came to the performance with Glynis Johns and Jean Simmons and introduced himself to me after the show. I kick myself to this day for begging off. I mean, looking back on it, so what if I had gone and fallen asleep in my soup? It was Richard Burton! Years later, in New York, I was backstage after attending the opening night of Mr. Burton's *Hamlet* and I bumped into Elizabeth Taylor. She looked at me and said, "You're the one who refused to have dinner with my husband, aren't you?" Oh my God, how did she know that? Was it really possible that my name had passed between Richard Burton and Elizabeth Taylor's lips? How exciting!

While I was abroad, I got the chance to do two Royal Command Performances, one at Windsor Castle and the other at the London Palladium. The Windsor Castle performance was a party given for the Royal Guards. Kay Medford, Jessie Royce Landis, and several other notable entertainers performed. I was beside myself with excitement at the opportunity to meet royalty. Then, of course, when I was introduced to Princess Margaret, I could not think of one intelligent thing to say, so I stammered, "Gee, I'm just crazy about your mother and father!" She smiled and told me that she had enjoyed a certain impression I did and added that she always thought she did a rather good Bing Crosby impression herself. I smiled, too. I'm sure as Margaret moved down the line we both thought, "Hmm, odd girl."

I also met Princess Elizabeth, who is nearly the same age I am. It's hard to imagine that she has been on the throne for more than fifty years! At the time, of course, she had no idea how soon she would be queen of England. But maybe she was in training, because I have to say, she seemed much more formal than Margaret did. Elizabeth's mother struck me as more down to earth than her daughter. Perhaps it was being born a commoner, but when the Queen looked at you, you had the feeling that she was greeting a long-lost friend. Who knows, she may have been thinking about what she was going to have for dinner, but I found the future Queen Mum to be very warm and inviting.

King George VI was in poor health at the time and wore heavy makeup in public to try and hide the seriousness of his condition. He would be dead less than three years later. Imagine, just like Roosevelt, he was able to hide an ailment from the public. Not possible these days.

What was it that impressed me so about England and the royal family? I guess it was the idea that their country, so rich in history, has a physical emblem right there to look up to for guidance, a symbol that is higher than the people. (Must be another part of my Catholic upbringing that stuck with me: No Italian home is ever without a picture of the Pope.) Our leaders in America serve for only a short period of time, whereas English monarchs might not have the power they once did, but they can rule over several generations. There is something to be said for the devotion and loyalty a reign like that can inspire.

The King and Queen were also impressive to me because they set the standard for graciousness and proper behavior. (Not a requirement for our leaders over here.) Although I have to admit, I once caught two members of the royal family in a less than gracious moment. I was standing in line in the drugstore of the St. Regis Hotel in New York, directly behind the Duke and Duchess of Windsor. They were buying a product to control bathroom odor when the Duchess absentmindedly scratched her behind. Well, she was American, after all.

Lately, both of our countries have been focused much too much on the failures of our leaders as human beings. Scandals are uncovered in order to bring the mighty down into the gutter with everyone else. I admit it, I read those gossip magazines, too. They are juicy forms of quick entertainment. But in the quest to know if Princess Diana was pregnant when she died, or how many interns Bill Clinton was involved with, we have lost something. We have lost our heroes. Do we really think the men on Mount Rushmore were saints? I am concerned that we have no more great heroes for our children to grow up emulating. I had heroes. As unrealistic as our images of people like Winston Churchill and Franklin Roosevelt might have been, they inspired me and gave me something to shoot for.

When *Touch and Go* closed, I made one of the biggest mistakes I ever made by not staying in England. I received an offer to perform in another show, but I was so terribly homesick that I turned it down. I had sailed to England on the *Queen Mary* and returned home on the *Ile-de-France*. As soon as the ship docked I called John Murray Anderson to say I was home. Instead of the fond greeting I expected, he was furious with me and yelled, "Kimmer, why on earth didn't you stay in England!?" "Go back," he demanded. "Go back!" I told him I was homesick and missed my friends, and he said, "Don't you know that once you are a success in England you will always be a success? In this country, you are only as successful as your last performance! Go back, Kimmer. Go back and call me transatlantic!"

John Murray Anderson was right about America. We have always been a throwaway culture. Maybe it's because we're such a young nation—this country is like an adolescent who doesn't yet know the value of hard work and perseverance. I think that's why we have such a huge fear of growing old in this country. We don't want to be discarded. Anyway, I was home, and so back to work I went. Remember my Bert Lahr experience? If not, glance back at chapter three. *Two on the Aisle* was the dose of reality that left me once again retreating to the nightclubs and to Greenwich Village, just as it was about to explode. But first I took a job touring with yet another vaudevillian comic in *Top Banana*.

Phil Silvers

Phil Silvers was one of the great burlesque comics. Later known for playing Sergeant Ernie Bilko on television, Phil had a short career in MGM musicals and success on the Broadway stage. One of those Broadway shows, *Top Banana*, was an upscale burlesque especially tailored for Phil's comic talents. *Top Banana* opened at the Winter Garden Theatre in 1951 and was an instant smash. It started as a few loosely written pages of material, but Hy Kraft wrote the book, with contributions from burlesque and vaudeville veterans like Phil, Joey and Herbie Faye, and Jack Albertson, and with original songs by Johnny Mercer to string these bits together. The show ran almost a year and won Phil Silvers a Tony Award.

Filling out the cast in the leading-lady role was singer-comedienne Rose Marie. Rose was another vaudeville veteran, having begun her career at age five, as Baby Rose Marie, with her own radio show on NBC. When *Top Banana* went on the road, Rose Marie didn't want to be away from her husband and small daughter, so they looked for a replacement. Audrey Meadows, who had stepped in for a few weeks during the New York run when Rose had surgery for vocal nodes, was offered the part. I'd just returned from England at the time, and Audrey called me and said, "Gee, Kaye, I have an offer to do a television show with Jackie Gleason called *The Honeymooners*." I told her to be happy and take it. Television was becoming the place to be. I didn't know that a short time later I'd be offered the same role in *Top Banana*!

I've worked with many male comics over the years, and as brilliant as they can be on stage, some can also make life miserable offstage. I'm sorry to say that was my experience with Mr. Silvers. Shortly after I began the tour with Phil he asked me to come to his place and go to bed with him. No subtlety, no wine or flowers, just a flat-out proposition. I replied, "Oh, gee, Phil, I can't tonight, I just ate onions!" As a young, single woman in show business, I had heard similar requests before and tried to make light of Phil's proposition. Well, Phil didn't take my refusal lightly. From that moment on, Phil Silvers did his best to make me unhappy and my job as unpleasant as possible. He couldn't (or wouldn't) get past my rejection.

As soon as we arrived in California, Phil wanted to fire me and have Rose Marie return to the show. I had been contracted for ten months, and I was determined to stick it out, no matter how cruel Phil became. He started to make nasty comments around me. Knowing I was insecure about my looks, he would call me over by saying things like, "Come here, boy."

The whole situation was such a shame, because I enjoyed doing the material in the show. I tried to take the high road and smooth the relationship over. I even cooked Phil dinner a couple of times, but nothing made up for my romantic snub. I suppose it didn't help the situation to be traveling with another strong-willed woman who wouldn't back down to Phil. You see, by this point, Liz Smith was my road manager, and I was extremely grateful to have her accompanying me. We were in Chicago one of the times I invited Phil over for dinner. We were all watching *The Sixty-Four Thousand Dollar Question* on television, and one of the questions was "Who discovered gravity?" "Isaac Newton," Liz answered without hesitation. Phil became enraged at her for answering the question so quickly. He was very chauvinistic toward women in general and resented Liz for being so smart.

Some men, especially comics with very little formal education (Phil began performing at the age of twelve), always perceive women with intellects to be threats. Since Liz is not the type to waste her time pampering Phil Silver's (or anyone else's) bruised ego, I played referee and did my best to keep Liz and Phil separated for the remainder of the tour.

I have to admit, I took guilty pleasure a few times watching Phil squirm when he'd get nervous backstage. One of those times was when Cary Grant came to see the show in Los Angeles. I had met Mr. Grant before, and he was always congenial and gracious. I once ran into him and Desi Arnaz at the Hollywood Park Race Track. He was so gorgeous and fit, yet every time I saw him he was eating! I asked him, "Mr. Grant, how in the world do you stay so thin?" His reply was, "Kaye, I think thin." I told him I'd already tried that approach and it didn't work.

The evening Cary Grant saw *Top Banana*, Phil was so petrified that he could barely speak his lines. I nudged him right before he went onstage and asked, "What's your problem, Phil?" I knew that realizing people could see his flop sweat would only make him more nervous.

Not very nice, I know, but it sure felt good. Recalling this experience reminds me once again that being a single woman in this business, especially at the time I was trying to establish myself (in the 1940s, '50s, and '60s), meant continually playing a role offstage as well as on. I'm sure it was the same for women trying to break into any other predominantly male profession, but in show business these games seemed to be particularly clichéd. You were always expected to have that strong man on your arm, protecting you. He could be a husband, an agent, a boyfriend—it didn't matter, as long as he was a man. It didn't even matter if he was abusive, or ended up taking all of your money. In order for a woman to be socially (and therefore professionally) acceptable, a knight in shining armor had to be there to rescue and take care of the helpless damsel.

I want to mention that this of course is only my experience with Phil Silvers. Rose Marie writes in her biography that Phil was nothing but charming and gracious to her and her daughter. Now, she was married at the time, so perhaps that made the difference. But I can't help thinking Rose would understand my predicament, because she also reveals in her book that when it came time to film the movie of *Top Banana*, her part (the same part I did on the road) was almost entirely cut out after she spurned the advances of the film's producer. Hmm . . . where was Phil to the rescue?

Chapter Six

The Village, Brando, and the Actors Studio

I n the early 1950s, the tough-minded independence I had acquired as a child was sure getting a chance to bloom again. By refusing Phil Silvers's advances, I kept my dignity intact. By leaving *Two on the Aisle*, I kept my integrity intact. But I also left the $550 a week paycheck that went with it, and now I had to worry about my bank account.

I have always been very proud of the fact that during all of my adult life I have never made a penny at anything other than performing. Not that there's anything wrong with waiting tables in a restaurant or temping in an office, but I wouldn't have lasted a day at those jobs. I'm very lucky show business has kept me employed.

As far as I can see, the 1950s were the last age of innocence, both for New York City and for the world. Back then, most people walked around town without ever giving a second thought to being harmed. I could walk from midtown to downtown Manhattan all by myself and never worry about being bothered by anyone.

After I left *Two On The Aisle*, I moved into an apartment in Greenwich Village. If memory serves me correctly, it was at 149 West Fourth Street. I knew that was the apartment I wanted when they told me that John Barrymore had lived across the street and that he would come home and fall down drunk on the steps. Any connection to Hollywood was good enough for me. I got a job appearing five times a week on Mel Tormé's daytime television show (the first TV show ever to be broadcast in color). I appeared for twenty-four weeks with Mel, and we did a running gag in which he would come up and ask me to play my flute just before they went to commercial.

The Village has always been a haven for creative people and controversy, and in the early 1950s it was an exciting, vibrant place to live. The Village also offered a lot of opportunities for a variety artist like myself to perform. (Artists from Barbra Streisand to Andy Warhol to Jimi Hendrix got their start in the Village.) While I waited for my breakthrough role on Broadway, I earned my food and rent money performing in the clubs. I worked all over the city, but my two favorite nightclubs, the Blue Angel and the Bon Soir, were in the Village. And oh, the people I met!

The Blue Angel was an extraordinary supper club owned by Max Gordon and Herbert Jacoby. Legendary impresario Max Gordon also owned the Village Vanguard. Herbert was an ultra-chic homosexual who had owned a nightclub in Paris. The Blue Angel, complete with quilted walls, resembled a very elegant and sophisticated coffin, and Herbert was the tuxedoed, superbly classy, very French undertaker. He was known to all the notable people in New York throughout the 1930s, '40s, and '50s as the Prince of Darkness!

Herbert Jacoby adored the performers in his club and demanded that they get the respect they deserved from the clientele. If anyone talked during the show, Herbert would calmly walk to the offending table, tear up the check, and ask them to leave. He was not, however, the best judge of talent. He once advised Lena Horne to get out of the business because she did not have what it took to make it as a singer, and he fired Sarah Vaughn for not staying on the melody! Oh, well.

Let me say a word (or several) about working in clubs. I have often thought that if I had chosen just one particular way to market myself, I might have gotten farther in this business. There is a tendency in show business to categorize talent. For example, you are a singer, a dancer, or an actor. You are the straight man or the comic. Producers, directors, and even the general public find it a lot more efficient to put you into a nice little cubbyhole and keep you there. There are advantages to remaining in that little cubbyhole. Someone might find the perfect role for you, and in that vehicle you might go straight to the top. The disadvantage is in trying to find work. By specializing, a performer cuts the possible job offers in half! Since I could work in any medium, from big bands to nightclubs to television, and I sang as well as did comedy, people didn't know how to categorize me as a performer. The fact that, when I needed to, I continued to make a living in nightclubs rather than use them as a stepping-stone, may have kept me employed, but I believe it hurt my ability to get roles on Broadway and in films.

Years ago, if you were a movie star and then you did stage work or, God forbid, a television program, it was a signal that your career was over. That hierarchy exists in the business even today. Now, however, the road to all things seems to be television first. But at the time I'm talking about now, back in the 1950s, work was work.

Just as in vaudeville, in the nightclubs you worked and worked on your act until you had it polished. You wanted your act to be original and fresh, so performers were naturally very protective of their material. I remember I did a number at the Blue Angel about five trained fleas that Mel Brooks helped me develop. One night Charlie Chaplin was in the audience, *the* Charlie Chaplin. I did my flea bit and it went over really well. Maybe too well. Someday, rent a copy of Mr. Chaplin's 1952 film *Limelight*, and you'll see that part of my act!

I worked several eight-week runs at the Blue Angel for nearly two years, doing two shows a night. There were no days off, but I got to meet some incredible people. It was not unusual to have Cole Porter and Josephine Baker in the audience and to share the stage with performers like Harry Belafonte, the Smothers Brothers, Jean Sablon, Pearl Bailey, Barbara Cook, Larry Storch, and many others. One of the famous faces in the audience with whom I became acquainted was Dorothy Parker. She asked me after a show one night, "Kaye, all these songs women sing are about how he beats me, he drinks, he screws around. Doesn't anyone ever do a torch song about a man because he's nice to you?"

One afternoon Dorothy asked me to accompany her to a Voice of Freedom luncheon. Voice of Freedom? Sounds patriotic; besides, I was still the star-struck little girl from Cleveland and could hardly believe my eyes when I saw celebrities like Jose Ferrer, John Garfield, and the famous poet Louis Untermeyer attending as well.

The next day a friend of mine, Dr. Eizenstat, called me and asked, "Kaye, were you at a luncheon yesterday with Dorothy Parker?"

"Oh, yes!" I answered, quite pleased with myself. "I met so many celebrities, it was great! How did you know?"

"Your name was in today's issue of the *Daily Worker*," he replied. "Now, Kaye, I know you're not involved in politics, and you're not smart enough to have become a Communist! So you'd better not attend any more luncheons with Miss Parker."

A Communist?! I had no political views whatsoever! It's just that I was always so absolutely enamored with interesting, provocative artists. And interesting, provocative artists are always the ones who seem to get into trouble.

Regardless of her politics, I was thrilled to know the witty Miss Dorothy Parker. I am reminded of the time that Robert Benchley, Dorothy's close friend, went to visit her in the hospital. Dorothy said, "Bob, ring for the nurse. That will insure us of forty-five minutes of complete privacy." Another time, she stole the sign off the men's room door and put it on hers because she wanted company!

I've always admired people for having the courage of their convictions. Was it innocence or cowardice to simply not have any convictions at all? Well, it wasn't long before that would change. I was living in Greenwich Village and was about to meet a group of people who had nothing but convictions—and strong ones!

I met Marlon Brando for the first time when I went to my friend Maggie Eversoll's home with the writer Sidney Shaw. Maggie was an artist who had a large apartment on Washington Square. About this same time I met Maureen Stapleton, who introduced me to Eli Wallach and Anne Jackson. Eli and Anne had recently married and lived in a basement apartment on Eighth Street. Imagine all these future icons of twentieth-century American theater struggling to make a name for themselves and living practically next door to me. It was an exciting time.

Maureen was a staunch Democrat her whole life. During the Kennedy campaign in 1960 she gave me a rocking chair (because John Kennedy liked rocking chairs). The night of the election we all sat around waiting for the results. It was freezing cold outside, but we had a lot of food and Maureen had bought several bottles of champagne. The first returns that came in showed the Democrats with only 14 votes in New Hampshire. Maureen shouted, "Okay, we're in trouble, let's open the champagne!" Any excuse to open the champagne! We lost a great actress in March 2006 when Maureen passed away at age eighty, and I lost a wonderful friend. I knew Maureen had been in poor health in recent years, and all that smoking and drinking had finally taken a toll, but she was someone I just figured would always be around. It may come as a shock to those of you reading this, but nobody is going to be around for-ever, so listen to me—live life to the fullest, and give one of your won-derful friends a call.

Maureen's apartment, on West Fifty-second Street, and Maggie's apartment were gathering places for just about anyone who aspired to be exotic and eccentric. And let's face it, we all did. One of Maureen's friends, Jane Forman, dyed her hair purple long before the punk rock craze.

The champion of these exotics was Janice Mars, a friend of Marlon Brando. She was a very good singer, but completely over the top as a personality. Janice shaved her hair in what looked like a bad scull cap and dressed as flamboyantly as she could manage. During the time I knew her, Janice was having an affair with a black man and, later, a white woman. I remember the woman bore a striking resemblance to Spencer Tracy. Maureen commented, "Tennessee Williams would think of Janice Mars as just plain folk!" Forget about Cleveland, I loved this place!

I don't know if it was a conscious decision, but somehow being around all these serious actor folks for the first time influenced me to try and seek some formal training. I mean, hanging out with people like Marlon Brando and Shelley Winters can play on your insecurities. The new Method acting technique was the rage. All anybody talked about was Stanislavski and Strasberg. I had never had an acting class in my life, but as I said, my insecurity got the better of me, and somehow both Janice and I auditioned and got into Lee Strasberg's class at the Actors Studio.

It would be ludicrous for me to criticize what people like Elia Kazan and Lee Strasberg achieved. They, along with their devoted students, changed the face of modern drama, both onstage and in the movies. But my experience with the Method was, shall we say, short-lived.

I remember the day when Marilyn Monroe got up in class, flailed her arms around, and jogged her torso while singing the loosen-up number "Look Down, Look Down That Lonesome Road." The rest of the class was mesmerized. Of course they were. It was Marilyn Monroe, for God's sake. Everything was bouncing up and down and left and right. I mean, who needed to warm up with a body like that?

Mr. Strasberg tried to get me to really visualize and internalize what I was doing. No luck. Okay, I'd try harder. One day the entire class was sitting and watching George Peppard rehearse a scene. He was holding onto an imaginary curtain as he stared off into space for what seemed an eternity. "What is he doing?" I whispered to the person next to me. "Shhhhh! He's watching the rain." I thought, "Okay, that's enough of this bullshit." Shortly after telling me that I wasn't *feeeeeling* the imaginary glass I was holding, Mr. Strasberg suggested that I was not taking the exercises seriously and that perhaps I didn't really have anything to gain from his class. I agreed.

This might sound egotistical, but over the years I have played many parts that made me realize I understood what people were trying to get to in those classes. I really connected with my roles in shows like *The Robber Bridegroom, A Murder of Crows, High Spirits*, and Ronald Harwood's *Quartet* (directed by one of the best directors I've ever experienced, Vivian Matalon). While playing one of the grandmothers in Joe DiPietro's brilliant play *Over the River and Through the Woods*, I knew that I was good. I poured everything I had into that role and it was easy, like a second skin. I knew this lady. She was my Nana. She came as naturally to me as waking up in the morning. If that is what Method acting is, then I completely agree with it. But how many great actors have there been who can just do it, without the classes? Paul Muni, Spencer Tracy, Katherine Hepburn, Jimmy Stewart, Henry Fonda, and the list goes on and on.

That leads me back to Brando. He was another actor who could just do it. But it took being enrolled in Erwin Piscator's Dramatic Workshop of the New School for Social Research (even the title reeks of pretension) to discover it. Marlon eventually studied acting with Stella Adler and, as everyone knows, became an overnight sensation as Stanley Kowalski in Tennessee Williams's *A Streetcar Named Desire*.

Marlon and I had known each other since the late 1940s, and he invited me to see a preview of *Streetcar* in Boston. He was unbelievably brilliant and magnetic, and this was truly one of the great evenings in the theater. I was astonished to find out that Marlon was so terrified on opening night that the director, Elia Kazan, had to literally push him onto the stage. Marlon also adored Maureen Stapleton and Maggie Eversoll and was a frequent guest at their gatherings. He played the bongo drums at the time, and like every other woman on the planet, I found him irresistibly attractive. And yes, he and I had a brief affair. When the physical part of the relationship was over, we became good friends and often had dinner together. I remember he took me to a Greek restaurant one evening and introduced me to baklava. I must have gained three pounds that night! We had a common love of food. He used to tell me, "Kaye, you are going to get fat." Well, my dear, you were right! But let's just say "heavy."

I was also with Marlon the first time I went to Fire Island. He wanted me to meet his sister, Jocelyn, and so we stayed the weekend. Marlon was absolutely brilliant at doing accents, and so for two days he pretended to be a member of the royal family and spoke in a perfect, crisp British accent. You know, from his later film roles and political causes, you might get the idea that Marlon was a very serious, brooding type of guy. I think the media eventually strangled him and turned Marlon into the recluse he became in later years. But that wasn't the Marlon I knew, especially that weekend on Fire Island. He was lighthearted and hilarious, and we had a wonderful time.

Marlon was also very loyal. He phoned one afternoon and said, "Come on, I want you to see a friend of mine." He took me to the Village Vanguard, where Wally Cox was performing. Wally became known for his television role as Mr. Peepers and later as a regular panelist on *Hollywood Squares.* His mild-mannered milquetoast persona was just a character. He wasn't like that in real life at all. Wally had a very well-developed body, but his neck was so small it made the collars of his shirts appear too large and gave him the appearance of weakness. He and Marlon were roommates and would often ride their motorcycles around the city together. Imagine, Stanley Kowalski and Mr. Peepers in black leather jackets—talk about the Odd Couple!

I don't think Marlon ever really enjoyed being onstage. For one thing, he was very uncomfortable with public adulation. And like so many actors who give everything to a performance, he probably got tired and bored doing the same show every night. I think that is why the theater lost Marlon to the movies. And what a loss it was.

One of the last times I saw Marlon was just before he left for England to star in Charlie Chaplin's *The Countess from Hong Kong.* Marlon said, "Let's go over to Maureen's house tonight. I'm having a few old girlfriends meet me there." I got to Maureen's and found at least thirty other women there. Marlon had dated us all! Marlon was the last to arrive, and when he walked in with his best friend, Christian Marquand, and four beautiful Asian women at his side, every woman in the room died instantly of jealousy. But you have to hand it to Marlon. How many other men could invite all their ex-girlfriends to the same party and have them leave still adoring him?

Marlon once said that he was the antithesis of his Stanley Kowalski character. In many ways this was true: Marlon was very intellectual and refined. However, there was an undeniably macho, even chauvinistic side to him. Marlon said that he did not believe that monogamy was natural. He believed that men were meant to sow their seed in many different directions. And my Lord, he certainly did. Well, it's not that (during our brief fling), I wasn't tempted to be one of those directions. I mean, come on, he was stunningly gorgeous. But on the off-chance that the baby would look like me, I just couldn't take the risk!

Marlon, Sidney Shaw, and I tried to make money composing poems for a guy who was paying a buck a poem. One of the deeper ones went:

> *We took a trip*
> *to the land of me*
> *A land so far away*
> *Although we haven't reached it yet*
> *When we get there*
> *we hope to stay.*

Shortly before his death, Marlon called my home in Rancho Mirage, but I was not in. A friend answered and asked who was calling. Marlon said, "Tell Kaye that Minnie the Moocher is calling."

"Well, Minnie," my friend replied, "you'll have to mooch around some other time because Kaye is at the casino!" I spoke to Marlon later that evening, and even after all the turmoil and grief he had gone through in recent years, he was just as delightful as ever. I told him I was busy writing this book and that I could still remember every moment I spent with him. Marlon replied, "Every little moment, Kaye? I can't even remember who I've slept with!" It's true, my darling Marlon, I recall everything. And I'm glad we had just a phone call, because I wanted us to remember each other just as we were. That way we'll both remain young, gorgeous, and thin! By the way, that phone call came about through Marlon's close friend George Englund, who wrote one of the better biographies of Marlon. Thank you, George. I sent Marlon a card for his eightieth birthday, and that was the last contact I had with him. The sensation of losing a friend is always unreal, even more so if the friend happens to be an icon and the world mourns along with you.

After performing at the Blue Angel, I went directly to the Bon Soir, where I did one show a night and two on the weekends, with Sundays off. A whole Sunday to myself. It was heaven. The Bon Soir was owned by Ernest Sgroi and Phil Pagano, who were reputed members of the Mafia. I can't say whether that is true or not, but I know that Vito Genovese was a frequent guest at the club. At the time I had no idea that Mr. Genovese's other name was "The Godfather." Oh, Marlon, how life circles around and mixes together! What I did know was that these men were always polite, well-dressed, and quite generous. Phil Pagano threw the greatest parties for us on closing nights, complete with dinner and gifts for everyone in the show.

The Bon Soir was in a basement on Eighth Street in the Village. One large room with every table facing the stage. I worked there with my friends Larry Storch and Alice Ghostley, along with Sylvia Syms, Tony and Eddie, a world famous pantomime team, Felicia Saunders (a singer, who like Bernadette Peters, could cry at the same measure of music every night), and a group called The Big Three, whose lead singer was Cass Elliot, later to be known as Mama Cass.

Just like the Blue Angel, the Bon Soir boasted more celebrities in the audience than onstage. At the height of the club's popularity, people like Anna Magniani, Gregory Peck, David Brinkley, Judy Holliday, and the Kennedys all came in. One night during my act, I looked down to see Shirley MacLaine sitting in front of me playing solitaire! (Where was Herbert Jacoby when you needed him!?) I sang three songs at the Bon Soir that went on to become smash hits—for other people. I did "Fly Me to the Moon" before Frank what's-his-name got hold of it, and another great song, "My Coloring Book," that was to be the first hit for the young songwriting team of Kander and Ebb. After singing "My Coloring Book" at the club, I wanted to sing it on *The Perry Como Show*, but Nick Vanoff, the producer, wouldn't allow it. Nick told me, "Kaye, you are not the singer on this show; you are the comedienne." This is a perfect example of how people want to pigeonhole you. So Nick had Sandy Stewart do the song, and it was a big hit for her. And later, it was an even bigger hit for another Bon Soir alumna, Barbra Streisand.

The third song I introduced really was my song. After my disappointment with "My Coloring Book," Fred Ebb offered to write me another song. (More on what happened to that one in a minute!) There would be many more nightclubs in my future, but now I was finally about to find *that role* on Broadway.

Fred Ebb

Now I am calm, safe and serene;
Heartache and hurt are no longer
a part of the scene.
Isn't this better? The way it should be?
Better for him, much better for him.
And oh so much better for me.

"Isn't This Better," from *Funny Lady*

F red Ebb wrote the most wonderful lyrics. He first came to my
attention while I was working at the Bon Soir in the late 1950s. I
was doing somewhat sophisticated comedy songs at the time, and
Fred was writing songs that were right up my alley—songs like "Merrill,
Lynch, Pierce, Fenner, Smith and Bean," about a wealthy society lady lovingly singing about her stock portfolio. His collaborator at the time was
a man named Paul Klein. After Paul, Fred teamed up with Norman
Martin and finally, a couple of years later, found just the right fit with
John Kander.

The right fit is an understatement. The team of Kander and Ebb is
among a small group of songwriters who have built on the great legacy
of people like the Gershwins, Rodgers and Hammerstein, Rodgers and
Hart, Jule Styne, and Lerner and Loewe. At a time when the American
musical was growing continually out of favor and harder to produce, these
two gentlemen helped reinvent musical comedy with a fresh dose of reality. In doing so, they have given us some of the last quarter-century's
most legendary and enduring songs. It's hard to remember that there
even was a time before the musicals *Cabaret* or *Chicago*—hard to remember a time when everyone couldn't sing at least the first line of "New
York, New York"!

I remember. As I have said a hundred times before, I have always been
attracted first and foremost to talent, and Fred Ebb had talent to spare!
Once I began singing his songs, Freddy and I became very close friends.
In fact, I have to admit, I was probably a little bit in love with him. His

material was so fresh and so exciting. I always went out of my way to help him get the attention I knew he deserved. Because of my celebrity, I was able to sing his songs on the *The Jack Paar Show, The Johnny Carson Show*, and *The Mike Douglas Show*, and when I did, I never failed to plug Fred's name.

Later, while I was working in *Carnival*, I was making a pretty good living, so I would give Fred money every week. Not because I had to, but because I respected what it took to be a writer. He did not have much income at the time, so I would pay him for special material that I would use in my act or on guest appearances.

I mentioned in the last chapter about not being allowed to sing "My Coloring Book" on *The Perry Como Show*, and how it became a hit for other people. Well, Fred felt very bad about that, so he offered to write me another song. I said something like, "Yes, maybe next time I'll be lucky!" (referring to my many experiences of almost making it in this business).

A few days later, Fred came to me with the song "Maybe This Time." I was delighted with it. It was a beautiful song, and Fred said, "Kaye, this is your song forever." I recorded the song on a single for Reprise Records, and I'm sorry to say, it didn't go anywhere. But, hey, it was my song.

Enter Judy Garland. Fred, of course, was a huge fan of Judy, just like everyone else was. He wanted to meet her, so I introduced them. A couple of years later, Fred and I went to see Judy's daughter Liza in her first off-Broadway show, a revival of *Best Foot Forward*. In the decade that followed, he shaped and guided and almost single-handedly gave birth to the legendary Liza with a Z. He helped that young girl with the abundance of raw talent and huge gamin eyes develop into a true triple-threat performer.

Fred broke my heart when he gave "Maybe This Time" to Liza to record. Adding insult to injury, my arrangement was copied. When I found out about it, Fred looked me straight in the eye and told me, "Tommy Valando, the publisher, gave it to Liza! I would never do that to you, Kaye." What Fred didn't know was that another publisher by the name of Frank Military (now the head of Warner Music) called me and told me that Fred was lying to me. He said, "We didn't even know that song existed until Fred gave it to Liza to sing." Like a fool, I went to Liza's opening night at the Plaza. Just before she sang "Maybe This Time," she announced, "This song was written especially for me." Fred Ebb and I did not speak for years. Even after all this time it hurts to recall this experience.

But that's show business. And that's why I include this story about a song. Anybody who gets into this business had better be warned that show business is just that—a business, and business is business.

But if you're lucky, sometimes friendships do stand the test of time (and money). Freddy and I patched up our differences. I could not remain angry at someone I truly loved and respected. I remember seeing him across the room at one of the performances of his show *The Rink*, and that was all it took; we were instantly back together. I forgave Fred right there on the spot.

I'm sorry to say I do not know John Kander the way I knew Fred. John is much more elusive. Nobody knows much about him, and I guess he likes it that way. Fred called his partner "the Christ Child" because he's like a saint who has managed to stay away from, and remain untarnished by, show biz. Good for him!

Up until the day Fred died, he and John got together every day to work. World-famous multi-millionaires who still punched the nine-to-five clock. Why not? They loved what they did and so did we—we always will.

The last time I saw Fred I was still working on this book. My co-writer and I had dinner with Fred in New York, and he seemed a bit frail. He told me he had taken a stress test recently and that the results weren't good. But anyone who knew Freddy knew that you had to take his health complaints with a grain of salt—he always had some ailment. That night I took him to see *The Boy from Oz*, the musical biography of Peter Allen, whom we both adored. I told him I had seen it before (as had he), and I went on and on about how terrific I thought Hugh Jackman was. I told Freddy that, of course, we would have to go backstage after the show or at least send a note. He said no and told me that if I tried to, he wouldn't go into the theater. We sat there listening to Isabel Keating performing so wonderfully as Judy Garland, and I remembered being able to introduce Judy to my gentle, talented friend sitting next to me. My friend who was now a bona fide legend, who had a show running just down the street, who'd just been honored at the Kennedy Center. My Freddy Ebby, who was too shy to meet Hugh Jackman.

Chapter Seven

My Golden Apple— The Cover of LIFE

I auditioned for the female lead in *The Golden Apple* seven times. Each time I wore a different fur piece, all borrowed from Eddie Cantor's daughter, Marilyn. I wanted the producers to think I really didn't need the job. Once I had been cast, they never saw me in a fur again.

Oh, those auditions! Lisa Kirk, known for starring roles in the original Broadway productions of *Kiss Me, Kate* (for which I had auditioned) and *Allegro*, and later for dubbing Rosalind Russell's singing voice in the film version of *Gypsy*, competed with me during the first six auditions. On one of the last callbacks, the director asked me to come back the next day and be funny and seductive. So I came in and bumped, and slinked, and strutted through my song, and when I was done:

Director: Uh, yes, Miss Ballard, but can you be seductive?
Me: That was seductive.
Director: *(Silence)* Oh.
Me: Who am I supposed to be in this anyway?
Director: Helen of Troy.
Me: Oooh, Helen of Troy! She's beautiful.
Director: Uh, she's a little . . . different in this.
Me: Different?
Director: Yes. She's seductive, but plain.
Me: Seductive but plain?
Director: Plain, but willing.
Me: Plain but willing. You mean ugly but kind?

Well, I must have done something right, because they asked me to return again the following day and sing something from the show. And this time Lisa Kirk was nowhere to be seen. I had the part! *The Golden Apple* had no dialogue. It was a musical fable based on classical Greek characters and stories, and set in Washington State between 1900 and 1910. All the makings of a smash hit, right? To make matters worse, critics claimed *The Golden Apple* was years ahead of its time. In other words, the show didn't have a chance.

The cast of *The Golden Apple* included many talented and interesting people. Jack Whiting played Mayor Hector, only a year after playing another soft-shoeing mayor in the musical *Hazel Flagg*. Bibi Osterwald, with whom I had auditioned for several of the same parts over the years, was terrific as Lovey Mars. She knocked 'em dead with her siren song, "By Goona-Goona Lagoon." Bibi came to be known as everyone's understudy. She understudied Carol Channing in *Hello, Dolly!* all those years and never got to go on. (She and another well-known understudy, Leanora Nemitz, have found a little bit of lasting fame in the musical *Nunsense*, as part of Dan Goggin's lyrics in a song about being an understudy.) Also on stage with me were Stephen Douglass, Portia Nelson, and Charlotte Rae.

Oh yes, and Jerry Stiller. Jerry had a bit part in which he just skated across the stage. He was even more adorable than his son Ben is today. (If that's possible.) I also remember meeting Jerry's girlfriend at the time, Anne Meara. They eventually joined a theater group called the Compass Players, which became the Second City Comedy Troupe. A short time after Jerry and I did *The Golden Apple*, the short, funny Jewish guy and the tall, red-headed Irish Catholic girl were married. Jerry and Anne and I were having dinner a few years later in Chicago, where they were doing a revue called *Medium Rare*. The two were talking back and forth, giving each other hilarious one-liners, and I commented that they should do an act together. So, in a sense, Ed Sullivan should have thanked me: I discovered Stiller and Meara!

Jerome Moross composed the astounding score for *The Golden Apple*. Jerry was a genius who began taking piano lessons at age five and was composing by age eight. At the ripe old age of eleven, he became the youngest student ever to graduate from a New York City public high school. Jerry Moross may not have been a household name like Rodgers and Hammerstein, but by the time he passed away in July 1983, just one month short of his seventieth birthday, he had managed to compose the scores for four musicals, seventeen films (including *The Big Country* and *Rachel, Rachel*), two TV series (including *Wagon Train*), five ballets, and one full-length opera based on *Sorry, Wrong Number*. For *The Golden Apple*, this man of many and varied musical talents used the popular song-and-dance forms of turn-of-the-century America, as well as waltzes, ragtime, blues, and burlesque/vaudeville styles to create a seductive, innovative score.

Everyone in the cast was so excited about the material, and I got to introduce the pop standard "Lazy Afternoon." What a thrill! Not only was the music in *The Golden Apple* wonderful, but the lyrics and book by John LaTouche were witty, the set by Bill and Jean Eckert was creative, and Hanya Holm's choreography was superb.

The show opened off-Broadway at the Phoenix Theatre on March 11, 1954, and ran there for forty-eight performances. I was extremely nervous and excited on opening night. I guess everybody was nervous that night, because seconds before I was supposed to sing "Lazy Afternoon," my biggest number, the conductor dropped the score. I pantomimed some ridiculous bit of business with a fan for a full two minutes. (It felt like an hour!) The next day in the *Daily Mirror*, Robert Coleman described my little performance during those two agonizing minutes as ingenious. He also said that our show was the most important musical since *Oklahoma!* The *Daily News* hailed *The Golden Apple* as the best thing that had happened in and to the theater in a long, long time, and the *Journal-American* said the show was a milestone in the American musical theater. We were riding high!

When *The Golden Apple* won the New York Drama Critics Circle Award for Best Musical, a couple of investors, in partnership with the Phoenix Theatre, decided to move us uptown. On April 20, 1954, at the Alvin Theatre, on Fifty-second Street (it's now the Neil Simon Theatre) I experienced my first opening night on Broadway! They say everyone has fifteen minutes of fame, and my clock seemed to be starting to tick. I was certainly at a high point in my career. I was finally on Broadway with a role in a show I was very proud of. People were beginning to notice me. What came next still seems almost like a dream—Richard Avedon took my picture for the cover of *Life* magazine. Avedon was already quite well known, and he eventually became one of the most respected photographers of the twentieth century. I was the second of just three covers he would shoot for *Life*. The others were a fashion spread he did in January 1954 and a 1959 shot of an actress I'd run into a couple of years before in acting class. In what has become a very famous photo, a gorgeous blonde holds a diamond earring between her teeth—the subject, of course, is Marilyn Monroe, promoting her film *Gentlemen Prefer Blondes*.

While I waited anxiously for *Life* to come out, I wasn't the only one enjoying fifteen minutes of fame. Senator Joseph McCarthy was on his way to being censured by the U.S. Senate. The editors told me that my cover could be scratched if anything happened in the McCarthy hearings. The waiting was agony, but finally there it was, on May 24, 1954—my face on the cover of *Life* magazine! Why can't anything ever be perfect? It rained all that week. I had envisioned crowds of New Yorkers rushing by newsstands and seeing my face, but instead they saw piles of magazines covered up so they wouldn't get wet!

Despite all the acclaim, *The Golden Apple* ran on Broadway for only four months and lost its entire investment. The LP cast recording released at the time of the show didn't become available on CD until 1997. The crime is that we recorded only fifty minutes of that gorgeous score. Back in 1954, even when so much of popular music came from Broadway, people wouldn't have bought a cast album that was two hours long.

Ken Mandelbaum summed up the fate of *The Golden Apple* in his wonderful book *Not Since Carrie: 40 Years of Broadway Musical Flops*:

> *The Golden Apple*, perhaps the most neglected masterwork of the American musical theatre, was simply caviar to audiences more attuned to *The Pajama Game, Kismet*, and *Can-Can*, all playing nearby. Most of the shows in this book failed their audiences; it was the audience that failed *The Golden Apple*.

The show has had several off-Broadway revivals, including a production at the York Theatre in 1962, but I'm afraid that, for the most part, it is destined to be one of those long-lost treasures waiting to be rediscovered.

※

Footnote: I would like to register my disappointment that the Richard Avedon Foundation recently turned down my request to reprint my *Life* cover in this book. I originally called Dick on October 1, 2004, to ask his permission, but nobody would let me talk to him. A day later I discovered why. He had suffered a cerebral hemorrhage and passed away while on a shoot in San Antonio, Texas, the very day I called.

Chapter Eight

CINDERELLA

Richard Rodgers was a musical genius who wrote brilliant melodies. I had been singing his songs since I was old enough to walk! When I got to meet him in person, though, he seemed a bit aloof, not the sort of guy you'd expect to get close to or chum around with. I've heard his daughter, Mary, say that he was not a man who showed much emotion, even to his children. While Richard Rogers might have appeared a bit cold on the outside, there's no doubt that he poured his soul into his music. The minute he sat down at a piano you could tell that was the place where he was most at ease with the world. Throughout his long career, he wrote with several different lyricists, including Stephen Sondheim and Martin Charnin (who later wrote the smash hit musical *Annie*). With each new collaborator, Rodgers's music took on a different feel. Very late in his career, he even tried his hand at writing his own lyrics. But he will always be remembered for the incredible works he created with two very different gentlemen.

Richard Rodgers's first partner, Larry Hart, was a witty, urbane, self-loathing homosexual whose alcoholism made him very difficult to work with, and eventually killed him. Together they wrote shows like *Pal Joey*, *On Your Toes*, and *A Connecticut Yankee in King Arthur's Court*. When Larry Hart became impossibly undependable, Rodgers began to work with another genius, Oscar Hammerstein, on a musical called *Away We Go*, and this partnership eventually brought the three of us together. (By the way, *Away We Go* was renamed before it came to New York; it became *Oklahoma!*)

Oscar Hammerstein II grew up in the theater. His uncle, Oscar Hammerstein I, had been a larger-than-life showman and entrepreneur. He was an inventor, a designer, a publisher, and a builder who loved the theater and also happened to write and compose music. The first Oscar Hammerstein built ten theaters in his lifetime, seven of them on or near a place called Longacre Square (a little piece of real estate today known as Times Square). The younger Oscar found success as a lyricist and bookwriter long before teaming up with Richard Rodgers. He had written with such giants as George Gershwin, Sigmund Romberg, Vincent Youmans, and Jerome Kern, with whom he wrote what to many people is still the greatest American musical of them all, *Show Boat.*

Larry Hart's lyrics might have made Rodgers' music crackle and sparkle with wit and humor, but Oscar Hammerstein's words drove those melodies straight into your heart with a truth and beauty that made the songs seem deceptively simplistic:

> *Do I love you because you're wonderful,*
> *Or are you wonderful because I love you?*
> *Are you the sweet invention of a lover's dream?*
> *Or are you really as wonderful as you seem?*
>
> "Do I Love You Because You're Beautiful?" from
> *Cinderella,* lyrics by Oscar Hammerstein

In stark contrast to the diminutive, businesslike Richard Rodgers, Oscar Hammerstein was a teddy bear, a large, burly, soft-spoken man with a bad complexion who really couldn't sing. Yet when he stood in front of me and the rest of the cast of *Cinderella* and recited those wonderfully brilliant lyrics for the first time, tears ran down my face. The year was 1957. CBS had been desperately searching for a response to NBC's musical version of *Peter Pan,* starring Mary Martin—a huge hit when it had aired two years earlier. CBS decided to make a musical of the fairy tale *Cinderella,* with twenty-one-year-old Julie Andrews in the lead. Richard Rodgers later said that the chance to work with Julie was what sold him and Oscar Hammerstein on the idea of writing an original musical for television.

It took Rodgers and Hammerstein only eight months to write the entire book and score for *Cinderella,* and from casting to rehearsals they approached it the same way they would a Broadway show. We rehearsed for several weeks, then did two complete run-throughs, which Dick and

Oscar called the New Haven and Boston tryouts. The cast for *Cinderella* was just perfect, and having my old friend Alice Ghostley to play off as Cinderella's other stepsister was a great treat. When I think back on the experience now, I was literally surrounded by some of the legends of the American theater. Ilka Chase played our mother, and was terrific. Like so many other wonderful character actors and actresses of the past, Ilka seems to have been forgotten, except as a television game-show panelist or talk-show guest. But in 1936, she created the role of Crystal Allen in the stage production of *The Women* (the role Joan Crawford did in the movie). Ilka also had several other impressive credits, and later went on to be quite a good writer. Edie Adams, a great singer who was married to Ernie Kovaks and had just completed a year as a regular on his innovative, groundbreaking TV show, played the Fairy Godmother.

Howard Lindsay and Dorothy Stickney were cast as the King and the Queen. Howard Lindsay was a producer, director, performer, and playwright who, with his frequent writing partner Russel Crouse, created the books for such shows as *Anything Goes, The Sound of Music, State of the Union*, and *Call Me Madam*. Dorothy was a fine actress who had created the role of Molly in another classic, *The Front Page*. (She passed away in 1998 at the age of 101!) Howard and Dorothy were two sweet people who, when Howard died in 1968, had been married for more than forty years. They were famous for playing another married couple, the father and mother in Broadway's longest-running nonmusical play, *Life with Father*, which was also written by Lindsay and Crouse. Every day during rehearsal, when we broke for lunch, they would sit together, Howard on the King's throne and Dorothy at his feet, and eat the sandwiches and fruit they had brought from home. There was not an ounce of pretense about these two professionals who had devoted their lives to each other and to the theater.

When you work on a groundbreaking project like *Cinderella*, not only are you surrounded by legendary figures, but also by young people who will become legends. Julie Andrews was the perfect choice to play Cinderella, and a delight to work with. I didn't get as close to Julie as I did to some of the other members of the cast, simply because we didn't have many scenes together. Most of the publicity and rehearsal time was devoted to scenes between her and Jon Cypher, who played the Prince. Poor Julie must have been exhausted, because in the evenings she was still performing on Broadway with Rex Harrison in the mega-hit *My Fair Lady*.

Julie was so beautiful and talented, and already well on her way to becoming a very important star. But I remember one strange little quirk about her performance. If you get a chance to see the kinescope, you'll notice that Cinderella, the girl of the cinders, is totally spotless. For some reason, Julie didn't want to have her face smudged. Now, maybe this had to do with the show being a live television event; it would have been difficult not to damage her makeup when wiping off the cinders for the ball scene. Or maybe since Julie was already playing a smudged-up, Edwardian Cinderella, Eliza Doolittle, eight times a week, she didn't want to become typecast. In either case, they ended up showing the plight of her character by sewing little patches all over her dress. It didn't help the typecasting. Little did Julie know that she would have years of Cinderella type roles ahead of her, from Mary Poppins to Maria in *The Sound of Music*. I'm sure that must have frustrated the actress in Julie, but what a gift it was to the rest of the world.

I've always felt that Jon Cypher got the short end of the stick when it came to his performance as the Prince. He went on to play lots of leading men on the stage, but poor Jon's handsome features photographed in a very angular way that was somewhat unflattering on television, and his moves were a bit too theatrical for the small screen. He had a wonderful voice, but the reviewers were not kind to him.

The future stars who worked on *Cinderella* were not limited to the people in front of the camera. Our stage manager was a young man named Joe Papp. He would often talk to Alice Ghostley and me about his dream of producing Shakespeare in Central Park. His dream not only came true but was a huge success, and Joe introduced many of today's movie stars, Glenn Close, Kevin Kline, and Meryl Streep among them.

I will always be grateful to Joe for, a few years later, bringing me back to New York after my television series ended. Well, okay, more than a few years (it was thirteen, to be exact) elapsed between the end of *The Mothers-in-Law* and my debut in *The Pirates of Penzance*. I had worked in the city a couple of times during that period with limited success, but Joe hired me to be in what became a bona fide Broadway hit, and I'll always love him for that. Also behind the scenes on *Cinderella* was Emmy Award–winning director Ralph Nelson, who was in charge of the production. A pioneer of live television, he went on to direct Sidney Poitier in the highly acclaimed 1963 film *Lilies of the Field*.

The rehearsal process went very smoothly. The most complicated part was the camera rehearsal, designed to determine the logistics of shooting what was essentially a full stage musical for a live telecast. Set and costume changes had to be done during the commercials, and the scenes were written with that in mind. As Oscar Hammerstein said in his biography, "Being ignorant of the medium, I wrote this show on the assumption that we could do anything, and nothing has been refused me yet."

Then there was the problem of how to transform Julie from her rags to the gown for the ball in front of the live audience. Special effects on television were rather crude, but the technicians and costume designers pulled it off with a couple of superimposed sparklers and a dress that sort of opened up into a ball gown. The filmed dress rehearsal helped avoid several disasters that could have occurred when we were on the air live. For instance, in the opening sequence Cinderella is following her stepmother and stepsisters on a shopping trip through the village and, of course, is loaded down with all their packages. The action was recorded in one, long traveling shot. We had to walk up and over staircases, down small passageways, and through crowds of people. In the rehearsal, Julie carried a tremendously high stack of boxes all tied together. This was great for a comic effect, but Julie couldn't maneuver the pile well enough to allow the cameraman to get a good shot of her face. So the prop was shrunk to half its original size for the live performance.

The production cost $375,000, which was astronomical for television at the time. The show was broadcast live and in color (for those seven or eight people who owned color sets) on the East Coast, and three hours later on black-and-white kinescope (a precursor to videotape) on the West Coast. If it hadn't been for that delayed broadcast on kinescope, the cast album we recorded two weeks before the broadcast might have been the only record of the production.

CBS got what it had wanted. On March 31, more than 107 million people tuned in to watch Rodgers and Hammerstein's *Cinderella*, at that time the largest television audience on record. An instant classic was born. The show was done for TV again in 1965, with Lesley Ann Warren, Walter Pidgeon, and Ginger Rogers. That version became known to several generations of children, because it was taped and could be replayed. A few years ago, Cinderella was updated again with a multiethnic cast, including Brandy, Whitney Houston, and Whoopi Goldberg. The script has also been turned into a successful stage musical. Just more proof that Rodgers and Hammerstein's songs are not only brilliant but timeless. It would be impossible to grow up in this country not having heard "In My Own Little Corner" or "Ten Minutes Ago."

It's been a long time since Alice and I got to be the first women to sing "The Stepsister's Lament," but I'll never forget that two of the greatest compliments I've ever received in this business were given to me on the set of *Cinderella*. One day Oscar Hammerstein pulled me aside and told me I was becoming a consummate professional. That made me feel ten feet tall. After watching me rehearse, Howard Lindsay said, "You know something, Kaye? You think funny." Wow. It's a shame, I guess, but I seem to appreciate what those gentlemen said more today than I did back then. For most of my life I have found it difficult to accept any kind of praise. Self-image is a tricky thing, you know? In November 2003, I was invited to the Museum of Television and Radio in New York. They had found the original kinescopes of both the dress rehearsal and the actual performance of *Cinderella*. Kinescopes were only black and white, and not quite of the same quality as video or film, but after almost five decades I got the chance to watch myself with all these wonderful people for the first time. I enjoyed seeing it, of course, but a friend sitting next to me told me that the only comment I made out loud and almost under my breath was, "I always thought I was fat." I guess I was amazed at how thin I actually looked—and, God forbid, pretty.

So all you people, actors or not, who see only the bad things when you look into the mirror, take note! Don't let fifty years go by before you start seeing the good! I am thrilled that CBS and the Rodgers and Hammerstein Organization released our original version on video and DVD in 2004. They asked me and several members of the original cast to do interviews that are included on the DVD as extra, bonus material. I am very happy and proud to have been part of Rodgers and Hammerstein's original *Cinderella*, and it gives me chills to think that something I have done will now have a chance to be passed down through the generations.

Carol Burnett

C arol Burnett and I have several things in common. Though I am a few years older, we fell into the same niche in this business— funny ladies with big voices, willing to do pretty much anything to please an audience. We both worked with, and admired, Lucille Ball. If it hadn't been for Lucy (and Martha Raye) leading the way, our careers, along with those of so many other comediennes, would have been a lot more difficult. On the personal side, Carol and I were both practically raised by our grandmothers, who gave the kind of unconditional love we couldn't get from our mothers. I know firsthand how that kind of devotion can inspire an awkward girl to do things she might never have dreamed possible.

Even with all those similarities, or perhaps because of them, at one time I was extremely envious of Carol and all that came her way. For instance, I had heard that lyricist Marshall Barer wanted me for the role of Princess Winifred in *Once Upon a Mattress*, and that George Abbott, the director, wanted Carol, who got the part. Even if it's true . . . so what? That wasn't the first or last role I'd miss out on. A little while later, Carol and I were both hired for guest spots on *The Garry Moore Show*. As a test for a regular spot on the program, we were each given three shows. Well, I never did them. I looked at my material and said, "This isn't funny." The response I got was quick and to the point: "If you don't like it, leave." And so I left. Smart, huh? Blame it on my Italian blood. (Whatever the cause, that kind of youthful pride and arrogance cost me a lot in my career.) I blamed my failure and Carol's success on my inferior sketches, and later assumed that it all had to do with Joe Hamilton, one of the *Garry Moore* producers at the time and her future husband. Jealous? Yes!

I am writing this to say that my youthful envy has long since disappeared. What is left in its place is admiration. I've always been amazed at Carol's discipline. She's worked very hard, and has never been anything but gracious to me. I enjoyed being a guest on her show, and I haven't forgotten how she even let me sing a song from my Broadway show *Molly* as sort of a backers' audition for producers in order to help find people to invest money in the show. Carol Burnett has been through a lot in the years since we last saw each other. And she's gone through it all with dignity, humor, and strength. She deserves everything she's accomplished in this business.

My first dinner with a star, Martha Raye, on my right. Martha and I got to know each other well over the years, and in the 1970s I took over her spot in 4 Girls 4.

Spike Jones, on the left, told me, "Kid, if you ever get to Hollywood, I'll give you a job." So I went, and he did. I played the flute and tuba, and sang with his band. Here we are with band member Mickey Katz, Joel Grey's father.

With my scarecrow, Ray Bolger. He was the star of the 1946 Broadway revue Three to Make Ready, *my first show, and what a pro he was.*

My first friend in New York, the great dancer Harold Lang, introduced me to a world I never knew existed.

I met Arthur Siegel (shown at top finishing one of the many pies we enjoyed together) in 1947, and we worked and laughed together for the next forty-five years.

Here we are, below, performing my show "Hey, Ma!"

In 1950, I played Touch and Go *in London with Desmond Walter Ellis. While there I rented a room from one of Sigmund Freud's daughters, met the future Queen Elizabeth, and turned down a dinner invitation from Richard Burton.*

When I was in London, the legendary ballet dancer Vaslav Nijinsky died, and I attended his funeral with The Debonaires, the dancers in the show I was doing. It seemed like every dancer in the world showed up for the service, a musical spectacle that was downright joyous.

In 1952, I worked with Phil Silvers in the road tour of Top Banana, *an upscale burlesque tailored to his talents. Funny as Phil was onstage, he could make life offstage miserable.*

When The Golden Apple *won the New York Drama Critics Circle Award for Best Musical in 1954, we moved from off-Broadway to Broadway, to the Alvin Theatre.*

Onstage in The Golden Apple. *Critics loved the show, but we ran on Broadway for only four months. That's Jonathan Lucas, opposite, who played Paris to my Helen of Troy. A musical based on classical Greek characters—no wonder we weren't a big hit!*

With Lou Costello, Morey Amsterdam, and Joey Adams at the Bon Soir, a nightclub in Greenwich Village where I often worked in the 1950s.

On The Jack Paar Show. *That's the young Hugh Downs next to me.*

In a 1957 made-for-television musical of Cinderella, *I was surrounded by legends (including Alice Ghostley and Ilka Chase) and young actors who would become legends— a twenty-one-year-old Julie Andrews played the lead.*

The Girl Most Likely, *1957, in which I worked with Jane Powell, was one of the last gasps of the big-budget Hollywood musical. The film sure didn't do much to revitalize the genre!*

*One of the perks of being in a Hollywood extravaganza
like* The Girl Most Likely *was this glam shot.*

Me and my flute: I wanted to play the clarinet, but when I joined the band back at West Tech High in Cleveland, they gave me a flute instead. Came in handy on my first big gig, with Spike Jones's band.

For sixteen weeks in 1958 and 1959, I performed at the legendary Hungry i in San Francisco, working with the likes of Shecky Greene (shown in front of me here). We are at a reunion, along with Jack Reilly and owner Enrico Banducci (top row), and Barbra McNair and Ronnie Schell (bottom row).

Peanuts *creator Charles Schulz (Sparky to those of us lucky enough to get to know him) gave me and Arthur Siegel permission to do an album of songs and dialogue based on his famous cartoon characters.*

Carnival opened in 1961 and ran for 719 performances, making my tenure as the Incomparable Rosie my longest run—to date. That's Henry Lasco with me.

I recorded Kaye Ballard, Live? *at the Bon Soir nightclub in 1961.*

*Handsome Jack Cassidy played Herbie to my Mama Rose
in a 1962 production of* Gypsy *in Dallas.*

*With my role in
A House Is Not a
Home, 1964, came a
friendship with star
Shelley Winters and
a comment from my
mother, who asked,
"Did you have to
look like that?"*

Chapter Nine

Bette, Lenny, Charlie Brown, and Communism at the Hungry i

I have to admit that I never particularly enjoyed the atmosphere when I was working in nightclubs. In many, audiences were often more interested in what was going on at their tables than what was happening onstage. A performer could devote all her time and effort to getting an act "just right," but it didn't matter when you were competing with someone's third round of gin and tonics!

Still, you know what? They're gone. The nightclubs are gone. And you know what else? I miss 'em. Not all of them, but in the late 1950s and early 1960s, the nightclub circuit around this country was comparable to the vaudeville circuit in the 1920s, '30s, and '40s. The club circuit included the Blue Angel and the Bon Soir in New York, the Hungry i in San Francisco, and Mr. Kelley's in Chicago. To my surprise and delight, one of the audience members I encountered at Mr. Kelley's was none other than Walter Cronkite! It was an even greater surprise when over the years Mr. Cronkite became one of my biggest fans. He continues to show up in the audience, regardless of where I am playing.

The clubs I've mentioned were terrific places to work. They were not like the comedy clubs of today, and the performers who worked them were not strictly what you'd call "stand-up." These were places you'd go to laugh, yes, but also to think a bit. Or to hear a great singer like Mabel Mercer interpret the lyrics to a song. Satire of all kinds was thriving. People were writing and performing witty songs and monologues with plenty of political and social commentary. Today only my beloved *Saturday Night Live* comes close to the sort of cutting-edge entertainment those places served up. By the way, while I'm thinking about it, I'd like to include a little note to *Saturday Night*'s creator, Lorne Michaels:

Dear Mr. Michaels,
I have been a fan of your show since it went on the air in 1975. As soon as I finish this book I am available! I realize I may not be a hip, up-to-date enough star to host the actual show, but how about a spin-off? Shecky Greene and myself can host, with Keely Smith or Andy Williams as the musical guest. We'll call it *Saturday Night and Still Alive!* I'll be waiting for your call.
Yours for the asking,
Xxxooo
Kaye

Anyway, by the time I started appearing in the clubs, they were in sort of a transition period. Entertainers like Bea Lillie, Keely Smith, and Noel Coward were giving way to Woody Allen, the Kingston Trio, and Peter, Paul and Mary. It was an alive and exciting time—before television killed off most of the interesting nightlife.

I spent sixteen weeks between 1958 and 1959 performing at one of the most legendary and innovative clubs of the era, the Hungry i in San Francisco (the "i" stood for "intellectual"). In the winter of 1958, San Francisco beat to the sound of bongo drums. Every corner had a coffee-house (not Starbucks, thank you very much), where people gathered to hear beatnik poets and sip tiny cups of thick, bitter espresso. A decade later, the flower children would arrive and plant themselves on these same streets. Then, soon after the upheaval of the late 1960s, nothing would be left of those coffeehouses but seedy, topless, or nude bars that marketed sex to attract tourists of a whole different sort.

The owner of the Hungry i, Enrico Banducci, was every bit as exceptional as the club. Enrico was a true eccentric with such zest for life that it was always fun to be around him. He wore a black beret and hung out with interesting and witty people like John Huston and Francis Ford Coppola. Enrico also owned one of those coffeehouses, where he would hold court, regaling his admirers with "tales of the city" long before Armistead Maupin coined the phrase. Sally Stanford, the infamous madam who owned a restaurant in Sausalito, was frequently a topic of discussion. These places were truly a reflection of the man who ran them, energetic and edgy. Working in the Hungry i was more like working in a theater than in a nightclub. The place was shockingly plain. I stood against a backdrop of a blank, brick wall, facing a tightly packed audience who sat on hard wooden benches. The "band" consisted of just a piano (on which was always displayed a vase of fresh flowers) and a bass. And though this wasn't a formal theater space, the sound and lighting were beyond superb.

I must take a little side trip here to mention the man who did the lights at the Hungry i. Maybe, in a way, he fit right in with this hotbed of creative people, but as brilliant as his lighting was (and it was spectacular), he shouldn't have been there. His name was Alvah Bessie. Not familiar? Alvah Bessie was one of the famous (or infamous) Hollywood Ten during the McCarthy era. He, along with men like Ring Lardner Jr., Dalton Trumbo, and Edward Dmytryk, refused to "name names" during the congressional investigations (or witch hunts) that Senator Joseph McCarthy led in order to flush out Communists. Alvah Bessie had been a novelist and an Academy Award–nominated screenwriter (*Objective Burma*, 1945) for Warner Brothers. In 1947 he claimed his First Amendment rights and refused to testify before the House Committee on Un-American Activities. For this, he was sentenced to twelve months in prison and fined $1,000, and he never worked in Hollywood again. By the time we worked together, he was a broken man. Such a darling, sweet, talented person running the lights for my act! He did his job with precision and integrity, and never once complained. He loved being around show people. God bless Enrico Banducci for giving Alvah Bessie a place to earn a living.

Back then, the Bay Area was just surging with bohemian-type artists and performers; they blanketed the coastline like the city's famous fog. Raw, new talent emerged—people who were willing to push the satiric envelope just a little further. I became friends with emerging talents Ronnie Schell, Jorie Remus, and a young, talented housewife-turned-comedienne, Phyllis Diller. They were all performing at another great club in San Francisco, the Purple Onion. I was so impressed with the talent of these people that I called Herbert Jacoby at the Blue Angel in New York. "Herbert," I told him excitedly, "you must book these people, they are all fantastic!" Eventually he did, along with another struggling unknown, Lenny Bruce.

Lenny was one of the sexiest men I had ever met. Extremely good-looking, with an incredible body, the man just oozed sex appeal (not a very common trait among most comics of the day). But Lenny was more than a comic. He had things to say. And a hell of a lot of those things were spelled with four letters. I went to see him at a local club called FACKS, where he was appearing with singer Jack Jones. I'd heard so much about him I just had to see this guy for myself. Like everyone else, I was shocked by his language. But Lenny Bruce was an extremely bright kid, an intellectual who used certain language only to make a point. His material was strictly for adults, but it was very funny and very powerful.

When, a little later, I was offered an engagement in Hollywood following Lenny on the bill, I told his agent that even though I thought Lenny was brilliant, with my material I could never follow someone with his kind of act. When we eventually did work together, it was at another club in Hollywood, the Interlude, and I opened for him. Despite our different performance styles, we became friends. One night in the dressing room, I asked if he would write some material for me. Lenny pulled out the cardboard from a shirt he'd just gotten back from the laundry and scribbled out this satire of the song "Autumn Leaves" for me right there on the spot:

> The autumn leaves pass by my window
> And then the trees, and then the buildings
> The automobiles fly by now
> The hurricane has finally come
> The river overflows
> I must prove my love
> A raft comes floating by, just room for one
> I will miss you most of all,
> My Darling, when autumn leaves start to fall.
> It's a dog eat dog world, right?

I wish I still had that piece of cardboard. I recorded his parody on an album called *Boo Hoo, Ha, Ha,* and Lenny received a royalty check for the sum of fourteen cents. When he showed it to me, I said, "So, you gonna cash it?" "No," he said gleefully, "I'm going to keep it and fuck up their books!"

By the way, I have recorded several albums in my life (including a version of *Oklahoma!* with Nelson Eddy, in which I sang the role of Ado Annie, that sold millions of copies) and never made a penny on any of them.

The tone of comedy has changed a lot since the days when Lenny Bruce shocked everyone with his language. These days the language you hear on television every night is much worse than any Lenny ever used. To tell you the truth, I think he would be disgusted by much of today's comedy.

Because the Hungry i was so popular, lots of wonderful people filled the audiences. *Peanuts* creator Charles Schulz came to see my act one night after he received a fan letter from me telling him how much I adored his cartoon characters. He loved the show and said he had decided to come down after seeing me on the *Tonight Show*, with Jack Paar. "Oh, Kaye," he said, "you're so lucky! You get instant approval and gratification when you perform onstage. I never get to hear the applause!" He had recently moved to the Coast from Minnesota and confided to me that he was very nervous about the price he had just paid for his new home in Marin County, $125,000! Today you couldn't buy a storage shed in Marin County for $125,000!

One day Charles ("Sparky" to people who got to know him) invited my musical director and accompanist, Arthur Siegel, and me out to see his house. We discovered that we had a mutual midwestern fear of California earthquakes and quickly became good friends. Sparky gave Arthur and me his permission to do an album of songs and dialogue based on his famous cartoon characters. He was also kind enough to do the artwork on the cover for no charge! Unfortunately, John Hammond with Columbia Records didn't want to use the songs that Arthur had written and hired Fred Karlin instead. Fred was very popular at the time and used the gimmick of all these little toy sounds underneath the dialogue. (I still believe Fred's sound effects didn't compare to Arthur's songs, but what are you gonna do?) Arthur Whitelaw, the producer, later admitted that he got the idea for the show *You're a Good Man, Charlie Brown!* from our recording. Foiled again! About the only place you can hear that album today is in my living room or at the Charles Schulz Museum in Santa Rosa, California.

While I was still out in San Francisco, I was delighted to introduce my new pal Sparky to the comedy team of Nichols and May, and to Bette Davis, whom I knew quite well. Bette and her then-husband, Gary Merrill, were in town doing a show called *An Evening with the Poems of Carl Sandburg*. I love introducing talented people to one another. Even if they don't always get along, it's never boring.

It will come as no surprise that Bette was a very strong, very opinionated woman. She always seemed much too willful to stay married, and yet she told me many times that all she ever wanted from life was to be a wife and mother. Well, one evening, Mike Nichols, Elaine May, Arthur, and I were invited up to Bette's apartment for dinner. We were having a very pleasant time when Gary made some inane comment regarding politics and Bette snapped at him, "Be quiet! You're a weak, weak, man!" "Oh, God, how awful!" I thought. "It's *All About Eve* in the flesh, and we really are in for a bumpy night!" After Bette had gone to bed and everyone else left, Arthur and I sat up until four in the morning with Gary. I finally got the nerve to ask, "Weren't you embarrassed when Bette spoke to you that way?" "No," he answered, "I understand her. She was the biggest star in Hollywood. The studio always gave in to her. Everyone always gave in to her. It's difficult for Bette now, acting on the stage for so much less money and feeling she no longer has the kind of power and mystique that go with being a movie star." Though Gary was very kind, the marriage didn't last. Strong women always seem to yearn for an even stronger man to take care of them. But when it comes right down to it, they choose men who will allow them to dominate, then turn on them for being weak.

I noticed another ironic twist in Bette's character. She could not stand sentiment. She was embarrassed at the emotions it brought out, and yet she was the absolute best at portraying those same emotions on the screen. I attended a sixteenth birthday party Bette gave for her daughter at the Plaza Hotel in the early 1960s. Everyone called the girl "Baby B.D." I was thirty-five years old and the youngest guest there! After we had finished dinner, B.D. stood up and announced, "Oh, Mummy, Mummy, I want to thank you for the most wonderful birthday party I've ever had!" Bette looked at her and, in her best Bette Davis voice, answered, "Bullshit!" Even still, I truly think Bette believed she was a good mother.

I know, I know, I'm off track a bit, but since I'm here I might as well finish up a few other morsels on the great Bette Davis. Bette once gave me tickets to the Actors' Fund benefit performance of *Night of the Iguana* in which she was appearing. I went backstage to visit with her and asked how she liked working with the people from the Actors Studio. She answered, "I could make an entire movie while waiting for them to speak."

Another time, I was waiting in the lobby of a theater to see *The Killing of Sister George*. Bette walked in with Viola Rubber, an agent, and very loudly announced, "Viola, you go and sit on the other side of the theater. I don't want anyone to think we're lovers!"

I remember taking Bette to dinner at Gavin MacLeod's beautiful home in Brentwood. The house had been decorated from top to bottom in a paisley motif. As soon as Bette walked in, she asked Gavin's wife, Patti, "Do you have a decorator?" "Why, yes," Patti replied proudly. As we walked on, Bette turned to me and said, "He should be shot!" (I guess she didn't like paisley . . . I do.) I also remember Bette telling me about another dinner she was invited to. Toward the end of her life, she was living on Havenhurst Avenue in Hollywood, and two very nice gay gentlemen lived downstairs. They were always after her to have dinner with them. "Oh, please, Miss Davis, we've always been such big fans of yours. Won't you please come down and let us make you dinner!" Finally she said, "All right, I'll come!" After dinner, she got up from the table and announced, "There! Now we never have to do this again!"

God, I loved Bette Davis. She said exactly what was on her mind. And she was so unpretentious. The first time I went to her house for dinner, I noticed an unusual doorstop—her Oscar! She was outspoken, but she also could be very generous and loving to those close to her. I happen to know she took care of her mother and sister all of their lives.

It's ironic that when Bette got sick, MCA, her agency, refused to give her a loan. She was largely responsible for making MCA flourish! When she was at her height in Hollywood, they used her to get work for their other clients, saying, "If you want Bette Davis, you'll have to use Errol Flynn and you have to use so and so." Bette had been such a huge box office draw that the studios would do anything to get her. When they abandoned her, she had a right to a certain amount of bitterness. One of the last times I saw her was in her New York apartment after she had undergone a mastectomy and had also suffered a stroke. She greeted me in true Bette fashion, "Don't ever have a stroke!" she shouted. "Did you hear? B.D. wrote a book about me! Why can't my daughter have the decency to wait until I'm dead?"

Think of it: Bette Davis . . . Alvah Bessie . . . Lenny Bruce . . . Charles Schulz. An odd list, isn't it? Smart, outspoken people, intellectuals, truly witty and bright. I've always gravitated toward people with talent. My way of schooling myself in show business, I guess. What a thrill just to have been in their company!

Chapter Ten

CARNIVAL

B elieve it or not, I was once considered to be a young Zsa Zsa Gabor. Please stop laughing and let me explain.

It used to be that Hollywood went to Broadway to find a lot of its material (and actors), especially for musicals. Nowadays, due to the lack of brave producers and the need to ensure financial success in advance of opening night, Broadway almost always goes to Hollywood for material (and actors).

One of the early exceptions to the old rule occurred back in 1961, when David Merrick produced a musical called *Carnival*. The show was based on the hit 1953 MGM film *Lili*, starring Leslie Caron, about a young girl who finds work and romance in a traveling French carnival. The movie, in turn, was based on an original story by Paul Gallicos, which Helen Deutsch developed into an Academy Award–nominated screenplay.

For the Broadway version, Michael Stewart (*Hello Dolly!, Mack & Mabel, George M!, 42nd Street, I Love My Wife, Bye Bye Birdie*) wrote the book, and Bob Merrill wrote the wonderful music and lyrics. Until then, Bob's biggest claim to fame had been writing the pop hit "How Much Is That Doggy in the Window?" With the score to *Carnival*, Bob proved that he could write delightfully romantic themes and wonderful character-driven songs, as well as cute and funny comic numbers. The musical theme "Love Makes the World Go 'Round" ran throughout the entire show and became a Broadway classic. Just a couple of years later, Bob Merrill would write the lyrics for *Funny Girl*.

The great Gower Champion directed and choreographed *Carnival.* Gower was also my personal champion, an extremely talented man to whom I'll always be grateful. In 1957, Gower had cast me in my first film, *The Girl Most Likely,* with Jane Powell (Carol Channing had backed out of that role). Though I had to go through a formal audition for *Carnival* in front of David Merrick, Gower told me that the part of The Incomparable Rosalie (which Zsa Zsa Gabor played in the movie) was mine.

The part of Lili, originally played by Leslie Caron, went to a beautiful Italian child prodigy who began her singing career in Italy at the age of six and had her Carnegie Hall debut at the age of thirteen! Anna Maria Alberghetti was blessed with a brilliant soprano voice and a childlike innocence that won her a Tony Award for her performance. To this day, Anna has that same amazing voice, with a multi-octave range, and is just a delight to work with. In the play, Lili gets caught between two men who compete for her affections: the troupe's beguiling magician, Marco the Magnificent, and Paul, the crippled, pure-hearted puppeteer. Jerry Orbach, an astounding actor, played Paul. Jerry was brilliant in everything he ever did, from El Gallo in *The Fantasticks* to his role on TV's *Law and Order.*

Jimmy Mitchell, another great performer, played my counterpoint in the show, Marco the Magnificent. Jimmy (or James) is probably best known now for the decades he's spent as Palmer Cortlandt on *All My Children* (I didn't get to work with him when I dropped by Pine Valley in 1993). But he started in the American Ballet Theatre in New York and became an extremely sought-after and accomplished dancer. He appeared in several classic Broadway musicals, including *Bloomer Girl, Brigadoon, Paint Your Wagon,* and *Carousel,* and was also in the movie musicals *The Bandwagon, Deep in My Heart,* and *Oklahoma!* (in which he played Dream Curly).

Vivian Vance once told me that she was in therapy every single day that she had to work with William Frawley on *I Love Lucy.* To millions of people they were Fred and Ethel Mertz, the bickering, loving married couple. But offscreen, they couldn't stand one another. Vivian had such a tense off-camera relationship with Bill that it became terribly uncomfortable just being on the set with him. I had a similar experience with Jimmy Mitchell.

Since I was the "comic" magician's assistant, I played most of my material with Jimmy. My character, Rosalie, kept threatening to leave

Marco and marry a doctor (who turned out to be a veterinarian). It was a great part and a lot of fun to play. In the second act, Jimmy and I got to do a hilarious number, "Always, Always You," in which he keeps thrusting swords into the basket in which I am enclosed. I have to say, Jimmy and I came off very well onstage, but our offstage relationship drove me crazy. I am the type of person who wants everyone around me to be happy and to like me. Sometimes I go to great lengths to achieve this goal. Jimmy, on the other hand, was the type of person who very rarely spoke offstage unless it was absolutely necessary. I did everything in my power to win him over. I greeted him cheerfully every day, I made conversation, I brought him little gifts, but nothing seemed to work. He remained indifferent to me throughout the entire run. It was infuriating, especially because we were so well matched on the stage. For almost two years I pretended to have this great relationship with a person I barely knew. That takes a hell of a lot of energy, and was the only negative aspect of my experience in *Carnival*. When we premiered in Washington, D.C., the reviews were all raves. The audience fell in love with the show from the beginning to the end. It was thrilling. This time around, we all just knew we had the perfect little musical to take into New York.

Well, art is never quite perfect to the artists who create it, and before we opened in Philadelphia, Gower Champion decided the play could be improved with a few minor adjustments. I did a number in the first act called "I'll Be Humming," in which my character admits to the carnival manager that though she hates Marco, she is hopelessly addicted to him. The opening line to the song is "Here's to the son of a bitch, tra-la-la." You get the gist of this song of "true love." Well, at one point the lyrics included the word "goddamn."

Gower decided to take it out. I did my best to explain to him that the profanity was what got the laughs, but he wouldn't listen. When we opened in Philly, the number fell flat on its face. Gower came up to me and told me to put the goddamn "goddamn" back in. Often in this business, questioning those in charge is a very dangerous thing to do. But not if those people truly know what they are doing. My being right about the song may have bruised Gower's ego slightly, but not enough so that he ignored what was right for the show. (And not enough to prevent him from telling me, after seeing me play Elsa Maxwell in a show called *Red Hot and Cole*, that I gave him chills and that if he wasn't busy working on *42nd Street* he would take over *Cole*.)

I loved Gower Champion. He was a true genius. *Carnival* opened on April 13, 1961, at the Imperial Theatre. At the time, the musical theater competition that year seemed no different or no more fierce than that of any other year. But looking back, it seems the musicals that year belong on a "Broadway Musical Hall of Fame" roster. Richard Rodgers returned to Broadway with *No Strings*, his first musical since the death of Oscar Hammerstein. *No Strings* is the one and only show for which he wrote both the music and the lyrics, and he ended up winning the Tony Award for Best Score. Also opening that year were Frank Loesser's *How to Succeed in Business Without Really Trying*, and Jerry Herman's first Broadway show, *Milk and Honey*. *Carnival* was nominated for six Tony Awards in 1962 and won two. Anna Maria tied for Best Actress in a Musical with Diahann Carroll from *No Strings*, and our set designer, Will Steven Armstrong, won for Best Scenic Design.

No, I wasn't even nominated. Phyllis Newman, who would later play a very significant role in my life, won in "my" category, Best Featured Actress in a Musical, for *Subways Are for Sleeping*. The other nominees were Elizabeth Allen, Barbara Harris, and that Streisand girl I had met at the Bon Soir, in her Broadway debut, *I Can Get It for You Wholesale*.

There's nothing quite like being in a successful Broadway show. I'd gotten my first taste of it with *The Golden Apple*, but now I was in a bona fide hit that might actually run! On the opening night of *Carnival*, a group of us went to Sardi's after the show for dinner. The entire restaurant applauded when we walked in! Then, of course, there were no tables available and half the cast had to stand in the corner waiting for people to leave. (Even being in a Broadway hit does not guarantee you a table at Sardi's!) Nonetheless, it's very heady being on the "A" list all of a sudden. Meeting all the most fascinating people, and attending or throwing wonderful dinner parties, was exactly what I had dreamed about back in Ohio. I was having the time of my life. I got very close to British actor and singer Tommy Steele, who was very hot at the time and performing in *Half a Sixpence* on Broadway. He and his wife, Annie, would come to dinner at my apartment nearly every Sunday. Many times we were joined by the likes of Dolores Gray, Fred Astaire's sister Adele, Eileen Farrell, Caterina Valenti, Eileen Brennan, and Liliane Montevecchi, and one Sunday there was a young, unknown actor at my table named Dustin Hoffman.

As I list these names, I can still hardly believe that this girl from Cleveland somehow got herself into the amazing position of being able to welcome such incredible people into her home. I even got to know the famous photographer Joseph Karsch and his wife. They became guests at my dinner parties and later visited my home in Rancho Mirage. Joseph once asked me to sit for him, but I refused because I thought he was just being polite. How stupid can a girl be?

I know it's not right, but the public recognition that turns you into a celebrity suddenly makes you feel that you have actually done something to deserve the attention. It can really play with your ego and emotions. Don't get me wrong. As I have said, it's very nice while it's happening. But the extraordinary attention and privilege (including the ability to get a good table at a restaurant) can vanish just as quickly as it appeared. As the closing of *Cats* finally proved, no show lasts forever. *Carnival* ran for 719 performances, and closed in January 1963. My tenure as The Incomparable Rosalie is still my longest run. In fact, it would take me almost twenty years to come close to that record when I played Ruth in *The Pirates of Penzance*.

I didn't realize at the time that it would be more than a decade before I had a chance to make my mark on Broadway again, in *Molly*, a show that would break my heart. I missed out on all the great musicals of the early 1960s. I was too old for *Funny Girl*, too ethnic for *Mame* (though I have never forgotten that after *Milk and Honey*, Jerry Herman wrote to me, "The next one is for you!"), not ethnic *enough* for *Fiddler on the Roof*, and Carol Channing made Dolly Levi her role for a lifetime.

As the 1960s wore on, it became harder and harder to find roles to play in musical comedies. Jazz and musical theater are the only artistic inventions we have created here in America. But unlike jazz, which can continue to grow and thrive as a reflection of its time, musical comedy loses its appeal in a world where people ignore their ability to imagine and to believe.

The golden age of Broadway musicals was just starting to wane as the country began to lose its innocence. By the time we started seeing actual scenes of war on television, we had gone through the assassination of a president, a struggle for civil rights that was both violent and nonviolent, and a sexual revolution.

It wasn't that the musical theater didn't make an effort to keep up with the times. A decade after *Carnival* debuted, this country's loss of innocence was reflected in Broadway shows like *Hair* and *Oh! Calcutta!* My type of entertainer just didn't have any place in these shows. I went to see *Oh! Calcutta!* with my friend Hermione Baddeley, the renowned

English comedienne. Her summation? "The sketches are too long and the cocks are too short!" After *Carnival* closed, I did do a few shows in New York. You'll find most of these in the chapter with "Flops" in the title. Well, I thought, I could always go back to doing my act. Plus, there were plenty of talk shows and variety shows on television. But now that my name was a little more high-profile, I dared to entertain the idea that maybe I could finally fulfill my dream on the other coast. Hollywood, here I come!

Fanny Brice / Barbra Streisand

One of the celebrities I idolize is Fanny Brice. I even performed a "Baby Snooks" routine as part of my act in my early days. One day in 1954, I had the idea to record a concept album telling the story of Fanny Brice's life through her songs.

Arthur Siegel did the major portion of work in collecting the material, then I presented it to Arnie Maxim, the head of MGM records. Arnie loved the idea and gave the songs to the great arranger Leroy Holmes to orchestrate the music. Two weeks later, I was recording my Fanny Brice album. We completed it after only two four-hour sessions. Today this would be a major miracle, since it sometimes takes months to record a single song. (Doris Day told me that when she recorded "Secret Love," she entered the studio at 4:00 in the afternoon and left at 4:16.) How times have changed!

I introduced my Fanny Brice album on Jack Paar's show to a very enthusiastic reception. I was excited when the producers told me that demand for the album was very high the next day. Then MGM took another four months to actually release the album and we lost all the momentum. The album was in print for many years, so I suppose MGM did well with it. I, on the other hand, received $500 and Arthur got even less.

I sent the album to Fanny Brice's son-in-law, producer Ray Stark. I thought it would be a fantastic idea to do a musical play about Fanny's amazing life. I also, of course, hoped to play the starring role, but Mr. Stark said it would "never be done." Then he added, "If it ever *is* done, Fanny will be played by Kay Kendall, not you." Okay, so I wasn't terribly Jewish-looking . . . but Kay Kendall!?

A few years after making the Fanny Brice album, I got to know Barbra Streisand when she started to work at the Bon Soir. I also remember that she and Jerry Herman came to see me in 1963 when I was doing *Wonderful Town* at City Center, and she couldn't have been nicer. This little girl with the big voice was beginning to make quite a name for herself around town. She'd even recorded Kander and Ebb's "My Coloring Book," the song they refused to let me sing on Perry Como's show, and had a big hit with it. I also followed her act at the Basin Street East, where we both worked with the Duke Ellington Orchestra. Those guys were great when they all showed up, but you just never knew who was going to be behind you until you stepped onto the stage.

Arthur Siegel adored Barbra and had given her a lot of sheet music over the years. She loved rediscovering older, obscure songs, and I must say she was brilliant at reinterpreting them. One night at Basin Street East, Arthur and I went backstage to say hello. We were told that Barbra was "much too busy" to see either of us. Hmmm . . . and not even a superstar yet.

Then, what do you know? One day it's announced that there is going to be a musical based on Fanny Brice. Ray Stark is producing and Jule Styne is doing the music, but no mention of Kay Kendall. I do know that at one point they offered the leading role to Anne Bancroft, because after she heard about my album, she came over and had breakfast with me, wanting to find out all about Fanny Brice. Well, we all know what happened. *Funny Girl* was the show that set the course of Barbra Streisand's career toward superstardom, and deservedly so. She was brilliant as Fanny Brice.

Sometime after Barbra Streisand became a full-fledged superstar, she and I happened to be having dinner at the same restaurant. A fan approached her during dinner and asked for an autograph. "Can't you see I'm eating my dinner?" Barbra snapped at the woman. The lady responded loudly, "Well, I enjoyed your *last* movie!" I can understand that to someone of Barbra's stature, fans, and especially paparazzi, can get very overwhelming at times. What I can't understand is how, once you've reached the "star" level, you can be rude to the people who put you there.

I am always deeply flattered and grateful that people would consider it worth their time to ask me to sign something. I was a hopelessly starstruck as a child (and still am), so I know how much seeing a celebrity and getting an autograph can mean to people.

In 2002, I was invited to perform in a benefit for the Actors' Fund of America, in which we staged a concert version of *Funny Girl*. There were thirteen fabulous young actresses portraying Fanny Brice and one actress (with a large fanny) portraying Mrs. Brice—me. It brought me to tears witnessing all those incredibly talented young women—Kristin Chenoweth, Sutton Foster, Ana Gasteyer, Idina Menzel, Jane Krakowski, Carolee Carmello among them—on their way to stardom. (I only hope that once they reach it, they won't mind signing an autograph or two.)

Chapter Eleven

Hollywood, My Dream!

Back at the RKO in Cleveland, back where my dreams began while watching Dorothy long to fly over that rainbow, I was longing, too—longing to get up there on that big silver screen.

Up there, where makeup makes you thin
I'll play a scene with Errol Flynn.
I'll show Carmen Miranda how to wear fruit in her hair
And finally get to go up there, up there!

And I'll leave Cleveland behind
Without a single regret.
They'll say they knew me when . . .

If Esther Williams resigns
I can be just as good wet.
I'll head the Oscar list.
Gable calls me "Kaye,"
Grauman's will insist that I put my feet in clay,
And I've just been kissed by Turhan Bey!

Up there, just give me one good break,
Then watch Deanna Durbin shake.
From the shores of Lake Erie gladly I'll soon disappear
And finally get to go

Up there, up there, up there . . .
Not here!

From my one woman show, *"Hey, Ma!,"* by Jerry Goldberg,
Leslie Eberhard, and David Levy

An artist puts paint to canvas or chisels out a figure in stone, and centuries later people still enjoy viewing the portrait or statue that has enriched generations. But performers in the theater, especially those of the early twentieth century and before, live on only in drawings, pictures, and the memories or writings of those who saw them on stage.

I have always wanted to create things that would last. Maybe that is why I was so drawn to the physical arts as a child. I could make something with my hands and have it right there in front of me to show for my efforts. Once the lights went down at the RKO, I realized that movies could also be tangible. Motion pictures gave me my first glimpse of how to dream. So, of course, one of those dreams was to be a famous movie star. Well, I never got my feet wet in cement outside Grauman's Chinese Theatre, but I consider myself lucky to have been part of the few films I *have* done. For good or bad, my performances are frozen in celluloid and will never change. It is one of my biggest disappointments that I have not had the opportunity to do a larger role on film. How wonderful it would be to create a part that people remember through the years. My friend Pat Carroll has been lucky enough to have one of those roles. Pat, who, incidentally, played my part in the Lesley Ann Warren TV version of *Cinderella*, was cast as the evil witch Ursula in Disney's *The Little Mermaid*. The role may be only a voice on a cartoon, but she will live on through it, in a film that will last as long as there are children to see it.

Television (ever since the late 1950s) lasts, too, but in film you have the luxury of time, good lighting, and camera work that, when edited well, can show you at your very best. As I mentioned, I got to be in my first film, *The Girl Most Likely*, when Carol Channing dropped out. Gower Champion, who was choreographing the picture, had seen me on the stage in *Great to Be Alive* at the Los Palmas Theatre in Hollywood. *The Girl Most Likely* was a well-intentioned remake of the musical *Tom, Dick and Harry* and starred Jane Powell in the Ginger Rogers role. (It was also the last musical RKO produced before being bought by my future boss, Desi Arnaz—strange coincidence.) Jane was extremely professional, and the quickest study I've ever worked with. MGM sure knew how to train 'em! The movie also starred Cliff Robertson, Keith Andes, and Tommy

Noonan, but I'm afraid it did nothing to help restore the luster of the old-fashioned Hollywood musical.

By the time I first got on screen, Hollywood was adjusting to the shock of the old studio system breaking apart. The moguls who had created "more stars than there are in heaven" were being replaced by businesspeople, New York "suits" who knew very little about filmmaking. The era of the big-budget musical that I had always dreamed about was nearly dead, and *The Girl Most Likely* was one of its last gasps.

My next film offer was not for a musical, and did not come until seven years after the first. I got a small part in *A House Is Not a Home* while sitting around the pool at the Beverly Hills Hotel. Producer Joe Levine came up to me and said, "Hey, kid, you want to do ten lines in a movie?" The film was based on Polly Adler's autobiographical story about becoming a famous madam. Shelley Winters played the lead role, and I played a factory worker who was her chum in the beginning. My mother said, "Did you have to look like *that*? Why couldn't you be one of the girls?" My mother was always disappointed that I wasn't Ava Gardner.

A House Is Not a Home also starred Cesar Romero, Broderick Crawford, and Robert Taylor. On the first day of shooting I was surprised to see Mr. Taylor's hands shaking. I said, "Mr. Taylor, you're not nervous, are you?" "Oh, yes, Kaye," he answered, "I'm always a nervous wreck on the first day of shooting." Can you imagine? Robert Taylor! He held Garbo up as she died in *Camille*, for God's sake—and he's nervous!

I also experienced my first bit of "movie star temperament" on that picture, from Shelley Winters. Actually, I am certain Shelley was just covering for the fact that she sometimes did not know her lines, because she'd say things like, "Everyone be quiet! I can't do my role with all this noise. I'm getting off the set, and don't call me until all of you can be quiet!" Shelley knew I caught on to her pretense and would smile at me as she stormed off. We became very good friends and spent many wonderful weekends together at my home over the years. In fact, when she was rehearsing for her role in *The Poseidon Adventure*, Shelley kept taking my flashlights into the pool and swimming underwater with them. It never dawned on her that the water might be ruining the flashlights until one day I ran out of them.

Keeping to my track record of making one movie every six or seven years, my next two efforts were *Which Way to the Front?*, with Jerry Lewis, in 1970, and Terrence McNally's *The Ritz*, in 1976. Jerry Lewis is a brilliant comedian when he has someone strong to guide him. He is also an excellent director, and after all the money Martin and Lewis movies made for Paramount, he was given carte blanche. Unfortunately, Jerry's movie career and popularity began to flounder once he became an *auteur* with total creative control. It's very dangerous to direct yourself. Even the great Orson Welles eventually found that out.

Which Way to the Front? probably made money only in France (where Jerry Lewis is revered as a comic genius). It wasn't the actors' high salaries that accounted for the poor financial returns on the film. Jerry insisted on paying everyone who worked for him scale (the least you can pay), but then he'd send flowers, candy, and champagne to us each hour we were on the set. In *that* way Jerry was very generous. He was very generous in general. One day I admired a lamp he had in his office and he pulled it off the wall and gave it to me. There are stories by others who have worked with him that paint Jerry Lewis as a monster. But this is my book, and he was never a monster to me. I know that Jerry never cared for female comics (which is curious, since he copied just about everything that Martha Raye ever did), but he was always very nice to me. Maybe it's because when I met him he said that people told him we looked alike!

The same year I did *Which Way to the Front?*, I also auditioned for a role in the movie *Lovers and Other Strangers*. At the audition, both Cy Howard, the director, and the casting director were in tears! They were so impressed that I was hired on the spot. Now this was more like it—a featured role in a first-class film with Gig Young, Anne Meara, Anne Jackson, Bonnie Bedelia, and a young Diane Keaton in her first role.

Lovers and Other Strangers is about a young couple who live together for a while, then decide to get married. It was written by the very talented husband-and-wife team Renée Taylor and Joseph Bologna. Even though I had to turn down a good deal of money working in Las Vegas, I excitedly flew to New York to start filming. When I arrived, Gig and Anne were already there, along with Rod McKuen, who was going to compose the music for the film. (Jimmy Griffin and Fred Karlin eventually did the music.) The producer, David Susskind, whom I hadn't seen in the audition, had me do a reading for him. I was horrified when he told me that I sounded too young for the part. Wait a minute, the part was perfect for me. I was the character's age, and as far as my voice was concerned, I sounded just like my mother! I told David this, and he repeated that he still thought I sounded too young. So I went back to the hotel and waited until I got a call from my agent.

"Go back to California," the agent told me, "they want to replace you." I was crushed. "Then I want to get paid the thousand dollars a week for ten weeks I was promised," I demanded. My agent said, "You can't. If you try and collect, David Susskind will blackball you and you'll never do anything in movies again." So I settled for five weeks' pay. They eventually gave my part to Bea Arthur. I was heartbroken. Anne Meara came back to the hotel to tell me how sorry she was about the whole thing, and when I got back home there was a huge bouquet of flowers on my doorstep from Rod McKuen. On the note was written, "To Kaye— Anyone who loses a role because they are too young has nothing to worry about!" The two of them will never know how much those gestures meant to me.

As I said, my next movie role didn't come around until 1976. (Gee, good thing I wasn't blackballed by David Susskind, huh?) *The Ritz* premiered on Broadway in January 1975, and Rita Moreno won a Tony Award in the tour de force role of Googie Gomez. The play is a wonderful farce written by Terrence McNally and set in the Continental Baths in New York. Along with Rita, the movie starred original Broadway cast members Jack Weston (as my husband), Jerry Stiller (my brother), and F. Murray Abraham, who later won an Oscar for his performance in *Amadeus.*

The film version of *The Ritz* was almost doomed from the start because of the choice of directors. A decade after I worked with him, Terrence McNally went on to become one of America's most important and successful playwrights. He has written such classics as *Love! Valour! Compassion!, Frankie and Johnny in the Claire de Lune,* and *Master Class,* and the books for the musicals *Kiss of the Spider Woman, Ragtime,* and *The Full Monty.* But *The Ritz* was one of Terrence McNally's first plays, and as a novice playwright he didn't have the clout (or maybe the willpower) to insist that it be directed by Robert Drivas, the man who had done such a great job with the play. Instead, Richard Lester, who was not gay and who hadn't a clue as to what the Continental Baths were all about, was given the job of directing the farce.

How could the director of *A Hard Day's Night* and *The Three Musketeers* be expected to understand the gay culture of the late 1970s? The same culture that discovered Bette Midler? On top of everything else, Richard cast very unattractive men. With the exception of a young Treat Williams, there was no one in the movie you actually wanted to see in a towel! The bottom line is that it takes a certain amount of delicacy and wit to handle material like this, and Richard just didn't identify with that crowd. (I remember hearing that when they had a famous opera singer perform at the baths all the men wore black towels! You have to hand it to gay men—that's funny!)

From the Continental Baths to Disneyland. My next venture into film was also in 1976, playing Jodie Foster's soccer coach in Disney's adaptation of the children's book *Freaky Friday*, by Mary Rodgers (Richard's daughter). I had a wonderful time making that film and working with the brilliant Barbara Harris. You could tell that Jodie Foster, then in her early teens, was going to do great things. She was very smart and very disciplined, and she had an instinctive talent for film. I guess that's not too surprising, considering that at age fifteen she'd already been in twice as many movies as I had. Ruth Buzzi played the coach of the rival team in *Freaky Friday*. I love Ruth and appeared with her in a couple of episodes on *Rowan & Martin's Laugh-In* during that show's first season. I wish I could have done more. I heard later that someone had gone to the producer and said that between Ruth and Jo Anne Worley, they could handle any material that I could . . . who knows?

Over the next twenty-five years I did small parts in a handful of movies, but only two that I feel are worth mentioning. In 1980, I met a brilliant young man who directed me in *Falling in Love Again*. Steven Paul produced, wrote, and directed the movie and later produced two other movies I did, *The Million Dollar Kid* and *Baby Geniuses*, both in 1999. This twenty-one-year-old kid ate, slept, and breathed film-making, and I just knew he would go on to bigger and better things. *Falling in Love Again* is about the midlife crisis of a man (played by Elliott Gould) traveling across the country with his family to a high-school reunion. Michelle Pfeiffer played my daughter. I was very proud of the work I did for Steven on that picture.

The other film was a decade later. Eight years after I had worked with Robby Benson in *The Pirates of Penzance* on Broadway, he asked me to play his secretary in *Modern Love*, a film he had written and was going to produce and direct. I adore Robby Benson, and he is a terrific director. While we were doing *Pirates* he met his wife, Karla DeVito (a former backup singer for Meat Loaf), and she played his love interest in *Modern Love*.

The rest of my film career is quite forgettable, but I am still holding out hope that someone will come to their senses and film Joe DiPietro's terrific play *Over the River and Through the Woods*, and that the wonderful Marie Lillo and I can once again play those beautifully written Italian grandmothers. Hell, if I win the lottery, I'll produce it myself!

My favorite pastime is still going to the movies. (I love getting in for free during Oscar balloting time!) The actors I see up on the screen nowadays are wonderful. Let's face it, many of them are better actors than ever appeared during the golden age of film. And the technology of film today? Forget about it! They can create visual images that I could never have imagined in my wildest dreams back at the RKO in Cleveland.

But still, something is missing. It has been said that at their peak the Hollywood studios had publicity departments that could keep any scandal the stars could get themselves involved in (traffic tickets, affairs, pregnancy, even murder) out of the papers. Those studios spent years creating their star products. They trained them in everything from song and dance to elocution and how to dress. The studios spent a lot of money on these people and fiercely protected their investments. I admit that everything Hollywood was feeding us during the 1930s and 1940s was about as real as the false facades of a back-lot set. But what do you know? It turns out that that reality was a lot more real than what most of our politicians and news channels offer us today. It was fantasy on the grandest scale, but it rang true. It was what we wanted to aspire to, not only in the beautiful films, but also when it came to the supposed real lives of the beautiful people who were in them. Stars became role models for a life that could never actually be achieved. But sometimes I wonder, did it hurt us? I miss the fantasy. I miss the heroes the studios created. If it hadn't been for Judy Garland, Bette Davis, Irene Dunne, Alice Faye, Gene Tierney, and Eleanor Powell, I might never have made it out of Cleveland!

The studios could also create an image of the world that you could believe in and fight for. During World War II they gave us movies that had a very clear "good guy versus bad guy" point of view, and it helped to unite us. The world is much more complicated today. And the audiences (for the most part) are much more sophisticated. But if we are serious about wanting a better world for our children, then what is wrong with someone like Jimmy Stewart showing us the way in *Mr. Smith Goes to Washington* or Spencer Tracy fighting for what is right in almost every film he ever made?

This sounds like I am a Republican running for office. I'm not. I'm just trying to say that we need to find our way back to common sense and the Golden Rule. The world could use some of those simple "John Wayne" type morals today. And our country could use some of the unabashedly blatant patriotism provided by immigrants such as Louis B. Mayer and Sam Goldwyn. That was entertainment! And that was the Hollywood I wanted so desperately to be a part of.

Billy DeWolfe

(That's *Mr.* DeWolfe to *You*)

I love nicknames. Maybe it was John Murray Anderson who started me on the kick (calling me "Kimmer"), but I like to find a suitable name for practically everyone I come into contact with. Some people might think this habit is a simple, disingenuous way to not have to remember people's real names. I think it is a sign of affection and kindness. A nickname makes you feel immediately friendly and close to a person. So when Billy DeWolfe christened me Miss Rose Boozey, I knew we would be friends for life! What a talented, funny, loyal, original gentleman. Today, Billy (Mr. DeWolfe) is probably most remembered as the voice of the phony magician in the holiday cartoon classic *Frosty the Snowman*, but he had a great career in television and films and on the stage for well over forty years.

All right, let me explain about the name. William Andrew Jones was a first-generation Welsh-American, born on February 18, 1907, in Wollaston, Massachusetts. His parents hoped he'd become a Baptist minister, but just like me, he got a taste of show business when he was very young. After hanging out at the local theater/burlesque hall, he got a job as an usher, just as I had back in Cleveland. When he was a teenager, he was fooling around doing some flips and rolls, and the head of an acrobatic team asked him if he wanted a job. Without hesitation he took it but was told by the theater manager that the name Billy Jones was not suited for the stage. His boss then gave him his own name, William DeWolfe.

Mr. DeWolfe's own story about the origin of his name is a little different, but much funnier. I asked him one time, "Hasn't anyone ever called you Billy?" He said, "Well, I'll tell you, I had an older brother named Bobby. And when my mother would call us she'd yell, 'Bobby! Bobby! It's time for dinner! (pause) Oh, Mr. DeWoooooolfe!'" God, he was a funny man!

Billy DeWolfe had a slightly nasal voice, and a very clipped manner of speaking with absolutely perfect diction. His meticulous style of dress, along with his trademark trimmed, pencil-thin mustache (created for him by famed makeup artist Wally Westmore), made him ideal to play high-strung, imperious, supporting comic parts to perfection.

Mr. DeWolfe learned his craft as I had, on the road. The acrobatic troupe he had joined eventually disbanded, so he became a dancer and impressionist in vaudeville and developed a cabaret act, with which he successfully toured all the smart supper clubs throughout Europe for five years.

Once Mr. DeWolfe returned to the States, the comic bit that really launched his career was a character called Mrs. Murgatroyd. The only "drag" he used was a simple flowered hat. Obviously tipsy, he'd hold up a martini. Licking the swizzle stick he'd hiccup and say, "It's my husband . . . he's drinking again." This routine became a smash in nightclubs and eventually got him into radio, movies, and television. Billy DeWolfe became a frequent supporting player in Hollywood during the 1940s and '50s. His movies included *Blue Skies*, with Bing Crosby and Fred Astaire, *The Perils of Pauline*, with Betty Hutton, *Call Me Madam*, with Ethel Merman, and *Tea for Two*, in which he worked with Gordon MacRae and Doris Day.

He got along so well with Doris (whom, by the way, he nicknamed "Clara Bixby") that she remembered him when she was putting her television show together and cast him as her boss. Though he and I had become friends years earlier, *The Doris Day Show* was the project on which Billy DeWolfe and I got to work together.

Every year, Mr. DeWolfe would return to Wales for a vacation. One year, Carleton Carpenter and I went down to see him off. As the boat pulled out, Mr. DeWolfe waved and smiled. We waved and smiled back, all the while teasing and shouting up to him, "Mr. DeWooooolfe, we have your passport!" Later, we took a trip to Europe together that was one of the greatest vacations I have ever had. Oh, did we laugh! There were certain things that weren't mentioned around Mr. DeWolfe. He wore a toupee, and when he would get a new one I'd say, "Oh, you got a new . . ." and that's as far as I'd get before he'd cut me off with, "We never discuss it." That became the name of his hairpiece: We-never-discuss-it.

I don't think anybody really knew much about Mr. DeWolfe's personal life. It didn't matter. In fact, the closest I ever came to even wondering about it occurred because of a chance meeting in an airport after he had passed away. A gentleman came up and introduced himself, saying, "I was Billy DeWolfe's friend."

Billy DeWolfe died of lung cancer in 1974. I can't believe he's been gone for more than thirty years. He entertained thousands of people without ever being offensive or uttering a dirty word. He was an original—a wonderfully funny, loyal man who never failed to make me laugh and lift my spirits.

So why write about Billy? (Sorry . . . Mr. DeWolfe.) I guess because he's yet another performer who falls into the category of brilliant "supporting players" who I feel left the public's consciousness much too soon after they passed away. Who knows, perhaps I have a fear that the same thing will happen to me. I think every human being hopes that they will leave something of value behind on this earth. As performers who never had children, Billy DeWolfe and I have a chance to be remembered through our work.

So look up Billy DeWolfe on the Internet. Find his old routines in films and on the radio and television shows in which he performed. There's a lot of wit and truth to be found there. And I'll bet that even if you never had a chance to meet Billy DeWolfe in person or never saw him perform, you'll begin to miss him, just as I do. You'll also discover that the world had much more style and class when Mr. DeWolfe was in it.

Chapter Twelve

Lucy, Desi, and THE MOTHERS-IN-LAW

By 1967, when *The Mothers-in-Law* TV series first appeared, I had been through burlesque, vaudeville, and nightclubs, starred on Broadway, and appeared on television in a variety of shows. I did everything from *Perry Como's Kraft Music Hall* and *The Mel Tormé Show* to *The Merv Griffin Show*, *The Hollywood Palace*, *The Jack Paar Show*, and, perhaps the greatest variety show of all time, *The Ed Sullivan Show*. But it takes a series of your own to become a household name. Once *The Mothers-in-Law* hit the air, I was suddenly everyone's relative, and I liked that feeling.

Late in the spring of 1966, Desi Arnaz was looking for someone to play opposite Eve Arden in a situation comedy about two very different families who struggle to get along after one couple's son marries the other couple's daughter and the kids move into her parents' garage. The comedy focused on the two mother characters, one a "white-bread" WASP and the other a stereotypical, loud-mouthed Italian.

A couple of years earlier, I was appearing at the Blue Angel in New York, where I had been booked several times with the likes of Barbara Cook, Harry Belafonte, and The Smothers Brothers. One night, Lucille Ball came in with her future husband, a former comic who loved to play golf by the name of Gary Morton. I knew Gary from the days when we were both playing the Catskill Mountain resorts. He was a very handsome, very mediocre comic who had never made it. After my act, Lucy called me over to the table and simply said, "You're funny." Two little words, but coming from her, well, I was so in awe of her I could barely speak.

Ann Sothern had originally been cast in my *Mothers-in-Law* part.

Ann was a good friend of Lucy's and had appeared with her several times on both *The Lucy-Desi Comedy Hour* and *The Lucy Show*. At the time, she was looking for a new project, having survived her role as another type of mother, the voice of the automobile on the ill-fated Jerry Van Dyke sitcom *My Mother the Car*. But, lucky for me, it seems the producers thought Ann and Eve Arden were too much alike to play against each other, so I got the role. As simple as that.

Well, not quite. Right before all this, I had been approached by two men, Bill Osbourne, a set designer, and Sal Mungo, some kind of businessman. They had also heard about Desi's new show and convinced me that they could get me on the pilot if I formed a corporation with them. We called it Carmella Productions, after a dog I had at the time. I loved that dog. She was the sweetest little toy poodle. Actually, she was a tiny human in a fur coat. She was so smart—smarter than me, it turns out. Trusting idiot that I was, I told Bill and Sal, "Oh, yes! Anything to get on a television series!" But it turns out my partners knew something I didn't: Desi Arnaz was already looking at me for the role!

After Lucy's recommendation, Desi sent Bob Carroll Jr., one of the writers of the show (he and Madelyn Davis, along with Jess Oppenheimer, were the original writers on *I Love Lucy*), to Detroit to see me. I was working at a club called the Act Four, and the night Bob saw the show I had a 103-degree fever. I guess it didn't matter. Bob called Desi and told him I was right for the part—and I was off to Los Angeles to audition, all the while thinking Bill and Sal had arranged the whole thing for me. For the next two years I gave away 40 percent of my earnings to them! What a shady deal it all turned out to be. The only good part of that production company was the puppy it was named for. No wonder I trust dogs more than people!

Desi Arnaz himself directed the pilot and most of the episodes. He was also the executive producer of the show and edited every script. As everyone now admits, Desi was a genius. Not only did he build the Desilu empire, he knew the art of situation comedy inside and out. Hell, he practically invented it. The three-camera system he pioneered on *I Love Lucy* is still used on situation comedies today. Of course, now technicians "sweeten" the soundtracks with extra laughter when the jokes don't get the desired response. And many times they don't, because the directors keep an audience captive for ten or twelve hours just to get eighteen or twenty minutes of tape. No matter how funny, a joke tends to wear thin on the fifth and sixth take. We would film *The Mothers-in-Law* like a play.

No retakes, and no canned laughter. What the live studio audience saw is what you got every week on your television set.

CBS, which had aired all of the Lucy shows, decided to pass on the project. But NBC wanted it. So *The Mothers-in-Law* premiered on NBC on September 10, 1967. We debuted as the number-two show that week, and for two seasons we were never out of the top fifteen in the Nielsen ratings. We were all delighted with the success. I remember Desi saying to me, "Kaye, remember, a series is only going to do well if you don't have too many people connected to it. A situation comedy shouldn't have more than four to six regulars on it, so the audience can focus on them and really get to know them."

Desi was never given the recognition he deserved. Vivian Vance also loved Desi. When she heard I got the job, she said, "You are going to work with the most tasteful man in show business." She also gave me a piece of advice I'll never forget. The night before I left for California, Vivian said, "Kaye, no matter what else you do, insist that your character's name be Kaye. I've spent a fortune in analysis because no matter what else I do, the entire world only knows me as Ethel Mertz!" As a result, we all kept our own names. Eve Arden and Herbert Rudley became Eve and Herb Hubbard, and Roger C. Carmel and I were Roger and Kaye Buell.

I was in heaven! On Mondays we did a read-through of the script with the writers, Madelyn Pugh Davis and Bob Carroll Jr., who were always on the set. Desi would immediately put the show on its feet with the script in hand. He would give us our blocking (where we were to move on the set), and by Tuesday we were expected to have some of the dialogue learned. On Wednesday we were expected to know it perfectly. Thursday was camera blocking day, and Friday we taped the show in front of an audience of 300 people. There wasn't a lot of time to experiment, and Desi pretty much told you what he wanted. But if you came up with something, he'd let you try it. We taped the dress rehearsal and the show, and that was it. No retakes, no doing sections at a time until three in the morning like they do today. It was like learning and performing a new twenty-three-minute (there were fewer commercials back then) play every week.

One of the great joys I had in doing the series was being able to work with the guest stars. Desi was a very loyal man and hired a lot of his friends for the roles, and many times I was able to suggest people and secure work for some of my pals as well. Some of the people who stick out in my mind are:

৯ৎ

ALICE GHOSTLEY Wonderful! Always wonderful! We worked together in *Cinderella* and have been friends ever since. They used to compare her to Paul Lynde, but she had that original persona down way before Paul came along. It was just an accident that they had the same sort of humor. In fact, I'm not so sure that Paul didn't copy a little bit of *her*!

৯ৎ

AVERY SCHRIEBER Funny man with funny looks. He was one of the "new" crowd that started coming in from the Second City comedy troupe. He had just been burned by *My Mother the Car*, along with poor Ann Sothern, and I had the feeling sometimes that he felt he was a little beyond playing with all us older "uneducated" comics.

৯ৎ

DESI ARNAZ JR. Adorable and very shy. I don't think he was ever given a chance to find the part that suited him, the role that might have carried him further. His sister, Lucie, was terribly talented and a little more confident. I always felt she would probably direct one day, but Desi Jr. got steamrolled a bit by having such famous parents.

৯ৎ

DON RICKLES A very funny man who was never offstage.

৯ৎ

JIMMY DURANTE The most precious man you'd ever want to meet. He was Desi's closest friend. All we did the week he was on the show was laugh. He didn't have to rehearse. All he had to do was say the lines and we were on the floor! Such an original talent. Many times when Jimmy was doing his act, he'd walk into a club and throw a stack of sheet music in the air and yell to the orchestra, "Here, play this!" He was just a joy to be around. I remember going to his seventieth birthday party with Desi and Desi's second wife, Edie. Jimmy sat down at the piano and did his famous "Inka Dinka Doo" as a ballad for all of us. I thought, what greatness, what simplicity. He was funny and endearing without ever resorting to being risqué. He and his wife, Margie, had adopted a daughter by the name of CeeCee, and Jimmy was just crazy about that little girl. One time CeeCee wanted to stay up to see a show on television that started at nine o'clock. Margie told her it was time for bed, but Jimmy intervened saying, "Aww, let the kid live a little, let the kid live!"

৯ৎ

JOE BESSER He was hilarious and a sweet, sweet gentle man. He used to tell me that he had all these Three Stooges films (he joined the Three Stooges in 1956 after Shemp Howard died) just sitting in his garage. Joe appeared on three episodes of *The Mothers-in-Law*. At that point in his life, he had no money. However, Desi remembered all the old-timers and would help them out whenever he could. (So many people I had admired growing up seemed to end up with nothing at the end.)

LARRY STORCH He has been one of my closest friends almost all my life. I first saw Larry when I was with Spike Jones. Spike took me out to a show one night and Larry was opening for, of all people, Desi Arnaz! Isn't it ironic that I met them both on their opening night at the Trocadero? Larry and I also did a revue together at the Flamingo Hotel in Las Vegas. This was back in the early 1950s, and the audience didn't understand a thing we did. We thought we were being quite sophisticated. Maybe too sophisticated. We bombed for four weeks straight. Larry was so funny. He was the emcee, and after I'd do something to a tiny smattering of applause, he'd come out and say, "Charming, completely chaaarming." We had a good time even if nobody else did!

ROB REINER Desi fired him. Rob wouldn't stick to the script, and Desi was a stickler for staying with what was written. To this day, I think maybe Rob is embarrassed that I was there when he was fired. I remember going up to him and telling him not to take it too hard. Poor kid. He's never hired me, but I think he is brilliantly talented!

OZZIE NELSON A wonderful man. A total professional who loved to rehearse over and over again. Harriet wasn't in the episode in which Ozzie appeared on *The Mothers-in-Law*, but she'd sit there on the side of the set watching him the whole time.

PAUL LYNDE I discovered Paul when I was doing *Three to Make Ready* at the Blackstone Theatre in Chicago. A boyfriend at the time took me to see a college show at Northwestern University. Paul Lynde and Charlotte Rae were in it. I called Leonard Sillman and told him he had to see this guy. I was twenty or twenty-one at the time, and Paul never got over the fact that I was in a Broadway show while he was still in school!

Paul was a very funny man who was never happy—not with his career (he always wanted to do more movies and be a serious actor), and not with his personal life. So, he drank to try and deal with his unhappiness.

And when he drank he became very mean, and he drove a lot of people from his life. Being funny and insecure seem to go hand in hand—especially with men. For instance, Sid Caesar was so insecure he once told someone that he went to both an analyst *and* a psychiatrist so he could check to see if they were sharing notes on him. Eventually, I was one of those people Paul drove away. The sad part is, toward the end he got sober and started to try and make amends with a lot of people, but by that time it was too late, the damage was done.

JOI LANSING In one of the funniest episodes, she played my husband's secretary. Joi was about as well-endowed as Anna Nicole Smith. I was sitting down looking up at her and I couldn't see her face. I kept trying to crane my neck or look around the side, but I still couldn't see her. My face started getting red, and finally Eve and I just kept breaking up! We couldn't get back to the scene. Here was this tiny girl with *huge* bosoms. I screamed, "Please, tell me, how does that happen? When I get fat, I get fat all over!" Sadly, Joi died of breast cancer about two years later.

We did between twenty-six and thirty episodes per season, compared to the eighteen or twenty they do today. Two of my favorite episodes were actually both my ideas. "The Wig Story" had my character borrowing Eve's blond wig. Suddenly my husband starts paying more attention to me and finds me irresistible, almost like another woman, and I get depressed because I think he doesn't love me for me. The other one, called "Who's Afraid of Elizabeth Taylor?" was based on a huge blow-up between my real-life brother, Orlando, and his wife, Grace. Orlando looked in the paper one day and saw an article about Elizabeth Taylor doing the movie *Cleopatra*. He said to my sister-in-law, "Hey, look, Elizabeth Taylor." She said, "Ugh! Elizabeth Taylor! How dare she break up a marriage like that! Would you sleep with her if you could?" (In the show, of course, we had to substitute "take her out" for "sleep with her.") So he said, "Yeah." Grace locked herself in the bathroom and Orlando shouted after her, "Wait a minute, don't worry, honey. . . . How am I gonna meet Elizabeth Taylor!?" Some businesswoman I am—I didn't get paid for either of those ideas. Today you'd get quite a fee! (By the way, Orlando and Grace ended up staying together for more than fifty years. That's longer than Elizabeth Taylor Hilton Wilding Todd Fisher Burton Burton Warner Fortensky's eight marriages put together!)

I adored Eve Arden and the actor who played her husband on the show, Herb Rudley. On the first day of filming, Eve came up to me and said, "Do you have a good side?" Totally confused, I said, "I don't know." "Well," continued Eve, "I do, so you'll be standing over here." I was just happy to be there. Deborah Walley played Herb and Eve's daughter, and Jerry Fogel played Roger's and my son. They were delights to work with. I always felt bad, though, because Kay Cole played my daughter in the pilot and was let go and replaced by Deborah Walley. To this day, I don't know why they got rid of her, but later I was thrilled for Kay when she got into the original production of *A Chorus Line* on Broadway.

Trekkies will forever remember Roger C. Carmel, who played my husband on the show, as Harcourt Fenton Mudd on two episodes of the original *Star Trek*. The series that turned into a multibillion-dollar franchise was one of the last projects Lucy herself green-lighted before she sold the Desilu studio to Paramount. Roger was a brilliant actor and we had a special chemistry together. But during the second season, a dispute arose between Desi and the cast. We had asked for a raise of $250 per episode. That's not a misprint, folks. All we wanted was an additional $250. Can you imagine? Today that would be a joke. Eve Arden, a very well-established star, was receiving only $6,000 an episode! Compare that salary with that of Jerry Seinfeld, who thirty years later got $1 million an episode for his show. Or Ray Romano, who was paid $2 million an episode for *Everybody Loves Raymond*. Oy!

I digress . . . Most of our cast really didn't care about the raise; we just wanted to keep working. However, with Roger the money became a real issue. The show cost approximately $90,000 an episode to produce. Even though the show was doing well, we were told that the company was in the red, and our request for a salary increase was refused. Roger said to me, "Toots," (he called me "Toots" and I called him "Cutes") "it's the principle of the thing. I want that raise!" Well, Roger ended up leaving the series and was replaced by another well-known character actor, Richard Deacon, who had just finished five seasons playing Mel Cooley on *The Dick Van Dyke Show*. Richard was also a marvelous actor, but the charisma that had been there between Roger and me just wasn't to be found with Richard. I also thought it was unwise to change husbands midstream in a series, but I wasn't the one making the decisions. Maybe we broke some new ground, though, because the following season, when Dick York had to leave *Bewitched* because of health problems, the producers pulled the now famous "Darren switch," replacing York with Dick Sargent, and the series lasted three more seasons. Oh, if we'd only lasted three seasons and been able to go into syndication! After the first year, I was delighted to know that I had a job the following year. I was enjoying both the recognition and the steady paycheck. After the second season we were all so certain we were coming back for another year that after we filmed the last episode we didn't even bother to say good-bye to each other.

Why were we canceled if we were such a success? Well, television, above all, is a business, a business run by advertising. Tastes change, and the advertisers like to try to be ahead of the trend so that they can cash in. This was the late sixties, and situation comedy was about to change forever with a little show called *All in the Family*. After two seasons of *The Mothers-in-Law*, it seems there were complaints directed at one of the advertisers, Proctor and Gamble, concerning the lack of black actors on television. This was a legitimate complaint when you think that just a couple of seasons before, *The Dick Van Dyke Show* took what was considered to be a dangerous risk with an episode that featured a black actor by the name of Greg Morris, later of *Mission Impossible* fame. So we were replaced in the NBC lineup by a gentleman I happen to adore. I first met Bill Cosby in Chicago right before he was cast on the *I Spy* TV series. *The Bill Cosby Show* (forerunner to the more successful *Cosby Show* in the 1980s), debuted in our spot in September 1969.

As I say, if we had lasted a few more seasons (long enough to get syndicated), my life might have been financially very different. The show was on just long enough to typecast me as a loudmouth Italian actress, but not long enough to ensure that I would earn the kind of money where I wouldn't have to *worry* about being typecast. I was having dinner one night with the great stage director Bobby Lewis, and we were talking about Henry Winkler. Bobby had taught Henry at the Yale Drama School years before he found fame as The Fonz on *Happy Days*. I said to Bobby, "Can you believe he's earning $200,000 a week for that part?" I was surprised when he replied, "And that's not nearly enough. Now no one will ever know what he is really capable of." Bobby meant that the public—and, more important, producers and directors—would forever see Henry as Arthur Fonzarelli, and so he would have difficulty being hired for anything else. He might never be able to show what he was really capable of doing. I'm sure this is partly why several famous TV actors have found their way into jobs behind the scenes as directors and producers.

I am grateful, though, that during the time I was doing *The Mothers-in-Law*, I became quite close to Lucille Ball. Well, as close as one could get to her. Lucy and Desi had divorced by then, and he was married to his second wife, Edie. Lucy was a very strong woman and, as others have commented, not a funny person offstage. One of the things I found fascinating about Lucy was that even with all her success and power, she was still impressed by great wealth. She had come from humble beginnings in Jamestown, New York. One day she took me to visit some friends who lived in a very chic home. I soon discovered that she wanted to show me the three different kinds of marble in their bathroom.

Lucy was used to being in control—and she was good at it. In fact, I think the only person she ever really deferred to was Desi. On another one of our outings, Lucy and I were riding our bicycles down a rather isolated street when out from behind a couple of palm trees came a ferocious looking dog, growling and barking and chasing after us. Unfazed, Lucy screamed at the dog in that baritone voice, "Get the fuck out of here!" The dog stopped in his tracks and ran away. "Lucy," I said, "that is why you are queen of the world." As her daughter, Lucie Arnaz, once said, "Even God is afraid of my mother."

While she was working, Lucy was all business and could come across on occasion as being quite cruel. Danny Kaye was on the set with Lucy during one of her shows, and they got into a disagreement. Danny was furious and shouted at Lucy, "Who the hell do you think you are?' Lucy shouted back, "You're full of shit, that's who I think I am!" Joan Crawford was a guest on *The Lucy Show*, and throughout rehearsal, she was sipping at a bottle of vodka she had hidden in her purse. Joan got drunk and Lucy was angry about it. She told me that she wanted to replace Joan and asked if I knew Greer Garson. I said that I did, and she asked me to call her to replace Joan. But Miss Crawford stuck to her guns and refused to leave the show. The taping went off without a hitch and Joan was wonderful. The audience went mad for her, and this annoyed Lucy to no end.

Lucy did sort of a mean thing to me once, too. One night, she invited me over to her house for a meal. *The Mothers-in-Law* hadn't aired yet, but Lucy had a copy of the first episode, and she was going to show it after dinner. I showed up at Lucy's house to find Milton Berle, Jack Carter, and several other famous comedians already there. Now, comedians are innately jealous of anyone who does comedy, and especially a woman. I don't think people like Jack Carter and Buddy Hackett believed that there was any place for a woman in comedy. Except Lucy. She was funny *and* beautiful. It is not often that you find a pretty woman willing to become "unpretty" in front of the camera.

They respected her. So, Lucy ran the episode, and there was no response at all from these men, nothing. They didn't laugh. I thought, "Oh my God, this is a flop!" I was so insecure that I kept interrupting and complaining, "I'm talking too loud!" I was still doing live-theater acting. Even though Lucy had recommended me for the part—a part that was full of slapstick comedy and shtick—I think she wanted everyone to know, especially me, that she was still the top, still the queen of comedy. So she was going to prove it in front of all those funny people. And Desi always, always let me know that no one was better at this game than Lucy. (But I have to say, he did laugh a lot at me.)

I believe that for the rest of her life Lucy was still very much in love with Desi, and he with her. There was always such a tremendous devotion between them, even after their divorce. You could not help but love Desi. He was always happy and had such contagious energy and a real joy for living. So why didn't it work? So much has been written on the subject, but I believe it's very simple. Lucy was a strong, proud woman, and Desi was a strong, proud man who drank too much and didn't know how to be true. He certainly was irresistible, and somehow when it came to women, he felt he had to service the world.

Even though it didn't run as long as *Friends* or *Seinfeld*, *The Mothers-in-Law* was the most fabulous job. To think that I was going to get paid every week and then get time off and get paid again for the residuals in the summer! To those who complain about working hard in television, I have one thing to say: You don't know what "hard" means! Try doing eight shows a week on the stage—now that's hard!

I think the most amazing thing about our little show is that even after thirty-six years, people still recognize me from *The Mothers-in-Law*. They come up all the time and say, "Hey, aren't you Kaye from the TV show?" It's a nice feeling. And thank you, Vivian, you were right! Oh. I got something else from it, too. Desi may never have made me rich, but he and Edie purchased a home near Palm Springs and were kind enough to let me use it whenever I wanted. I found such serenity in the desert that I eventually bought the house from them and have lived there since 1970!

Doris Day

One afternoon in 1966, I was browsing around an antiques shop in Beverly Hills when I spotted Doris Day riding her bicycle down the street. Being a brazen, star-struck girl from Cleveland, I rushed outside to talk to her. She was so gracious. I told her I was doing a pilot for a new series with Eve Arden, and she crossed her fingers and said she hoped it would go well. Over the next couple of years, I got to know Doris a bit better, and she told me that when she did a television series, she wanted me to be in it!

The Doris Day Show eventually appeared in the fall of 1968, which just happened to be the last year that *The Mothers-in-Law* was on the air. Doris had never really thought of doing a television show, but she had found out that her manager/husband, Martin Melcher, had squandered away the vast majority of her considerable fortune, and she needed to go back to work.

In the five seasons *The Doris Day Show* was produced, the format and story line changed four times. In the first season, Doris played a widowed mother of two who settles in the country, with her little boys, her father, and a farmhand, to escape the pressures of city life. Maybe the success of *The Beverly Hillbillies* and *Green Acres* had an influence on the location for the series. But *The Doris Day Show* soon got caught up in the tide of change. The same world-shaking turmoil happening in this country in the late 1960s that helped get *The Mothers-in-Law* taken off the air made it difficult to find the right "modern tone" for other situation comedies as well. If you think about it, when it came to defining women's roles on television, at least in situation comedy, *The Doris Day Show* was probably the perfect transitional link between shows like *I Love Lucy* and those like *The Mary Tyler Moore Show.*

Because of all the changes in the story line over the years, *The Doris Day Show* was chock-full of recurring guest-star characters. These guests included myself, Denver Pyle, Rose Marie, Larry Storch, Jackie Joseph, McLean Stevenson, Billy DeWolfe, and even Peter Lawford. In the second season, Doris takes a job at a magazine in San Francisco and commutes back and forth to the farm. The third season finds Doris and her kids moving into a small apartment in the city. Her father and the hired hand stay in the country to run the farm. This is when I entered the show. I played Angie Palucci, one of the owners of the Italian restaurant (what else?) downstairs. My husband was played by Bernie Kopell, who had been a semi-regular on both *That Girl* and *Get Smart*, and later found his claim to fame playing Doc on *The Love Boat*.

Though I was extremely grateful for the work and I absolutely adored working with Doris, I really believe her show hurt my career. Here I was, coming off a successful series and being cast as another loudmouth Italian. That role only served to solidify the public's impression of me. And to make matters worse, though I did only fourteen episodes, people in the business thought I was a regular. As a result, just a year after *The Mothers-in-Law* ended, at the point when I was probably my "hottest" careerwise, nobody thought of casting me because they assumed I was committed to *The Doris Day Show*. By the forth and fifth seasons, the story line concentrated almost exclusively on Doris as a beautiful young bachelorette, and I was out of work again.

That show was probably a mistake for me professionally, but personally it was wonderful to do. I got to work with terrific people like my buddy Billy DeWolfe, and I became good friends with Doris. She made it an awful lot of fun to be on that set.

One afternoon Doris and I went into a restaurant to have lunch. It's funny, we'd go shopping in the Topanga Canyon Mall and nobody would recognize her. They'd recognize me, but wouldn't give her a second look. She wasn't disguised or anything; it's just that nobody would ever expect to see a huge movie star like Doris Day out in public. But me . . . they were pushing papers under the door in the restroom for me to sign while Doris was peeing in the next stall!

Anyway, one day at lunch I spotted Diana Ross sitting at a table near ours. I said, "Oh, Doris, go over and say hello." "No," she said, "I don't want to bother her." "Oh, go on," I kept after her, "it'll be a thrill for her." So Doris got up and walked over to the table. "Hello," she said, "I'm Doris Day." Diana turned to her, said "Hello," and turned back to her meal, leaving Doris just standing there. Doris came back to the table and said, "That is the last time I ever listen to *you!*"

Doris once told me that the biggest heartbreak she ever had over not getting a film part was when they turned her down for the starring role in *South Pacific*. It had been the one part she really wanted. (And come on, she *was* Nellie Forbush!)

While we were still filming the show, I remember Doris and Mr. DeWolfe went to see *Last Tango in Paris*, and they came by to visit me afterward. "Well, Clara," (the nickname Billy DeWolfe gave her) "what did you think?" I asked. "Interesting," she said. "Oh, you can talk plainer than that," I coaxed her. "Well, they go too far in movies now. They try and make everything too real. Diarrhea is a part of life, too, but I don't want to see that on the screen, either." That was in the early 1970s. I can't imagine what she thinks of some of the things up there on the screen today!

There has been an effort underway in recent years to give Doris Day an honorary Oscar. I can't think of a more deserving recipient. She was such a huge part of American pop culture throughout the second half of the twentieth century. She influenced and entertained generations! How many other people had million-selling songs on the charts and number-one movies at the box office (from dramas to light comedies to thrillers to musicals, I might add) and then managed a successful five-year run on television?

Many people are curious about how Doris has managed to stay happily retired and out of the spotlight, except for a brief return to TV in the mid-1980s. I can tell you: her dogs. Doris and I found we had a common love for animals, especially dogs. Nowadays, she is well known and respected for her devotion to animals, but at the time of her retirement, people thought she was crazy.

Doris Day has been through a lot in this business, and I think that is another reason we bonded. When people you trust disappoint you or, worse, take advantage of you, you begin to lose your faith in human nature. That is what is so special about the love you get from a pet, especially a puppy. It is unconditional devotion and loyalty. At a certain point in a show-business career, that kind of love becomes indispensable.

P.S. The last time Doris called, we talked for over an hour. I am always so thrilled just to hear her voice, because I still can't believe Doris Day is calling *me!* The funny thing is, she called to tell me how excited she was that Paul McCartney had called her to say what a big fan he was of her work. Show business is such an odd "round-robin" of a food chain.

Chapter Thirteen

Headaches, Heartaches, Backaches . . . Flops

T here is nothing quite like the thrill and exhilaration of being in a hit show on Broadway, and nothing like the terror and heartbreak of being in a flop. One show in particular nearly killed me. But before I tell you about that one, let me mention several other bombs that have fallen on my delicate career.

PLEASURE DOME should have been successful. It previewed and closed while still in rehearsal in Washington, D.C., in 1955. *Pleasure Dome* was basically a revue billed as a "musical holiday." I costarred with Josephine Premice and Jimmie Komack, who later went on to direct *Welcome Back, Kotter* and *Chico and the Man*. Ira Wallach, Coleman Jacoby, and Arnold Rosen wrote the book, and later Tallulah Bankhead, Bea Lillie, and Carol Burnett would perform sketches from the show. In fact, Dean Fuller and Marshall Barer, who wrote the music and lyrics, collaborated on the book for Carol's *Once Upon a Mattress* four years later. We did weeks and weeks of auditions in a large open rehearsal room. As a result, everyone in New York had seen most of the show by the time rehearsals started.

George Abbott, the legendary writer, producer, and director, sat in and saw me performing one day and said, "Kaye, if this opens on Broadway, you've got it made." The producer, Jack Segasture, was very cordial, and once the show was cast, he took the entire company out to lunch after every morning rehearsal. Josephine Premice was very chic and beautiful and had a wonderful voice. Josephine thought quite highly of herself, and one day I told her, "Honey, if it were possible to have a relationship with yourself, yours would be the greatest love affair of the century!" Josephine just laughed. And agreed! This was an instance when the show's cast, book, and music were all very good. The problem was the producer. He ran out of money. I guess he spent it all on auditions and lunches.

સ

REUBEN, REUBEN was scheduled for Broadway, too, also in 1955. Bobby Lewis (*Brigadoon, Teahouse of the August Moon, Witness for the Prosecution*) directed the show, and Marc Blitzstein wrote the book and musical score. The show starred Eddie Albert, George Gaynes, and Evelyn Lear, the magnificent opera star. Eddie Albert was a fine actor, but when he felt at all insecure, he relied on his "good old boy" personality. Everything was great in rehearsals. Eddie was performing brilliantly under Bobby's superb direction. Then Bobby decided not to have a "gypsy" run in front of an invited audience and instead to open cold in Boston. That was a mistake. Eddie got nervous and lost his entire character. Granted, the subject matter—the play was about a man who couldn't speak—was rather depressing (and difficult to write songs for), but Eddie's character had to carry the show, and without a character . . . well, let's just say *Reuben, Reuben* received the worst reviews to appear in the *Boston Globe* in thirty years.

On opening night, several hundred people walked out, right past producer Cheryl Crawford, who stood in the middle of the aisle angrily defying them to walk around her. Bobby Lewis tried to call several people, including Arthur Miller, to come in and help fix the show, but Marc Blitzstein wouldn't hear of it. Marc was one of those brilliant men who seem content with failure. Or perhaps he was just daunted by past success. A lot of people in this business are guilty of that, including myself on occasion. Success can be frightening. As a result of success you become insecure, afraid of risk and the unknown. You rely on old habits to protect yourself from criticism. Success comes so much more easily when you don't know any better and have nothing to lose.

સ

ROYAL FLUSH opened in New Haven in 1964. The book, music, and lyrics were by Jay Thompson, a wonderful writer, arranger, lyricist, and composer who, among other accomplishments, also collaborated on the book for *Once Upon a Mattress.* The show had a lot of possibilities. Jack Cole (Gwen Verdon's first mentor) did the staging and directed. He was a great choreographer but hadn't directed before and, as a result, never quite got around to giving the show a second act. He also drank a lot and was very temperamental. Jack would go to lunch and buffer himself with several martinis before returning to work. I think he must have been terrified. He tried to hide the effect of the liquor, but when a director stands rigidly in front of you screaming out orders that make no sense, it becomes rather obvious. When he didn't know what to do next, which was frequently, he would shout, "All right, everybody get out! Go take a sh**!" I finally turned to someone and said, "Wouldn't it be funny if we all did? If we all just left a great big pile for him in the middle of the stage?"

I had top billing in that show, alongside the great Eddie Foy Jr., who'd been starring onstage since 1929. People have said that Eddie was fired, but I'd like to set the record straight. He quit. Eddie could see the handwriting on the wall. He'd listen to Jack Cole ranting and say, "Kaye, this man is crazy. I don't think he has all his marbles." Eddie was replaced by comedian Mickey Deems, and when we went to Canada, Martin Green was hired to direct. When that didn't work out, June Havoc was called. No one could save the show. Hey, it was about a queen who is imprisoned in an underground bathroom—*Royal Flush*? At least none of us were hurt by too much bad press—we closed while we were still out of the country! As a side note, Julie Taymor (*The Lion King*) took a stab at the same eighteenth-century source material and made it to Broadway in 2000 with a show called *The Green Bird.*

THE BEAST IN ME opened at the Plymouth Theatre in New York City on May 14, 1963, and closed on May 18, 1963. James Thurber and James Costigan wrote the show. Bert Convy, who appeared on Broadway in *Fiddler on the Roof* and *Cabaret* before becoming a popular TV game show host in the 1970s, was one of the stars. Ruth Gordon came backstage the night before we opened and told me, "Kaye, honey, you're in a bomb and there's nothing you can do to save it. You're wonderful in it, but it's still a bomb, so I want you to go out there opening night and just have fun with it." That was fabulous advice, because I did just that and received great notices for my performance. I felt a little guilty because other people were out there working their asses off to save the show. I just sat back and didn't try to make the show something it wasn't. Walter Kerr gave me a glorious review, thanks to Ruth Gordon.

·ᴅ·

MOLLY, a brand-new musical comedy about the matriarch of the Goldbergs opened on Broadway at the Alvin Theatre on November 1, 1973. Every new theatrical project requires a great amount of hard work and commitment just to get the show up and running. Still, some shows may come and go without too much heartache. (The four I've just mentioned, for example.) That was not true of *Molly*. It was the first time my name would appear above the title. The first time I had an entire production riding on my shoulders. (Or so it felt, anyway.)

I adored the performer the show was based on, Gertrude Berg. Anyone who lived through the Depression and the war years remembers her show, *The Goldbergs*, from both radio and early television. The indomitable Molly Goldberg, along with her husband, Jake, children Sammy and Rosie, and their Uncle David, lived in the Bronx. *The Goldbergs* was the Yiddish version of *I Remember Mama*. Even though I was not Jewish (and believe me, many prominent Jews objected to that fact), she reminded me of my grandmother—so funny and loving and down to earth. I felt I knew her. The musical was really an extended version of one of the episodes of the radio and TV series. The story had to do with Jake losing his tailoring job just as the Depression hit and Molly's attempts to make everything all right. Eventually Molly (Mrs. Fix-it) looks over the remnants of cloth in the tailor shop and comes up with an invention to make some money and save the day: the two-piece bathing suit!

Molly had a solid cast, a very good score by Jerry Livingston and Leonard Adelson, a so-so book by Leonard Adelson and Louis Garfinkle, and an inept director who had no idea what he was doing! Paul Aaron wanted the cast to play games before every rehearsal to relax us. I can see how some of those exercises might be beneficial . . . in class. But when game time takes the place of working on the show, believe me, it has the opposite affect of relaxation. Eli Mintz, re-creating the part of Uncle David, which he had originated on the Goldberg series, would come over to me and say, "This is *meshugga* (crazy) now!" And he was right. It was insane. We would spend weeks rehearsing only one number and ignore the rest of the show. I don't know how, but a few years later Mr. Aaron found some success in television. He directed Patty Duke and Melissa Gilbert in the TV version of *The Miracle Worker*, Glenn Close in the movie bomb *Maxie*, and Chuck Norris in *A Force of One*. (I hope Chuck liked to play patty-cake!)

While we were still in rehearsal, Leonard Adelson suddenly passed away. It was a terrible blow to the company. Mack David (*Cat Ballou*, *It's a Mad Mad Mad Mad World*, and Disney's *Cinderella*), Jerry Livingston's sometime song-writing partner, was brought in to help. Mack had been nominated for an Oscar eight times without a win. Six of those nominations were consecutive, from 1961 through 1966. It's too bad, but the man who had written "Bibbidi-Bobbidi-Boo" seemed to bring the same amount of questionable luck along with him this time!

We opened in Boston to terrible reviews, and that night our "leader," Paul Aaron, deserted the show and disappeared. He never returned to Boston. Turns out he had packed up and gone to New York to start doing some re-writes—but without telling anyone. The bright side is that we were finally free to actually start playing the material, and toward the end of our three-week run in Boston the show began to gel. In fact, at the final performances, the audience stood and cheered. A glimmer of hope. On to New York.

Two days before we were to preview on Broadway, our wayward director decided to return. Paul not only had the audacity (or maybe just ignorance) to return, but he also threw an entirely new first act at us right before our first New York performance. Well, I blew up. Maybe it was not professional to scream at the director in front of the entire cast, but the pressure was too great. I could not stand the idiocy any longer. I called him a f***ing idiot and worse. "Don't you realize that the first preview is the test of whether this show is going to make it?!?" I was absolutely furious, and screamed, "Where were you the last three weeks? Now you dare come back with a new first act!?!" Paul replied, "Yes, but we've got three weeks to fix it." "We don't have three weeks!," I shouted in frustration. "The first preview tells people exactly what is going on, and the word 'bomb' spreads like wildfire!"

Okay, tantrum over, and somehow we actually managed to learn the new first act. I also called in another writer, Norman Martin, to do more songs for the show. I learned one of the numbers Norman wrote, "I See a Man," in one afternoon and put it in the show that night. I had to sing it holding a cheat sheet of paper with the lyrics, but it stopped the show. Norman also wrote a new opening number, which was perfect. He did all this without any credit.

It seemed like everyone in New York showed up for the first preview of *Molly*, and my prediction came true. By the next morning, word was out that the show was a disaster. My great pal, Billy DeWolfe, came to see the show, and in my dressing room afterward he confided, "Miss Boozey, you must become Debbie Reynolds and fire the director!" (She had done just that on her recent Broadway show *Irene.*) The great producer Alexander Cohen, his wife, and Ethel Merman were in the first row that night and walked out after the first act. This not only hurt me personally but also damaged the show. When I saw Ethel later, I told her that leaving before it was over had been a rotten thing to do. She replied bluntly, "Ballard, get out of this thing." I got the same advice from Maureen Stapleton.

It wasn't that easy. My name was on the play and I felt a responsibility to the company. I was in a lot of emotional pain. Everyone working on *Molly* was doing their damnedest to make it a success. It was almost impossible to keep up with the (now daily) changes being made to the script, and Paul Aaron was too busy being esoteric to direct anything. The whole thing was now beyond a nightmare. We needed a miracle.

Michael Bennett was invited to see the show in the hope that he would take over. It was still almost two years before he would create the blockbuster musical *A Chorus Line*, but he was a very well-respected choreographer who was on his way to becoming the new Bob Fosse. Fifteen minutes into the show, Michael walked out without saying a word to anyone. He may have proved to be a genius, but I say he was a rather insensitive one. He didn't even have the courtesy to call the producer and explain why the show was not to his liking.

Finally, Alan Arkin was hired to try and fix the show. With so little time left, he understandably didn't want his name appearing anywhere on the program. Lucky him. But Alan really stuck with *Molly,* and he was fantastic! Funny and bright. And, you know, he almost succeeded in making the show work. But we had run out of time and out of money. When Alan asked for one more week, the producers refused. I remember the night before we officially opened, Alan told us all how proud he was of the show and that he wanted to put his name on it. Everyone in the cast worshiped him.

As if fixing the script and the score hadn't been enough to deal with, the scenery was very dark and gloomy—the play was set during the Great Depression. On top of that, there was a gas crisis in New York at the time, so it was difficult for people to get to the theater. The only thing saving me from insanity was Gertrude Berg's son, Chaney, who told me that I had really captured the essence of his mother in the role. Her daughter helped me, also. I asked her if there was something I could have of her mother's, some little personal item for luck. She gave me a scarf that

Gertrude had worn, and I kept that scarf onstage with me throughout the show. Every once in a while I'd look at it and think "Oh, Gertrude Berg is with me."

Despite all the bad publicity and all the other troubles, *Molly* closed to standing room only houses . . . during the matinees. You see, it was really a woman's show that appealed to the average person rather than the more socially elite, just as *The Goldbergs* shows on radio and television had done decades before.

As I've said, the early 1970s were the beginning of tough times for old-fashioned musical comedies on Broadway. Not only was subject matter getting more sophisticated (and risqué) with shows like *Hair* and *Oh! Calcutta!*, everything was getting too expensive. Naturally the cost of the production was passed right on to the ticket buyer and ticket prices jumped to record levels. Today the average price of a ticket runs between sixty and a hundred bucks. *Molly*'s top seat cost around thirty dollars and we thought that was outrageous!

On closing night I believe I suffered a slight nervous breakdown. I had to sing a reprise of "Go in the Best of Health" to end the show. During the middle of the song, I began to shake so badly I could barely stammer out the words. It was as if the four months of stress, trauma, and worry had caught up with me in one single instant. It was very frightening. I have always been so at home on the stage, and in that one moment I thought I was going to die right there in front of the audience. Everyone thought it was just part of the show and congratulated me on the "powerful dramatic emotion" I delivered. If they only knew. I think my heart was breaking.

We closed to a huge, appreciative audience, but the producer was so broke by then he didn't have enough money left over to buy orange juice the morning after closing night. I'll never forget, I was frozen in what I guess some sort of shock when the final curtain came down and Gertrude Berg's daughter came up onto the stage. Was she there to offer sympathy? Support? She looked at me, she grabbed my good luck scarf, and she left. Such a thin line between comedy and tragedy.

For months after *Molly* closed, I would suddenly find myself shaking uncontrollably. I've heard it said about motion pictures that it takes just as much blood, sweat, and tears to make a good movie as a bad one. The same applies to the theater. You never start off a project thinking you're going to fail. It takes too much hard work to create something. Why bother! And, believe me, when a show you've given your heart and soul to doesn't succeed, the tears flow freely. Those few months were perhaps the most devastating experience of my career. But after the tears, you pick yourself up and go on to the next project. I'd do it all again for a show that I believed in as strongly as I believed in *Molly*.

SHEBA belongs in this chapter on flops, too. As I said, I would have gone through an experience like *Molly* again if it had been for a show that I believed in. Well, just one year after *Molly* closed, I heard about another great part. A musical was being made from William Inge's first Broadway success, *Come Back, Little Sheba*. I was offered the part of Lola, which won Shirley Booth an Academy Award. The musical starred myself, George Wallace, Kimberly Farr, and Gary Sandy (later of *WKRP in Cincinnati* fame). We worked for three weeks with a director who was sick and a leading man who was eventually fired, and we opened in 1974 at a Chicago bank, in an auditorium with a set that had to be taken down every night so meetings could be held the following day! *Sheba* was another "shoulda-woulda-coulda" show that might very well have worked under different circumstances. The book was by Lee Goldsmith, with lyrics by Clinton Ballard Jr. (which, of course, I thought was a sign). I got Ralph Burns to do the arrangements.

Sheba turned out to be a really good show, but we never made it out of Chicago. Not too long ago, Donna McKechnie worked on a version of *Sheba* at the White Barn Theatre in Westport, Connecticut, and recorded the score. Now, at the very least, there is a musical record of the piece. Maybe someday *Sheba* will find its way back to the stage.

Footnote 1: We had a wonderful cast of actors in *Molly*. Besides Eli Mintz, there was Lee Wallace as my husband, Jake, Swen Swenson, Connie Day, Lisa Rochelle, and Ruth Manning. But the best thing to come out of doing *Molly* was my friendship with Camilla (Cam) Ashland, who played the Irish woman in the show. We have been close friends ever since. Cam is a brilliant, Tony-nominated actress who never got what she deserved in this business. Her husband, James Russo, was co-owner of the Bucks County Playhouse at one time but lost all his money producing a show for Bette Davis called *Two's Company*. Cam is now ninety-five years old and as sharp as can be. She lives very near me in California, and we've hatched many schemes of opening a restaurant together. We've thought up some terrific names (great ideas, no down payment!):

> Your Just Desserts
> Omeletique
> and
> Lettuce Eat in the Past
> (restaurant/antiques shop)

Footnote 2: Al Hirschfeld did a caricature of me as Molly Goldberg that is absolutely wonderful. But if you ever see a program or poster of *Molly*, you'll notice that my name is spelled "Kay." The reason? Well, let's just say that I will never go to a numerologist for advice again!

Footnote 3: There was a young actor named Daniel Fortus in *Molly*. I first met him while doing a production of *Minnie's Boys*, the short-lived musical biography of the Marx Brothers and their mother. After the New York company closed, I played Minnie Marx in Pittsburgh with the same cast Shelley Winters performed with on Broadway. Danny played Harpo and sang the wonderful Larry Grossman/Hal Hackady ballad "Mama, a Rainbow." He was a beautiful young man with a gorgeous tenor voice, and I loved him dearly. When it came time to cast the son in *Molly*, I happily brought him on board. I used to look into his eyes and think, "My goodness, only nineteen years old and already on Broadway. This talented kid can go anywhere. He has his whole life ahead of him." But he didn't.

Danny was never promiscuous, yet he was one of the unlucky young men to contract HIV before anyone knew much about it. Danny's mother simply couldn't face the tragedy and her son's suffering. Though she was not there when Danny passed away, he had his brother and several close friends (including Bob Mackie) by his side. All that talent and sweetness gone, for no good reason. Today, since we know how to prevent this horrible disease, stories like Danny's don't have to be repeated. And I hope sharing Danny's story gives meaning and purpose to the life and death of this beautiful young man. The struggle to cure AIDS is ongoing, and it would be another tragedy if we became complacent simply because we have found some horribly expensive drugs to manage the disease.

Several years after *Molly*, I recorded a few of my favorite songs from that show on a CD entitled *Kaye Ballard, Now and Again*, partly because an original cast recording of the show had never been made. The gentleman I chose to recreate Danny's voice on the recording, Mark Sendroff, is very special to me, as he was to Danny. I first met Mark through Danny several years after *Molly* closed, and he has been my dear friend and lawyer ever since. Every once in a while Mark moonlights as a singer, so I call him my singing lawyer. Usually I am ambivalent about lawyers, but I have to say that I will always love Mark Sendroff for standing by Danny, and for stepping in and taking care of all his medical and funeral expenses. It was a noble thing to do.

Virginia Graham

Besides Billy DeWolfe, there was one other person in my life whom I could always count on to give me a laugh, and that was my dear friend Virginia Graham. She was truly one of the wittiest, most intelligent women I have ever met.

Virginia told me that her father was Jewish and her mother was Norwegian. When she was little, the family had a car accident and her mother pushed the kids out of the way to get out of the car first! We were once out to dinner with a friend of ours (who was not particularly known for picking up a check), and when this friend actually paid the tab, Virginia said, "Did you see that? She opened up her wallet and three generations of moths flew out!"

Virginia Graham lived to be eighty-six years old. She had graduated magna cum laude from college at a time when very few women even considered getting a higher education. Until the day she died, Virginia was never at a loss for words, and she never repeated herself. She was positively brilliant. So brilliant, in fact, that her quotes are featured on a website!

For those of you who are too young to remember, Virginia Graham was a pioneer in the television talk-show field. She hosted three talk shows throughout her career, including *The Virginia Graham Show, Food for Thought*, and the most notable, *Girl Talk*, which is where we first met when she had me on as a guest. Because of Virginia's background, I think she was very hurt not to be asked to participate in some of the talk shows that became popular in the years after she went off the air, like *The View*, for which she had blazed a trail.

And blaze a trail she did. *Girl Talk* may sound like the perfect opportunity for a bunch of women to get together on television and do nothing but gossip. But Virginia had very high standards and a sense of propriety, which is so sorely missing in today's world. All her guests had something intelligent to say, and on or off the air, Virginia was the perfect host.

There was something almost European in the way Virginia conducted herself. Whether it was a small faux pas in a dinner party conversation, or a cataclysmic event that affected the rest of her life, Virginia handled the situation with class and dignity. For example, very late in life, when she was working on her memoirs (and I would never have revealed this while she was still with us), she discovered that her husband was gay—she walked in and found him in bed with the butler. I asked, "Virginia, why don't you put that in your book?" She said, "No, I couldn't." I asked, "Why not?" To which she replied, "I don't want to ruin my image."

When I had an apartment in New York, Virginia lived above me, and we shared the same maid, a wonderful woman named Estha Jeffers. Estha was a great maid but had very protruding upper teeth. Virginia used to say, "Estha's teeth arrive in the room five minutes before she does."

I don't mean to give the impression that Virginia was not a kind woman, but she did not suffer fools gladly. One day I inquired about our building's superintendent, and Virginia's reply was, "Well, Kaye, he's doing better. He just graduated to pencil sharpening!"

Like Gypsy Rose Lee, Virginia Graham was a total original. And to be a total original in this world, you have to have the courage of a lion. Besides her work on television, Virginia was a syndicated columnist and wrote several books. She even tried her luck on the stage (with varying degrees of success). I remember one time she was playing the mother in a production of Neil Simon's *Barefoot in the Park*. Anita Gillette was cast as the daughter. One evening Virginia came on stage and began doing the second act instead of the first. No one seemed able to stop her, until finally Anita glared at her and said loudly, "Mother, would you please just *leave*?"

Virginia was one of those people who are truly connected to the world. Her knowledge and interests were so varied that she could have an in-depth conversation with anyone on any topic. But she worked at it. I suppose how far you go in life is partly luck and partly the way you are born and raised, but it is also determined by how hard you try and how long you stick with it. Virginia worked at life. She never stopped being interested in learning.

The year Virginia Graham died, Roseanne Barr had a new talk show on the air for a little while, and after a guest appearance, she offered Virginia a regular segment. Virginia swore all her friends to secrecy about her illness, telling them, "Don't let Roseanne know I'm sick or I'll be out of a job!" Right up to the end, Virginia was a real participant in life, not just a bystander. She called me one day, shortly before she passed away, and said, "Kaye, I'm eighty-six years old, my body is falling apart, and I just ordered slip covers!" I miss her dearly.

Another of her quotes reminds me again of her wit. She said, "When some people retire, it's going to be mighty hard to be able to tell the difference." Well, Virginia never retired; her work and her life were intertwined. And when she left, the world could certainly tell the difference.

Chapter Fourteen

THE PIRATES OF PENZANCE— The Times They Were a-Changin'

I
n this business, it's not uncommon to be ignored by people for whom you've done favors—or to be dropped by old friends who become more famous than you. One of the exceptions to that rule was Joseph Papp.

In the 1970s Joe achieved the dream he had talked about years earlier when he stage-managed *Cinderella*: He started doing Shakespeare in Central Park. One of the shows he produced brought Linda Ronstadt and Kevin Kline to the stage in a highly acclaimed production of Gilbert and Sullivan's *The Pirates of Penzance* that eventually moved to the Minskoff Theatre for a long run on Broadway.

In 1981, Joe called me to ask if I would like to take over the role of Ruth. I was thrilled and ended up doing the show for fifty-three weeks. I loved the show and the role. The part was perfect for me both vocally and in terms of the style of comedy the production called for. But the thrill of returning to the Great White Way was diminished by changes I found in the business—and in some of the people, too.

Everything was about money. Ticket prices had soared to the point that seeing Broadway shows with any regularity was possible only for affluent people who could afford $80 a ticket (and that was before Mel Brooks broke the $100 barrier with *The Producers*!). Live theater, which in the early 1900s had been a vital art form for the masses, had by the end of the century become a luxury, one demanding that each show become a huge spectacle—through either star power or scenery, or both. You had to see a ship sink or a helicopter fly onstage in order for a show to be worth the money you had to shell out. These limitations also started to have an impact on the producing side. Theater was now big business, and very few people could afford to play.

Even more disappointing to me was the attitude and work ethic I encountered among my fellow actors. Not all, mind you, but stars were being hired from television and movies who didn't have the background, discipline, or professionalism to handle a live performance eight times a week (if they even knew what the word "professionalism" meant).

Toward the end of the run of *Pirates*, things really began to get bizarre. Joe Papp and Graciela Daniele, who was the choreographer, began hiring people like Jim Belushi strictly for their drawing power at the box office. Mr. Belushi was just one of four different Pirate Kings I worked with (I also went through seven Frederics and three Mabels) and was perhaps the most unprofessional person I've ever been onstage with. At times, he was downright vulgar. Mr. Belushi (who does not lack talent, only taste) would never do the same thing twice on stage, and he soon began doing pretty much whatever he felt like. Had this production really come from the New York Shakespeare Festival? Or was it now a Second City Comedy Club show? One night Mr. Belushi turned to George Rose, who was playing the Modern Major General, and said, "Did you just f-a-r-t?" I couldn't believe my ears! This was in front of an audience filled with children! When I inquired why such inappropriate behavior was allowed, I was told that I was free to leave if I didn't like it.

It disturbed me a lot to see the downward turn that professional theater had taken by 1982. You never knew which cast members were going to show up for the performance. There was hardly any "the show must go on" attitude among the cast and crew. People would take a day off if they had to break in a new pair of shoes!

Before I make you lose all hope, there were some company members who did do their job. George Rose was absolutely great and the only one who stayed in for the whole run (except for the few weeks he took off to make the film version of *Pirates*). I also met Robbie Benson and the woman he would eventually marry, Karla DeVito. They were wonderful to work with, as was Maureen McGovern. I felt that it was such a shame, though. After my experience on *Pirates*, I had no desire to return to the New York stage—the stage I had been trying to get onto for fifty years!

Critics

R eceiving a public critique for your work can be one of the most gratifying parts of this insane business. And, more often than not, it can also be one of the most infuriating. When I first start-ed out, I read all my notices. (And several times I was crushed.) But after the reviews for *Molly* came out, I just couldn't take it anymore and tried to stay away from them. When an artist has given his or her sweat (and sometimes blood) to create a performance, a painting, a statue, whatev-er it might be, a little piece of the soul goes with it as well. And if that work of art is torn to pieces, so is that little piece of the artist's soul. Not so hard to understand, is it?

After giving a synopsis of the play, many critics will offer an insight-ful comment like "She was great" or "She was awful." Unless, of course, they start to get nasty and talk more about a person's physical attributes or deficiencies than his performance. And forget about those "other peo-ple" who had sat in the same theater that night. I realize that the art form in which I've chosen to make a living is a very subjective one, but never once have I heard a critic write, "I didn't particularly care for the per-formance, but the audience was rolling on the floor!"

Though I don't think that any one reviewer today has the power to make or break a show, my biggest pet peeve is that so many theater crit-ics seem to have no background in the theater. How does one graduate from food editor to drama critic? I realize that reviews are a necessary evil in this business, but couldn't the people writing them be required to know a little something about what they are seeing?

That having been said, everyone involved in the theater is indebted to critics for their ability to advertise our product. But good criticism should make for better theater, just as good news reporting should make for a better world. And in both departments we are sorely lacking.

After all my years in this business, there are three theatrical critics for whom I have great respect:

❧

BROOKS ATKINSON Yes, he gave me one of the greatest reviews in the world (he called my performance of "Lazy Afternoon" in *The Golden Apple* a triumph in the theater), but that's not the only reason I respect him. The man knew his business and didn't wield his power in the press with a self-righteous ax, as if he wanted you to know he could make or break careers (even though he could).

❧

WALTER KERR Walter was part of the business. He and his wife, Jean, were both playwrights and really "theater people." Not only did Walter have a fantastic eye for the stage, but he could also be very constructive. These days only "de-struction" seems to sell papers or get you noticed. When I was doing *The Decline and Fall of the Entire World as Seen Through the Eyes of Cole Porter*, I was so proud of the review he gave me. He was very precise and accurate in his evaluation of my performance. He understood that I never did "impressions." He said that when I paid tribute to my favorite performers, like Bea Lillie or Mabel Mercer, I found the "essence" of the person, which is exactly what I've always tried to do.

❧

REX REED Rex has given me good reviews and bad reviews. He has an unabashed love for tradition. Most important, Rex has a love for the craft of acting and for the astonishing actors, like Kim Stanley, Judy Garland, Geraldine Page, and Julie Harris, who have excelled at that craft. Rex is simply the most qualified critic of both theater and film to come along after the golden age.

❧

I guarantee you that if some of the theater critics out there today had to sign their column "anonymous" instead of trying to make names for themselves as celebrities, there would be a lot more true critique and a lot less scandal-sheet slander.

P.S. And though she was strictly a film critic, I also liked Pauline Kael.

Chapter Fifteen
....

"HEY, MA!"

T he year was 1982. My stint in *The Pirates of Penzance* was over, and instead of being able to rest after my success, I went into a terrible depression. Looking back, I see that many things had conspired to bring me to one of the lowest points in my life.

Professionally, I didn't know where to turn. I felt that my television career had peaked with *The Mothers-in-Law*, and opportunities for Broadway shows were almost nonexistent, especially for a fifty-seven-year-old singer-comedienne who had never really been given the chance to prove she could act. In the past, whenever I needed a job I'd dig out the sheet music and head for the nightclubs, even though I hated doing so. But where were the clubs?

I wasn't sure what my next move should be. And things on the personal front weren't much brighter. I was angry, and I didn't know how to do anything about it because much of that anger was directed at myself. My whole life I had fought feelings of inadequacy—as a woman, a daughter, a performer, you name it. Now I found myself frustrated with my own weakness and insecurity, and I resented living in fear. I had always feared everything, from men, to failure, to show business, to death. And the reality of my own mortality was beginning to hit home.

One of my sisters, Rose, lost her husband at the age of fifty and went a little "cuckoo." At the funeral she suddenly announced that she "had no family." We eventually became strangers, and to this day I still don't know why. Then, in the late 1970s, after thirty years of dreading when it might happen, my beloved Nana died at the age of ninety-three. I was devastated.

A few years later, in 1981, my father also passed away, leaving my mother and me to deal with each other one on one.

The relationship between mother and daughter has to be one of the most complicated a woman will ever experience. Throughout my years of analysis, I fought with and tried to come to terms with the feelings I had for my mother—resentment, love, guilt, admiration. I never even got close to resolving them. It's funny how you can understand the things you feel intellectually, and yet never deal with them emotionally. Now it was time to try.

Leslie Eberhard and David Levy were two very talented gentlemen who had come to me with the idea for a one-woman show. I had previous commitments at the time, so Dolores Gray ended up working with them. But I loved what these two guys could do with a lyric, and a little while later, when I was looking for a project, I asked Leslie and David, along with Jerry Goldberg, to write a show specifically for me. When it came to the subject matter for the show, it suddenly seemed obvious. I could explore my relationship with my mother, tell the story of my career, and provide myself with employment—all at the same time. The show was called *"Hey, Ma!"* It opened in New York at the Promenade Theatre on February 27, 1984.

> *Hey, Ma, you said my face looked funny.*
> *I never would go far with a face that looked like mine.*
>
> *Hey, Ma, you said my face was homely*
> *And homely girls should stay in the home, where they'd be fine.*
>
> *You said that stars were always pretty.*
> *And pretty was just not my lot.*
>
> *You said that it was just a pity this Katey was not.*
> *"Homely" was the word I got.*
>
> *Hey, Ma, you said I wasn't special.*
> *I never would succeed 'cause my features were too blah.*
>
> *Hey, Ma, you said I should forget it*
> *'Cause with a mouth like mine who was likely to applaud?*
>
> *You said performers should sing softly.*
> *You said my voice was much too loud.*

I prayed if I told some jokes that some folks would be "wowed."
I even hoped that you'd be proud.

You weren't, Ma.
I went out into the world and I kept on trying.
I went on the stage, Ma!

I sang a song, I did a dance.
I had them clapping to the beat.

I did a bit, I did a take.
They even jumped up to their feet.

It was for me, Ma, the me who wasn't pretty.
For me, Ma, the me who wasn't special.
They made a part of me complete.

I had gone onstage as "myself" many times before in countless night-clubs. But *"Hey, Ma!"* was the only time I used my real life as material. I set the show's opening in the seats of the RKO Palace movie house in Cleveland, where I was inspired by all those wonderful old movies. I went through my years with Spike Jones, the nightclub acts, and eventually my big chance on Broadway in *The Golden Apple.* The show got spectacular reviews and ran for sixty-three performances! I was hailed as "a tri-umph!" I was even nominated for the Drama Desk and Outer Critic's Circle Award. (If it hadn't been for Jon Pareles, a "rock and roll" reviewer for the *New York Times,* the show might have run even longer.)

Hey, Ma, they thought that I was pretty.
You should have heard 'em laugh when the punch line finally came!
Gee, Ma, I started feeling pretty.
I knew I could get by though my looks were still the same.

But you really want to know what's funny?
You're my mother, that I won't erase.
You looked at me through those mornings without an embrace.
And, Ma, you never saw my . . .
Never really saw my face.

My mother saw the show when I took it to the Cleveland Playhouse. Her response? "I was never like that," she said. And I'm sure she probably truly didn't realize she was. Parents of my mother and father's generation and economic level were much too concerned with putting a roof over their family's head and food on the table to worry about the effect a harsh word or two would have on their children.

As I've said, I came from a very traditional, non-show-business family. My parents weren't impressed by the cover of *Life* magazine or a starring role on Broadway. And if they were, it was not in them to brag about it. I knew my father was proud of me and loved me very much, but his way of showing it wasn't by coming to the dressing room after a show. In fact, when I played Las Vegas, Papa didn't even watch the show—he greeted people on the way in and out of the theater to make sure they had a good time.

I also understood and accepted the fact that this attitude wasn't just toward me. It wasn't in my parents' nature to offer overt positive feedback on my sister's cooking and housecleaning either. But that didn't stop me from wanting their approval—from wanting a sign of their love. I suppose when I felt I wasn't getting that approval I resented it, and so later I took that resentment on the road with me and applied it to my future bosses, critics, friends, and lovers. All those years I wasted in analysis. Well, that's not quite true, it did help. Through all those sessions, I was able, little by little, to release some of the pressure I put on myself. I never got to that catharsis point, though. But isn't catharsis what good theater is supposed to provide?

Hey, Ma, you're calling me long distance?
I hope there's nothing wrong, hope the family's all okay.
Ma, it costs a lot, long distance, are you sure there's nothing wrong?

Oh, you got something to say?
You saw me where?
Some TV show? On Perry Como?
Oh, that's swell. Yeah, Perry's great.

You liked me, too? You thought that I sang just as well?
Do you mean me, Ma, the one who lost her stutter,
Me, Ma, you don't mean Dinah Shore?
You'd like to see me do much more?!
Gee, Ma, all the neighbors called?
And in the A&P they all said they liked my song?

Aw, Ma, you really felt important, huh?
And told them how you knew I would make it all along!?!

I'm glad my singing really got you.
Your telling me is awfully sweet.
Yes, I'll say hello to Frank Sinatra . . . if we ever meet.
Hey, Ma . . . you've made my day complete.

What, Ma? You thought that I was funny?
Thanks, Ma.

From my one woman show, *"Hey, Ma!,"*
by Jerry Goldberg, Leslie Eberhard, and David Levy

I did it. I made peace with my mother. But not quite the way the song says. As great as it was for the show, that last verse with the phone call never really happened. When my mother died, just a couple years after my dad, I was at her bedside. The last thing she did was hold her arms out to me. There was a look on her face that I can never erase from my memory. It was then that I realized she had done the best she knew how to do. My mother was a good woman, a truly good woman who was born into a world where she was given very little choice or opportunity.

And did I learn to accept myself a little bit more, too? I don't know. After we closed in New York, I took *"Hey, Ma!"* to Los Angeles and received a hideous review from Don Shirley in the *Los Angeles Times*. We played the Henry Fonda Theatre, and he said that I belonged in a night-club like the Cinegrill at the Roosevelt Hotel! That really kept the audiences away in droves!

Then a writer for *Variety Review* came to see the show and wrote, "When I walked in here today I felt sorry for Miss Ballard (because of the lack of audience), but by the time the show ended I felt sorry for all the people who had not seen her." God bless him for that. But you see? I remembered the *bad* reviewer's name, didn't I?

I never really fought with my mother, never would have thought of sassing back the way kids do today. She showed me her love by cooking. She was incredible in the kitchen and served all the food that I craved and that made me fat. I competed for my mother's love, and she yearned for my independence. And neither one of us had any clue as to how to show the other what we felt. Sounds oh so tragic and complicated, doesn't it? But maybe . . . maybe it's just what children and parents do.

On The Ed
Sullivan Show,
1963.

Royal Flush, *about a queen imprisoned in an underground bathroom,
opened, and quickly closed, in 1964. For me, the best thing to come out
of the show was this cartoon.*

I was in heaven doing The Mothers-in-Law. *I got to work with Eve Arden and other wonderful regulars, as well as Jimmy Durante and a long roster of other guest stars, many of whom were pals. If only the show had lasted more than two seasons and gone into syndication!*

I met Eve Arden in the 1940s when I was performing with Spike Jones at the Trocadero in Los Angeles. Who could have guessed that we would be costars in a television series?

Which Way to the Front?, *1970, was a big hit—well, in France, where Jerry Lewis is idolized.*

Molly, *1973, based on the radio and early-television show* The Goldbergs, *had a solid cast, a very good score, an inept director, and a* Playbill *with me, as drawn by Al Hirschfeld, on the cover—what an honor!* Photo courtesy of Playbill

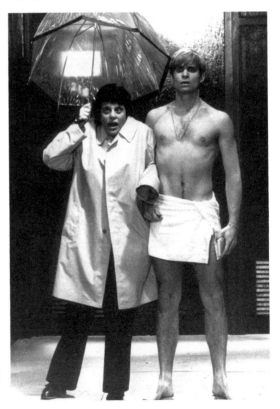

Treat Williams was the only man in The Ritz, *1976, a farce about gay bathhouses, you wanted to see in a towel.*

Doing Pirates of Penzance, *1981, I learned that some of the big names from television and the movies didn't have the background, discipline, or professionalism to handle a live performance eight times a week. But I worked with some real pros, too—George Rose, Maureen McGovern, Treat Williams, and Robby Benson to name a few. My cousin Paul Bellardo, on my left, made the ceramic apples we're holding.*

Sandy Dennis and I did the The Female Odd Couple *in 1988; she was a sweet, gentle soul who lived with forty cats. I can still hear her saying, "Nooo."*

With Tovah Feldshuh, E. G. Marshall, and Nathan Lane off-Broadway in New York in She Stoops to Conquer, *1984.*

*In 1987, Mel Tormé,
June Allyson, Patti
Austin, and I performed*
An Evening with Cole
Porter *at the White
House for President and
Mrs. Reagan. Whether
or not you agreed with
Ronald Reagan's politics,
you have to admit that
the man had grace and a
great sense of humor.*

To Kaye—
with so many thanks— My best
Nancy Reagan

In the early 1960s, Liliane Montevecchi was a regular guest at my New York dinner parties, and in 1998, I shared a dressing room with this ageless, tireless wonder during the Paper Mill Playhouse production of Follies.

Singing my showstopper, "Broadway Baby," in the Paper Mill Playhouse production of Follies, *1998.*

"Here they come, those . . . beautiful girls." The Follies *cast on the staircase, from bottom to top: Laura Kenyon, Donna McKechnie, Carol Skarimbas, Natalie Mosco, me, Mercedes Patterson, Dee Hoty, Liliane Montevecchi, Meredith Patterson, Ann Cunningham, Phyllis Newman, and Ann Miller.*

For the Nunsense *twentieth anniversary all-star tour in 2003 I spent six months on the road with Lee Meriwether, Darlene Love, Mimi Hines, and Georgia Engel. You're not going to come across as much combined experience anytime soon.*

In the spring of 2006, I reprised my role in Ronald Harwood's Quartet *in Sag Harbor, New York, working with director Jack Hofsiss and actors Paul Hecht, Simon Jones, and Siān Phillips. The thrill of being around such excellence!*

Chapter Sixteen
....

4 GIRLS 4

I love watching the news every night, but it seems that (especially
nowadays) the broadcasts give you a very limited and negative view
of the world. Those so-called "unbiased" reports can leave you feeling so isolated and depressed about the state of the world that you want
to bury yourself under the bedcovers and never come out. But then I
remember the people I've met around the country in places like Green
Bay, Wisconsin, and Providence, Rhode Island, and I have hope again.

One of the great things about touring with a show or a nightclub act
is the opportunity it gives me to see not only the great cities of the world,
but the little towns and places I'd never have thought of visiting if I hadn't
been working there. I've met so many wonderfully warm people over the
years, dined in fabulous restaurants, and been inspired by the thousands
of small communities that keep this country (and the world) going.

But when you're on the road you also discover that you can be at your
loneliest in a crowd of people. You come to depend on those traveling
with you for friendship and support while you are away from home. I
really hit the jackpot in terms of traveling companions when I joined the
cast of *4 Girls 4*.

4 Girls 4 began in the late 1970s as a vehicle for Rosemary Clooney,
Rose Marie, Helen O'Connell, and Margaret Whiting. Each of them was
approaching that wonderful age for women where everyone assumes
you're either dead or in a home somewhere. If anything, these women
were at their peak as performers, but they found it very hard to get work.
So they got together and created a sort of vaudeville show in which each

of them would take the stage for one-quarter of the evening, and then they'd all get together for a big number at the end. It was a brilliant idea because it increased their drawing power threefold at the same time that it reduced their workload.

The show became a big hit in California, so the ladies decided to make some money taking it out on tour. After they had been doing the show for a while, Rose Marie left and was replaced by Martha Raye. When Martha left, I took over her spot. Doing the show was a very happy experience simply because these women were all true stars.

Along the way, Rosemary Clooney left, and Kay Starr came in. Kay was one of the most popular female singers of the late 1940s and 1950s, known for hits like "Side by Side" and the number-one song "Wheel of Fortune." Her 1956 hit "Rock and Roll Waltz" was the first number-one single by a female in the rock era.

Kay is a real Oklahoma cowgirl, very country. I'm always being confused with her. Once a woman approached me and said, "Oh, Miss Starr, sing 'Wheel of Fortune'!" I replied, "I'm not Kay Starr, I'm Kaye Ballard." To which the lady replied, "Don't you get snippy with me!"

Helen O'Connell was one of the most popular girl singers of the Big Band era. Discovered in the late 1930s, she was best known for her work with Jimmy Dorsey and her hits "Green Eyes" and "Tangerine." Helen was a cantankerous but adorable person and a fantastic performer, but she would argue with everyone about everything. If I said, "Let's leave at four o'clock," Helen would say, "No, we'll leave at five." If I said, "How about leaving at five?" she'd say, "No, we're going at four." But I loved her. She was a tiny, dimpled lady who couldn't have weighed more than ninety pounds, but she could drink a martini and a beer before going onstage and never miss a note. She amazed me.

Margaret Whiting, known for hits such as "Moonlight in Vermont" and "It Might as Well Be Spring," was not only a great singer, she was (and is) a very, very funny lady. Maggie would sing everything back to you. When I asked her if she wanted to go to dinner, she would sing, "Do I want to go to di-i-i-i-nner?" I'd say, "How about six o'clock?" She'd sing "How about six o'clo-o-o-o-ck?" I guess it was her version of an easy way to warm up.

I suppose women can be a little harder on each other than men, but they can also bond more tightly. I was very proud to be invited to join the talented group of ladies who were doing 4 Girls 4. And you can't have any better conductor than Frank Ortega. He was a big reason everything went so smoothly. For my part of the show I came out and yelled, "One more time!" and then went into several songs I had done in my act for years. I sang "The Very Thought of You" and "This Is My Love," and included all the material about my grandmother (Nana) from *"Hey, Ma!"*

I stayed with the tour for about four months. And though it was try-ing at times—we drove through the night in a bus—we each had our own lounge chair and our own stories to tell, and we made the best of it. There is a funny little sidelight to this story that I want to mention. I can't say that the singer/comedienne Rose Marie, one of the original members of *4 Girls 4*, and I have ever been close friends, but I find that throughout my career I seem to have had a strange professional connection to her.

Though we have never really worked together, Rose Marie and I have been in three of the same shows. We were both semi-regulars on televi-sion in *The Doris Day Show*. In 1952 I took over Rose Marie's role in *Top Banana* when the show went out on the road, and twenty-five years later I slipped into her position on *4 Girls 4*. (And what about Richard Deacon? He played producer Mel Cooley on *The Dick Van Dyke Show* with Rose Marie, and my husband on the second season of *The Mothers-in-Law*.) Recently I heard that Rose had said to someone that she and I don't get along. If that is true, I have no idea why. I have always liked Rose Marie. I think she's wonderful. The only thing I can think is that maybe she got upset because I wouldn't allow them to buy me out of my *Top Banana* contract once we got to California. I knew Phil Silvers wanted her back, and I'm sure she would have loved the chance to play the show at home, but at that point I wasn't about to go through everything I'd gone through with Phil, play all the dates that nobody cared about, and then give it up before we got to Los Angeles! The reason I bring this up at all has to do with the way personal relationships are twisted and manipulated in show business, and most of the time you have no control over it.

It's funny (and aggravating) that rumors fly about so quickly and sometimes keep people at odds with each other for years. And often when these people finally meet again they end up finding there's no basis at all for the perceived animosity!

For example, before I met her, Louise Lasser (of *Mary Hartman, Mary Hartman* fame) had heard that I didn't want her on the bill with me at the Bon Soir nightclub because I knew that she was a comedienne who also sang. Well, that was a total fabrication on someone's part, but it colored Louise's opinion of me for years—and I had nothing to do with it. It wasn't until much later when we had become close friends that she told me this story.

By the way, Louise Lasser is one of the most innately funny people I have ever come across. One of the last times I was in Manhattan I wanted to get together with her, and she suggested, "Let's meet at Bloomingdale's in the couch department." I said, "Why the couch department?" Like a perfect yenta, she said, "We'll sit, we'll talk."

After I had spent four months touring with *4 Girls 4*, the show was booked to go on a cruise to Hong Kong, but I opted to head back to Palm Springs. And who took my place? Rose Marie.

A few years went by, and then in November 1988 I returned to the cast for a little while when the girls played the West Coast, and I got this very nice review from Dan Heckman in the *Los Angeles Times*:

> Kaye Ballard added an unrelentingly contemporary point of view—in fact, added a jolt of up-to-date spice—to a program that might otherwise have become mired in its own reminiscences. Numbers like "My Son, the Stripper" and "Don't Ask a Lady" combined with Ballard's devastatingly pointed impressions (of everyone from Joan Crawford to Nancy Reagan) to give *4 Girls 4* an energy it has not always had in the past.

The act was a brilliant concept and stayed together (sometimes as *3 Girls 3*) through several different combinations of women for more than a decade. By the end of the 1980s *4 Girls 4* just faded away. But not before it had proved that a group of ladies who really know their craft can still knock an audience on its ear whether they are forty-two or seventy-two. As jazz singer Anita O'Day told a reporter who stupidly asked whether she thought she was still improving, "You dig a hole, it gets deeper, don't it?"

Chapter Seventeen

A "Broadway Baby" in Jersey

I n his 1998 review of *Follies* at the Paper Mill Playhouse, New York drama critic John Simon wrote:

> I ashamedly admit that, like some colleagues, I did not in 1971 recognize the greatness of *Follies*. Much depends on the right cast, and here we have seven great luminaries of yore: Kaye Ballard, Eddie Bracken, Donna McKechnie, Ann Miller, Liliane Montevecchi, Phyllis Newman, and Donald Saddler. They act, sing, and dance with untarnishable bravura and mastery that should speak equally loud to established fans and astounded new audiences. Do not think for a moment that the Paper Mill Playhouse, in Millburn, New Jersey, peddles some nice but provincial, reflected glory production for memory-chewing old-timers but small beer for newcomers. This staging has Broadway written all over it, and the sooner it gets there, the better.

We never made it to Broadway. We also didn't know at the time that Paper Mill's *Follies* would turn out to be Ann Miller's last great perform-ance. One of her last great regrets was that she didn't get to deliver it in New York.

For those of you who aren't familiar with *Follies* (*is* there anyone?), back when it debuted in 1971 it was the proverbial "show ahead of its time." It was written by Stephen Sondheim and James Goldman.

Follies takes place in an old theater that is about to be torn down. The entire show was inspired by a picture of Gloria Swanson in *Life* magazine. In the photo, Gloria is all made up in glitz and feathers, standing in the ruins and rubble of the Roxy Theatre in New York City as it was being demolished. In *Follies,* Dimitri Weisman, a Florenz Ziegfeld-like Broadway producer, stages a reunion of his old follies girls. It is a ghost-filled pageant about life, told with a brilliant mixture of celebration and regret. The complicated staging (originally conceived by Hal Prince and Michael Bennett) involves the ghosts, or "memories," of these aged performers, particularly the two leading couples, sharing the stage simultaneously with their younger counterparts. It is a remarkable concept, and a thrilling show to do.

Even though it won seven Tony Awards and the New York Drama Critics Circle Award for Best Musical, *Follies* is legendary because of its standing with the critics and its cult following rather than its commercial success. It ran a little over a year on Broadway but was so expensive to produce that it never paid off its original investment.

After closing, the original Broadway cast spent a little time on the road, and then *Follies* just seemed to sort of fade away. The original cast album is a very abridged version of the score, and with the exception of the highly acclaimed 1987 Lincoln Center concert version, the show had never been revived.

Then in 1997, executive producer Angelo Del Rossi and artistic director Robert Johanson decided to include *Follies* in their 1998 season at the Paper Mill Playhouse. And I must say, they did it right.

In addition to the stellar cast, the sets and costumes were every bit as good, if not better, than the original Broadway production. When I stood in the wings and watched each of those wonderful women appear at the top of the grand staircase and then parade down as the tenor sang "Here they come, those . . . beautiful girls," I got chills.

I was cast as Hattie Walker, originally played by Ethel Shutta in 1971 and reprised by my old friend Elaine Stritch for the Lincoln Center concert. My big number was "Broadway Baby." Just to rehearse with this cast and be in the dressing room with them every night was a thrill.

I "roomed" with Liliane Montevecchi, who'd been a dear friend since back in my *Carnival* days. She was reprising the role of Solange La Fitte, which she had done at Lincoln Center ten years earlier. Liliane is selfish, self-centered, and an absolutely perfect person. I love her so much that I named one of my puppies after her. "Gorgeous" does not begin to describe Liliane Montevecchi. She is an ageless, tireless wonder who gives

180 percent at every single performance. I used to watch her in the dressing room sewing a few new sequins onto her gown or adding another feather here or there. Watching her tireless quest made me laugh. She never stopped thinking about how to improve things in order to give the best performance she could give. That's true of all the ladies in the show—as well as the gentlemen. Eddie Bracken, Donald Saddler, Tony Roberts, and Vahan Khanzadian also gave it their all. I'm sure that's why these people have all endured and are still performing. And the senior company members' everlasting "star quality" came through in each performance, and helped give the show its magic.

Every night, from the dressing room next door, Liliane and I would hear "I'm still . . . HEEERE!!" sung at the top of our next door neighbor's lungs. That's all, just those three little words and the centerpiece of our glorious production, Miss Ann Miller, was warmed up and ready to go. Annie just wanted to know that she could still hit that note. "I'm Still Here" was the perfect song for the trouper of all troupers.

When our *Follies* opened, the positive response was unanimous. There had been talk of a Broadway revival of this show for years, and now here it was, fully realized and ripe for the picking. Audiences and critics absolutely raved about our production. We sold out the house at each performance, and rumors started to fly about taking the show to New York.

How could we miss, right? We had Robert Johanson's wonderful direction, Jerry Mitchell's great choreographic tribute to Michael Bennett, and all these true legends up there on the stage. We even made what is thought to be the first complete, definitive recording of *Follies*, with Jonathan Tunick conducting his brilliant orchestrations and Stephen Sondheim himself producing.

But hold on. I forgot to mention what is fast becoming known as the "Paper Mill curse." Over the years, many shows that originated at the Paper Mill Playhouse have been rumored to be on their way to Broadway, and only one that I know of has made it. In the 1980s Jason Robards and Colleen Dewhurst took *You Can't Take It with You* to the Kennedy Center and then on to Broadway for a limited run.

Why, when there were theaters empty all over midtown Manhattan, couldn't a production with the prestige our *Follies* had earned make it to New York? Expense had a lot to do with it, but so did egos—egos that apparently feel there is a stigma attached to having a show produced by a regional theatre.

Since 1934, Paper Mill Playhouse, which has been honored by being made the State Theatre of New Jersey, has consistently produced exceedingly high-quality work. It has given New York performers a place to work when there was nothing for them in the city. And yet because the Paper Mill is so close to the city, it is still thought of as Broadway's "community theater."

I first worked at Paper Mill the season before *Follies*, doing *No, No, Nanette* with Helen Gallagher, Eddie Bracken, and Lee Roy Reams. I was amazed to see that almost everyone I mention in this book and many more had played on that stage! Forgive me for this tangent, but I think it's important to show just a sample of the wonderful actors who have performed on the stage of the Paper Mill Playhouse over the years: Eva Le Gallienne, Uta Hagen, Billie Burke, Geraldine Page, Jean Stapleton, Celeste Holm, Chita Rivera, Bert Lahr, Ginger Rogers, Shelley Winters, Lillian Gish, Dorothy Gish, Tallulah Bankhead, Elaine Stritch, Basil Rathbone, Carol Channing, Liza Minnelli, Sandy Dennis, Eve Arden, Gene Wilder, Dom DeLuise, Jane Fonda, Shirley Booth, and Anthony Perkins. Not to mention Gloria Swanson herself! Some community theater!

I have been told that the real reason our production of *Follies* was not transferred to Broadway was because the widow of one of the authors, James Goldman, did not approve. It seems to me that Stephen Sondheim must have had the power to persuade Mrs. Goldman to reconsider if he had wanted to. I always got the feeling from Stephen that we were a bit too "second class" to be considered worthy of Broadway—even though we'd all starred on the Great White Way at one time or another.

As I said, it broke Ann Miller's heart not to be able to make a triumphant return with such a great show. I think it hurt even more when a revival eventually turned up in New York a couple of years later and was greeted with less than stellar notices. Inevitably, that production was compared rather unfavorably to the glorious revival at Paper Mill Playhouse.

Oh, well, we still have the recording—and our memories. After we closed, something else that John Simon said in his review of our production took on even greater meaning. He said, "I now see that *Follies* is the kind of show irresistible to anyone who has lived long enough to fathom the meaning of aging, lost youth, mortality, and the magnificent, though Pyrrhic, victory of not going gentle into that good night. The show potently accumulates meaning from all our losses, from all our gallant last-ditch stands."

Palm Springs

Throughout my career, I lived most of the time in either New York City or Hollywood, because that's where the work was. I enjoyed California, but New York had my heart, and I was always sad to leave my friends and the excitement of the city.

But then, in 1970, I found the place where I knew I would spend the rest of my life. I purchased Desi Arnaz's house in Rancho Mirage, California, just outside Palm Springs. There is something about the serenity of the desert, with the mountains in the background, that makes me happy and puts me at peace. (Plus, a keno machine is never too far away!) Soon after buying Desi's house, I was driving down Palm Canyon Drive on a beautiful Sunday afternoon with a friend of mine when a black Mercedes pulled up next to me. I did a double take, because there in the car was Elvis Presley. I shouted out the window, "I love you, Mr. Presley!" Elvis yelled back, "I love you, Miss Ballard!" I was as giddy as a teenager! My name had crossed Elvis Presley's lips! I guess I haven't changed too much over the years; you can tell by the hundreds of autographed pictures hanging throughout my house that I'm still that star-struck kid from Cleveland.

Many friends have visited me here in the desert over the years. One of my frequent guests was the actress Hermoine Baddeley. (Perhaps best remembered for playing Ellen in *Mary Poppins*, she also appeared in the film version of *The Unsinkable Molly Brown* and as Mrs. Naugatuck on the TV series *Maude*.) Hermoine loved what she called the "dimpled mountains." She was always quick-witted and often quite poetic. One time she told me, "You know, Kaye, rattlesnakes are awfully good sports." "Why?" I asked. "Because at least they warn you when they are about to strike, unlike most people I've known!"

Hermoine was a funny, tough lady brought up in the English music-hall tradition, just like the "other" Hermoine, Hermoine Gingold. Both ladies had great wit. Hermoine Gingold had been married to a struggling songwriter, Holt Marvel, whom she later divorced. After they called it quits, Holt wrote "A Nightingale Sang in Berkeley Square" and "These Foolish Things (Remind Me of You)," which made him quite successful. Hermoine ran into him on the street one day and said, "What about some alimony?" Holt looked at her in shock and said, "I could never accept money from a lady!"

The Palm Springs area began as a haven for Hollywood stars and their families when there was only one small road to get out here from Los Angeles. Jack Benny, Bob Hope, George Burns, Alice Faye and Phil Harris—all the legends bought property out here and literally camped out until they built houses. The trend kept on going, and my neighborhood was home to celebrities like Mary Martin, Carol Channing, and Ginger Rogers. (Ginger had a large cartoon of herself on her refrigerator that I loved. The caption read, "I did everything Fred Astaire did—only I did it backwards, and in heels!") Many of the streets in Rancho Mirage are named for these people, and in September 2003, Mayor Hobart gave me the honor of renaming my street after *me!* I love giving directions and telling people to go down Bob Hope, past Dinah Shore, and past Gerald Ford, but don't cross Frank Sinatra!

President Ford and his wife, Betty, also have a home near mine. The first time I met them was at the annual Bob Hope Dessert Classic golf tournament. I wanted to thank President Ford for moving here, because before he did, my home was considered a cottage, and now it's an "estate"!

Chapter Eighteen

NUNSENSE

Before Whoopi Goldberg ever donned a habit in *Sister Act*, another group of singing, dancing, wisecracking nuns were entertaining people around the world. Danny Goggin, creator of the theatrical phenomenon known as *Nunsense*, is really a sort of genius. He was the first to think of taking a group of Catholic nuns (in full uniform, the way he remembered them from his Catholic upbringing in the Midwest) and put them onstage to sing and dance. Danny's original version, along with the six subsequent sequels, has generated hundreds of millions of dollars.

When I first saw *Nunsense* off-Broadway in the 1980s, I didn't think the music or the book were great, but I laughed a lot and enjoyed myself very much. More than that, I knew this was a show I wanted to do. I've always thought it would be fun to play a nun. I grew up with nuns in Cleveland, just as Danny had in Alma, Michigan. Besides, the costume was perfect for me. A black robe that would cover up my legs, and comfortable shoes! What more could a girl ask for? I've always hated changing costumes in a show. It's the only thing I dislike about being onstage. I remember Lucille Ball told me that she did *Wildcat*, her first and only musical on Broadway, for the same reason. Her character wore blue jeans for the entire show!

Arnold Middleman, the producer of the Coconut Grove Playhouse in Florida, called me and told me to look around and see if there was any new show I wanted to do. If I could find a show, he would produce it for me at his theater. I was sort of "hot" at the time and always sold out the room whenever I took my act to Florida. They loved me down there. It was my crowd. By that I mean that many people my age sooner or later migrate there..

So I told Arnold I would like to play Mother Superior in *Nunsense*. Up until that time, the show had played only smaller venues, and never with a known personality. I told Arnold I thought it could play very well in a bigger theater if we coaxed some other "name" entertainers into the cast as well.

And, boy, did we get the right people. Besides me, we had Marilyn Cooper, Marsha Lewis, Jaye P. Morgan, and Helen Baldassare, who had done the show in New York. From the moment rehearsals began, we knew we had something special. The show opened and became a smash hit. It's only the second time in my career that I've won an award for best actress (Florida's Carbonell Award). The show was so good that even before we opened, Arnold began to think he should take it on the road. I said I would agree if I could play it in California. Sadly, that was not meant to be.

Like many other deals I lost out on, I will probably never really know what happened to the West Coast tour of *Nunsense*. When I first met Dan Goggin he seemed to be a sweet little Irish guy with a very winning way and a great sense of humor. But I blamed the loss of the West Coast tour on Danny. I was told that before our show had even opened, Danny had given the rights for a West Coast production to Shirley Herz, who just happened to have been my publicist in previous years! I was furious. I felt I had really, in a sense, given birth to this production. I was the one who had suggested the show to Arnold Middleman in the first place, and had helped round up our great cast. Not being allowed to bring it home to California was like a slap in the face. Someone had screwed me once again. (Believe me, I know how Ann Miller felt when we couldn't get *Follies* to New York!)

So, after that production of *Nunsense* closed in Florida, Danny and I didn't talk for almost twenty years. And in all those years, every time I was offered the chance to play Mother Superior again, I turned it down.

Fast forward twenty years. In early 2003, I got a call from, of all people, Dan Goggin. He wondered if I would be interested in playing Mother Superior in the twentieth anniversary all-star national tour of *Nunsense*. I was more than a little surprised and taken aback. At first I thought he was crazy. Taking a show like *Nunsense* on the road? A show that had played every nook and cranny of the universe for two decades? Who would come and see it? But the money was good, the tour was going to be playing major cities for a week at a time (including my hometown), and most intriguing of all, the cast was sensational. So, in a move that I'm sure shocked Mr. Goggin (who had told everyone I would never accept), I put my twenty-year-old bad feelings aside and accepted the job. But I still didn't trust him. We began rehearsals in November 2003 at the Nola Studios in New York City with a cast that included Georgia Engel as Sister Mary Leo, my dear friend Mimi Hines as Sister Mary Amnesia, Darlene Love as the gospel-singing Sister Hubert, and Lee Meriwether, the former Miss America, as the butch Sister Robert Anne. Two novice nuns, played by a pair of extremely talented young actresses, Deborah Del Mastro and Bambi Jones, joined the cast to help us old broads out in the big numbers and understudy all the parts. I turned seventy-eight years old during rehearsals. Nearly sixty years had passed since I stepped onto the *Blue Goose* (my first tour bus) and here I was, on the road again—unbelievable!

I spent almost six months on the road with these ladies, and for the most part we got along great. I don't think there has ever been a cast of seven more diverse women traveling together on a bus across the country, including any incarnation of *4 Girls 4.*

This tour was unique. Very few actors who have had any success on television, Broadway, or in the movies will bother to go on tour anymore—it's too much work. So I don't think you'll run across a touring cast with as much combined experience as we had anytime soon. After all, in what other show will you see the likes of Lee Meriwether or Georgia Engel coming down into the audience to shake hands? Each performer brought something special to the show, and night after night, the audience got to reap the rewards of all that talent.

Although everybody in the show had her featured moments, we also did a lot of group songs and scenes. It was a very physically and vocally demanding show, and I'm sure we all wondered privately to ourselves after the first few days of rehearsal if we were actually going to be able to pull this off. As far as rehearsals went, all I can say is, thank God, we had all experienced the peaks and valleys of show business. I was working with professionals. Everybody had a firm grip on the reality of touring, and there were no unwanted egos.

Many times in interviews the press asks what the people you are working with are really like. For what it's worth, here are my thoughts on each of the ladies.

※

MIMI HINES was the only cast member I knew well before we started rehearsals. She and her partner and former husband, Phil Ford, had toured the country for years, performing in nightclubs and musicals.

Their big break came on *The Jack Paar Show* when they sang "'Til There Was You" from *The Music Man* and made Jack cry. The next day they were the toast of New York and were invited back on Paar and several other shows regularly. Eventually Mimi took over the role of Fanny Brice in *Funny Girl* when Barbra Streisand left the New York production for London. Mimi and Phil played the show on Broadway for more than a year, and Mimi really made that part her own, no easy feat. Mimi is the dearest combination of innocent little girl, sophisticated lady, and saloon singer I have ever met. She can do the hammiest shtick one minute and break your heart with a song the next. What a character! In every city we went to, Mimi would splatter the stage with holy water during sound check before the first performance. One day, she forgot to bring the little bottle of water from her dressing room, so she sent a technician to get it. I didn't have the heart to tell her, as I later discovered, that the technician had grabbed the wrong bottle and we'd been doing the show all week on a stage blessed by mouthwash! Oh, she makes me laugh. But only after 2:00 p.m. Until then, she is in her bed fast asleep until room service arrives! The woman spends more money on food brought in on a tray than anyone I know. But it makes her happy, so whatever she wants she should have. I adore her. Plus, she loves puppies as much as I do!

LEE MERIWETHER, or Leemer (my nickname for her), has never known an ugly moment in her life. I know as she reads this, she is rolling her eyes and shaking her head, but it's true! She's gorgeous! If I could look like her for an hour I'd be happy. Lee is one of the hardest-working overachievers I have ever met. When the rest of us would take a break during rehearsals, Lee would grab someone to go over a song or dance step and work right through it. She is a wonderfully sincere person, and that shines through in her acting. I don't know whether it is the decorum that comes with being Miss America or the fact that she is also such a ter-rific mother (and grandmother—sorry, Catwoman, but it's true), but Lee is the only one who never had a tense moment with anyone. Let's face it, all of us on that stage were strong and opinionated, and at times we had no reservations about letting such traits show. But not Lee. She has the amazing ability to remain everybody's buddy. Miss America? Please, how about Miss World! God bless you, Leemer, and I hate you.

While the tour was in Minneapolis, I thought Lee might benefit from seeing my brilliant ear doctor, Bill Austin. I have been deaf in one ear since my childhood and now I wear a hearing aid in the other. Dr. Austin is world-renowned and has always given me the very best hearing aid you can buy. Anyway, since I was getting a new one, I arranged a free examination for Lee, who I was sure had sustained some sort of hearing loss, or at the very least, some horrible wax buildup. Well, her hearing was purrrrfect and her ears were absolutely immaculate ... ahhhh! I asked her how that could be, since on several occasions she didn't answer me when I asked her something. I was sure she didn't hear me. She said in that genuinely sweet way that makes you want to slap her, "How do you know I was listening?"

DARLENE LOVE has a voice that only God can create. You cannot get it from training—it's just a God-given gift. Every night she blew the roof off the place with her gospel number at the end of the show, and she always gave it all she had. Darlene is, like me, very opinionated. What is that rule about friendship that says to stay clear of discussing religion or politics? Well, we ignored that rule and got into some lovely fights! I can't remember now if we made up after the last one, but who cares—we know how we feel about each other. I love Darlene because she calls a spade a spade. She is just one more of those exceptionally talented women who have spent most of their careers in the background. Phil Spector, the record producer, saw to it that while she worked for him (doing songs like "Da Doo Ron Ron") she would have a very hard time ever coming into her own, but she's a fighter. I think she is just now entering her prime, and she deserves everything that comes her way.

I have to tell a little story on Darlene and Mimi. We old veterans may have fluffed a line of dialogue here and there or mixed up the words in a song now and then, but for the most part we knew how to cover and nobody could tell. Plus, the fabulous band headed by Leo Carosone could follow us anywhere in a split second! Anyway, one night, Darlene and Mimi were backstage discussing what time the following evening's performance would begin (the curtain times changed from week to week). I was onstage doing "Turn Up the Spotlight," my big number in the first act, and they had an entrance together directly following me. Well, Darlene got onstage (mind you, this is well into the run) and went totally blank. She didn't have a clue what to say. So she turned to Mimi and whispered, "What's my line?" Mimi, obviously still engrossed in the backstage conversation, responded, "Eight o'clock!" Darlene repeated in a whispered frenzy, "What's my line?" "*Eight o'clock!*" Mimi said. I just stood there watching what looked like an old Abbott and Costello routine, with no idea of what was going on!

GEORGIA ENGEL is a very fine performer. I had wanted her to play Sister Mary Amnesia in the Florida production twenty years earlier. She would have been terrific, especially since the audience had been used to seeing her as the sweet, innocent Georgette on *The Mary Tyler Moore Show.* But she said she didn't think she wanted to do it. A few years later, she took over that character for Vicki Lawrence when Vicki had to back out of the national tour of *Nunsense Jamboree,* the country and western version, to host a new talk show. Georgia is a wonderfully positive person, but very private. I have to say that after six months on the road, I still don't know her. But I truly love and respect her.

BAMBI JONES AND DEBORAH DEL MASTRO are every bit as good or better than most of the actors I see today on Broadway. All they are missing is that one good break. I hope they get it! I have so much admiration for these two fantastic young women. They were ready to go on at a moment's notice, and eventually they did—for everyone but me. I was very proud of the fact that we logged more than 150 performances and I never missed one!

And, of course, Danny and Scott: Scott Robbins produced the tour and, through many obstacles, did a fantastic job. (Thank you, Scott-a-Lotta!) Danny Goggin is a very hands-on type of guy, and most of the time he was out on the road with us. He makes props, irons costumes, drives the van, you name it. I think he is the happiest enjoying time with the company, listening to the laughs backstage or telling jokes in the van. He and I would sit in the van waiting for the other ladies (I was always ready on time) and tell dirty jokes until the tears rolled down our faces. Danny's tour generated a lot of money in salaries for many people and never failed to send the audience home with smiling faces. He should be very proud of both of those facts. No matter what the truth of the first *Nunsense* experience was, I have to say I love Danny. I wasted twenty years being angry over something that may have been totally out of his control, and that was stupid.

In March 2003, the tour played a week in Cleveland. After all those years I was extremely nervous to be playing my hometown again. But I was excited, because my sister Jean and her husband, Jerry, were going to host the entire company at their home for a real Italian dinner. When the day came we all piled into our enormous tour bus and pulled into their driveway. The neighbors must have thought that Loretta Lynn or some rock band had turned up for lunch. My sister has a basement full of games and slot machines (and my memorabilia), and we had a wonderful time. And of course there was food enough for 300! One of my greatest joys is seeing people I love getting to know each other and having a good time. While we were in Cleveland, I was invited to see what they'd done to my old high school. I have to admit, I didn't really want to go. Though I enjoyed school at the time, today when I think of those years, I mostly think of my constant yearning to get out of Cleveland. But then I realized that I never took the time to appreciate what West Tech had given me.

Built in 1914, West Tech High is a beautiful old school they took care to build right, with huge marble hallways and wonderfully stained woodwork. The school was scheduled to be torn down, but some of the alumni felt so strongly about the place they helped turn it into condominiums. (Classy condos that allow pets!) I never realized that people from the West Side of Cleveland had such class! And I don't mean this as a put-down—after all, I'm one of them. One of the city council members gave me a citation from the city and a wonderful little wooden replica of the school, then I went on a tour. The building was much bigger than I remembered. I was filled with pride at the care they had taken to preserve the memories of the past. They had totally redone and refurbished the interior, with a reverence for years gone by that you don't see very often today (especially in America). I saw the auditorium where I had first performed, and was delighted that they had turned it into a little theater. I was astonished to see that they left the old lockers in the hallways, the blackboards where they were in the classrooms, and even the principal's portrait alongside his "track team." (If you were late for school, he made you run around the track—believe me, I was a member of the team!)

After all those years, seeing West Tech filled me with a new respect for the education I had been given. I cried when I thought about how lucky I was to have gone to a school with such superb teachers. They not only taught us the basics, and taught them well, but they inspired young people to keep learning long after they graduated. I realized that I must have had the equivalent of a college education.

Throughout our week in Cleveland, my entire extended family saw the show and came to the dressing room afterward. In a strange way it was like performing for my mother and father again, and getting acceptance in my hometown at the same time—very nerve-wracking, but very rewarding. Life is really a crazy series of circles, isn't it? Some complete circles, and some left hanging open, unresolved. There I was, back in Cleveland, onstage at the Ohio Theatre, right next door to the old RKO Palace, where all my dreams began.

I haven't talked an awful lot about my brother and sisters. I love my family, and I know they love me. For years I would send everybody a hundred dollars for Christmas (a lot of money at one time). Then an analyst told me that I was trying to buy their love. I don't necessarily think that was the case, but there might be a little grain of truth in there somewhere. As I have said, I grew up in a hard-working, upper-lower-middle-class family where loud voices prevailed and true emotions were seldom talked about. We loved each other and we knew it, so what was the point of expressing it?

Of us four kids, Orlando, Rose, and Jean got married and had families, and I went off to my career. We stayed in touch, and to this day Jean and I talk on the phone every week. She and Jerry come out to Palm Springs to visit a couple of times each year. She loves the casino as much as I do and spends the rest of the time making Italian meals that take me right back to my mother's and grandmother's cooking.

Orlando and I also talk every once in a while, but he has his family and sticks pretty close to home. Years ago when I was still living in New York, Orlando and his wife came to visit and I got them tickets to the big musical hit at the time, *The Pajama Game.* I told them to watch for Carol Haney, because she was so brilliant. That night they got home and said, "Carol Haney wasn't in the show." I asked, "What do you *mean* Carol Haney wasn't in the show?" Instead, they said, they saw somebody named Shirley MacLaine!

My sister Rose lost her husband when she was relatively young, and it affected her deeply. Well, Rose came to the performance of *Nunsense* one night in Cleveland and I didn't recognize her. I thought she was my childhood friend Carolyn Vanucci. When she walked into my dressing room I said, "Carolyn?" And she said, "I'm *Rose!*" I know I hurt her feelings, but I hadn't seen her in twenty years! I felt so bad and embarrassed about it that I haven't called her since. Shame on me, I guess.

I send her Christmas cards but never hear back. I know she was stuck living across the street from my mother all those years and had to deal with a lot, and maybe she still resents the fact that I wasn't around. Whatever the reasons for our estrangement, I love her and I always will . . . but families are complicated, and the one I grew up in didn't equip us to deal with our emotions easily.

We all have trials and tribulations in life. We all experience hurt and loss. Sometimes we are the victims, and at other times we are the ones who inflict the pain. Somewhere along the way, if we've learned from these experiences, we get the opportunity to resolve past hurts and make things right. Sometimes we succeed at mending fences (I made peace with Danny, my hometown, my mother, my career), and sometimes, as with Rose, we hope that we'll be around long enough for another opportunity.

Maurice Chevalier and me, in 1965. When I was a kid, I would put on a straw hat and dance across the kitchen floor imitating him singing, "Mimi, you funny little good for nothing, Mimi!"

With Gypsy Rose Lee and Paul Lynde in my Los Angeles apartment. I envied Gypsy's strength, confidence, tenacity, and joie de vivre. Paul was a very funny man who was never happy.

June Havoc, sister of Gypsy Rose Lee and "Baby June" of Gypsy fame, is a talented actress and director. Plus, she gave me the best financial advice I've ever received: She told me to buy property.

I've known world-famous columnist Liz Smith, my Bibba, since 1950. Back in those days she worked as my road manager. She can read faster than anyone I've ever met and still teases me about the fact it took me a year to read Kon-Tiki.

Bette Davis— sometimes with her you really were in for a bumpy night, but she could be very generous and loving to those close to her.

Cris Alexander and me with trumpet and flute. Cris and I roomed together way back when, in New York in the 1950s, and are still good friends.

I adored working with my lovely "Clara," aka Doris Day. In the late 1960s, I played (what else?) a loudmouth Italian on her Doris Day Show.

My dear friend Billy DeWolfe (that's Mr. DeWolfe to you) and I got to work together on The Doris Day Show, *in which he played Doris's boss. He was also one of the many friends I brought on to* The Mike Douglas Show *when I was guest host.*

Sid Caesar, Gavin McLeod, Karen Valentine, and I all appeared in TV's The Love Boat. *Gavin, one hell of an actor, also played Herbie to one of my Mama Roses in* Gypsy, *this one in San Diego in the early 1970s.*

With Edie Adams, who had worked with me in Cinderella *(she played the Fairy Godmother), and Virginia Graham, a trailblazer in television talk shows and one of the wittiest, most intelligent women I have ever met.*

Fred Ebb, my Freddy Ebby, was a brilliant songwriter. I sang two of his songs, "My Coloring Book" and "Maybe This Time," that went on to be smash hits—for other people!

With Mary Martin and Carol Channing—look who's paying attention to the camera. I got to be in my first film, The Girl Most Likely, *when Carol dropped out.*

Larry Storch is one of my closest friends. We've sure made the rounds on the nightclub circuit. In fact, we met when he was opening for Desi Arnaz at the Trocadero in Los Angeles in the 1940s. In the early 1950s we did a real bomb of a revue together at the Flamingo in Las Vegas, and later we both worked at the Blue Angel and the Bon Soir in New York.

Gwen Verden, Jerry Orbach, Liza Minnelli, Liliane Montevecchi, Joel Grey, Chita Rivera, and I gather for a tribute to John Kander, behind Joel, and Fred Ebb, behind Lisa. Even after they became world-famous and very wealthy, John and Fred still got together every day and worked.

Friends Phyllis Diller and Burt Reynolds worked for free in my ill-fated, never-aired TV special, Hello, Kaye, *1987. They really pulled together for me.*

Joining me in Rick McKay's brilliant documentary Broadway, The Golden Age, By the Legends Who Were There, *2003, were, back row, Janis Paige, Robert Goulet, Carol Lawrence, Rick McKay, Gretchen Wyler, Charles Durning, and front row, Carol Channing, Patricia Morison, and Jerry Herman—just some members of the cast of thousands.*

*Phyllis Newman,
here with
husband Adolph
Green, was a
great ally when
I was battling
breast cancer,
and gave me the
best advice.*

*Visiting with my
old friend Alice
Ghostley recently.
People often com-
pare her to Paul
Lynde, but she had
that persona down
long before he came
along.*

*With Rex Reed—one of
the few great critics!*

Chapter Nineteen

How My Big Mouth Kept Me Out of the Big Time

You know, I'm better than I used to be, but discretion has always taken a back seat to my emotions and my varying ability to keep a tight rein on them. I tend to tell the truth. Sometimes, though, it really pays to shut up—I just never did. I found a prime example of this while looking through my scrapbook the other day.

In 1968, Rex Reed interviewed Eve Arden and me for an article called "Two Hot Mamas in Hot Water," which was published to coincide with the premiere of *The Mothers-in-Law*. Our interviews ran side by side, Eve sweetly recalling her career, her family life, her new home, and what it was like living in Europe. I, on the other hand, held nothing back: "There's this big dum-dum at CBS—you don't have to print his name, just say big dum-dum and everybody will know who I mean—who didn't want this show. I mean they were paying Desi Arnaz $50,000 just to think, and then when he came up with this show and both of the original writers from *I Love Lucy* to write it, this dum-dum says, 'Who cares about mothers-in-law?' Desi says, 'Everybody who has ever had or is about to have one, which includes most of the human race,' so we did the pilot anyway and CBS turned us down. There was no loyalty to Desi or even Eve Arden, who had both made so much money for CBS in the past. Even with the sponsor insistent on the show, they still said no. I loathe people who are not loyal. So we went to NBC. That'll snap their garters."

This was all true—but so what? Is it any wonder I was never offered a series at CBS?

And my opinions were not limited to show business. Around the

209

same time, I was making a guest appearance on a talk show in San Francisco with Angela Davis and the Black Panthers. They were saying, "Three hundred *years* you've put us through this. Three hundred *years* we have suffered. Three hundred *years* we have been slaves." I said, "Wait a minute! How old are you?" One of them said, "Twenty-three." And I said, "*That's* how long you've suffered. Don't give me three hundred years. I had nothing to do with three hundred years, so don't shout at me." And the whole audience went, "Ooooh," meaning I was going to be killed at any moment. How to win friends and influence people, huh?

I did a lot of talk shows around this time. Maybe the big mouth helped. I was on a show in Detroit and the people on the panel were discussing smog control. Smog control in the automotive capital of the world. The car companies were trying to separate themselves from their responsibility and even deny the simple fact of air pollution. Again, I said, "Wait a minute! Do these executives think *they* are going to live through that smog while we die?" Again the audience went, "Oooh." I never got a free car.

I did *The Perry Como Show* for about a year and a half. To his credit, Nick Vanoff, the producer who stopped me from singing "My Coloring Book," had told me right up front, "Look, I don't like lady comics. The only lady comic I like is Martha Raye, and you're not Martha Raye." Okay, the ground rules were pretty clear. So what did I do? I knew Perry liked me, which was why I got the job in the first place, and I wanted to do a number called "Rags." So I went to Perry and said, "Listen to this song." He loved it and said, "Hey, Nick, put this on the show!" When the song went over, Nick hated me even more. Nick went on to produce *The Julie Andrews Hour, The Sonny and Cher Show*, and several of the Kennedy Center Honors ceremonies. Needless to say, you haven't seen me as a guest on any of those shows!

Chapter Twenty

Afterthoughts

As I told you at the beginning, my mind does not work in strict chronological order when it comes to recalling events of the past. I suppose this can be confusing for someone reading an autobiography, but memories are confusing.

After eighty years of living, I have found that many moments I initially thought of as life-shattering faded away quickly, and others that might have seemed at the time to be an insignificant few seconds come back as clearly as if they happened yesterday. For example, the horrendous moment the doctor told me I had cancer can be relegated to one spot among many on the list of my life's events, yet I will forever treasure in my soul that certain look on Arthur Siegel's face while he played for one of the hundreds of shows we did together.

So here are a few additional people, places, shows, and moments from my life that don't fit in any particular order.

ON PARLOR GAMES WITH THE STARS Leonard Sillman, the producer of all the *New Faces* shows, invited Arthur Siegel and me to dine at his home one evening. It was a small dinner party, and I was delightfully surprised to find Shirley Booth, Judith Anderson, and Bea Lillie in attendance.

We spent the evening talking about the usual—the ups and downs of show business. I was astounded to discover that all their careers paralleled mine with regard to going through periods of being "in favor" or "out of favor." I have to say, it made me feel a bit better knowing that these ladies, who, in my opinion, should have never gone out of favor, didn't really have any more control over circumstances than I did.

Later that evening, we all played a game called "attraction," which Maureen Stapleton had originated. You had to answer "yes" or "no" to the question "Would you move over in bed for . . . ?" It didn't matter if the person was living or deceased. I almost fell on the floor when it was Shirley Booth's turn and she said "yes" to everyone, even the women!

I had played the game previously in Bette Davis's apartment with Maureen, Shirley, Gig Young, and his wife, Elizabeth Montgomery. There were three names that everyone answered "yes" to that night: Cary Grant, Lena Horne, and Simone Signoret! I believe that was also the night I arm-wrestled with Olivia de Havilland, and lost.

⁂

ON BABE RUTH Those of you who are sports enthusiasts may be interested to know that in the late 1940s I met Babe Ruth. We were both in the Manhattan office of Dr. Simon Ruskin, an ear, nose, and throat specialist. Babe was so chic and dapper in a camel-hair coat with a belt and a little cap. He couldn't say much because he was having trouble with his voice. I shook his hand and told him how thrilled I was to meet him. My father and brother were more impressed by this meeting than with any other thing I had accomplished. Pa and Orlando couldn't have cared less about my meeting Clark Gable, but Babe Ruth—*now* I had really "made it." Sadly, Babe Ruth died a short time later from throat cancer. He was a legend back when you had to earn the title.

⁂

ON MRS. WILLIAM RANDOLPH HEARST Elsa Maxwell once asked me to perform at a party she was giving in Mrs. Hearst's New York apartment on Fifth Avenue. I had met Hearst's longtime mistress, Marion Davies, when she invited me to lunch at her beach house in Santa Monica, so I knew a little about what Mrs. Hearst had gone through. Hearst never divorced his wife, and she never publicly acknowledged Davies. What is fascinating to me is that no matter how far you come in the eyes of the world, I guess you never really shed the skin of the person you were when you were growing up. As Mrs. Hearst showed me around her home that evening I don't know who was more impressed: Me seeing the priceless paintings and the mink bed cover, or the former chorus girl who was showing them off.

⁂

ON RED SKELTON Red gave me some very good advice on how to equip myself with a relatively inexpensive home-security system. He said, "Kaye, go out and buy an old, beat-up car and leave it in your driveway.

Then every once in a while, move it around and park it in different places. That way, people will always think you're home."

⁂

ON CECIL B. DEMILLE I just happened to be there on the set of *The Ten Commandments* (the talkie, not the silent one) when DeMille was filming his famous "parting of the Red Sea" sequence. The singer Pat Morrissey and her husband, Gil Kitt, and I were touring the lot—Gil got us in somehow. We were standing there enthralled in the midst of thousands of extras as the famous director yelled, "Cut!" Pat and I looked at each other wondering what had happened. Then we heard Mr. DeMille say, "Will the two ladies in modern-day sweaters please get off the set!" I'll never get over the fact that not only were we spotted among so many thousands of extras, but we gained the dubious distinction of being kicked off a movie set by Cecil B. DeMille!

⁂

ON JOHN SCHLESINGER I met the film director in New York in 1965 when he came to see *The Decline and Fall of the Entire World as Seen through the Eyes of Cole Porter* at the Square East Theatre. He was riding high on the success of his film *Darling*, with Julie Christie and Laurence Harvey. I made him laugh and we got along very well. We stayed in touch through the years, and while he was creating the script for what would become his masterpiece, *Midnight Cowboy*, he was very, very lonely. *Far from the Madding Crowd*, the film he made after *Darling*, was not a success, and he was being shunned by the Hollywood elite. (What a bunch of phonies. I've said it before: L.A. is truly a "tinsel" town. It's built on a foundation of papier-mâché!) Anyway, John was feeling so down at the time that I called my press agent, Jay Allen, and asked who we could set him up with. (John later called me the "Dolly Levi of the desert.") The first name Jay mentioned was Michael Childers. Oh, he was so cute and talented! Michael was twenty-two years old and had blonde hair. I was a little concerned at first about the sixteen-year age difference, but they hit it off immediately. I was so happy to have been part of that little bit of matchmaking! Michael became a fabulous portrait photographer, often compared to Joseph Karsch, and ended up producing many of John's films.

More of life's little circles: I happened to have dinner with John in Palm Springs in December 2000, and the next day he had a stroke from which he never fully recovered. He died just as I was putting the finishing touches on the first edition of this book. John was such an eloquent man. I remember him floating in my pool and giving me some advice. (He never employed me, but he did give me some fabulous advice.) He said, "Whatever you do, do not sell this house!"

⋙

ON RONALD REAGAN I will always be grateful to Marvin Hamlisch for putting together a show called *An Evening with Cole Porter*. In 1987, Mel Tormé, June Allyson, Patti Austin, and I got to perform the show at the White House for President and Mrs. Reagan. My eyes filled with tears to think that I was going to meet the President of the United States! I was a staunch Democrat at the time, but as soon as Ronald Reagan walked toward me I immediately became a Republican (at least while he was still in office). The President's secretary took us on a personal tour of the family's private quarters, and Nancy Reagan could not have been more gracious.

My cousin Paul Ballardo accompanied me on the trip and had brought a small ceramic globe for me to give to President Reagan. I asked the secretary if he would be kind enough to take it to the President. I wanted to let him know how much we appreciated being there; the globe was meant to say he had the whole world in his hands. Everyone thought it was silly of me to give such an inconsequential gift. The Reagans got so many things from people all over the world that they could hardly be expected to notice it. But as I stood in the receiving line, President Reagan came by, said hello, kissed my cheek, and whispered in my ear, "I love the globe, Kaye." What a wonderful man! Now that he is gone, I hope history will be kind to him. Whether or not you agreed with his politics, you have to admit that Ronald Reagan had a tremendous amount of honor and grace, as well as an incredible sense of humor.

⋙

ON MY TELEVISION SPECIAL One of the several times in my "checkered" career that I got my hopes up was in 1987. A TV producer named Joe Peterson convinced me that if I could get Burt Reynolds, he would do a television special for me. It actually sounded pretty simple. I would fly to Las Vegas and perform in front of a live audience for a week. The idea was to film my act and add a few guest stars and some cartoon graphics, and I'd have my very own television special. (Lucky was definitely back in town!) The show was to be entitled *Hello, Kaye* and was intended to be an hour of me and my friends in Las Vegas. So, I gathered my friends. Burt Reynolds, Phyllis Diller, Debbie Reynolds, Gavin MacLeod, Rip Taylor, and concert pianist Leonard Pennario all agreed to do it for free. (Milton Berle and Joan Rivers got paid). The material went over fine, but that was about the only good thing about the experience. A dancer named Paul Godkin, who had been in *That's the Ticket* with me way back in 1947, said he had just finished a Shirley MacLaine special and convinced me he could direct. Bad decision. He had not directed but choreographed the MacLaine special, and not only could he not direct, he hired a crew that was as inept as he was. The finished product was just terrible. It had been filmed with the wrong cameras, and the film and cameras were kept in an RV when it was 110 degrees in the shade. The film was *melting*! Did I need this!? The editing was slipshod, the sound was horrible, and the overall quality of the tape was totally unusable. I felt so bad, because Burt Reynolds (who was at the height of his career) had put in several days' work and was just wonderful about the whole thing. Phyllis (who is a gifted concert pianist) and I did a great comic duet for piano and flute. What a friend she was—and is! Everybody really pulled together to help me out and I never saw a dime. I didn't even get paid for the live shows I put on. Now I hear someone is making money from selling badly dubbed copies of the show on eBay, in a faked-up box and shrink-wrapped even! Oh well . . . that's show biz!

ON SANDY DENNIS In 1988 I was privileged to appear in a production of *The Female Odd Couple* with the incomparable Sandy Dennis. She played Florence (Felix) and I was the messy Olive (Oscar). In real life this probably would have been the other way around, but given our public persona and physical types, the casting worked out great. Sandy was a sweet gentle soul and a bit eccentric—she lived with forty or so cats (I love animals, but come on!). One day I killed a spider on the set, and she almost burst into tears! "How do you know who you're killing in another life!?" Oy! Though we were doing a Neil Simon play, I remember she told me that she and Neil didn't get along. I thought that was strange, since she'd done such an incredible job as Jack Lemmon's wife in the film *The Out-of-Towners*. It seems that her running gag line throughout the film, the whining "Ohhhh, my God!" (one of the funniest lines in the picture), was her own ad-lib. How could someone as brilliant and successful as Mr. Simon have such an easily bruised ego? I couldn't believe it when the producers wanted to give me billing above her. I said, "What? Are you crazy? She's an Academy Award–winning actress!" Sandy was a successful Method-acting graduate of the Actors Studio, but even so, we got along beautifully and our acting styles complemented each other perfectly.

Sandy Dennis died of ovarian cancer in 1992 at the age of fifty-four. Who knows how much brilliant work was ahead of her? I can still see her in the opening scene when she comes in the door of Olive's apartment wearing a big hat and dark sunglasses with tears running down her cheeks. I could barely keep it together. "Anything wrong, Florence?" I'd ask. "Nooo," Sandy would reply. At one point in *The Odd Couple*, Olive says, "I love you, Florence," and that line couldn't have been more true in describing how I feel about Sandy Dennis.

ॐ

ON LOSING WEIGHT There is not one weight-loss regimen I have not explored at one time or another throughout my long career as an eater. In 1965, while I was doing *The Decline and Fall of the Entire World as Seen through the Eyes of Cole Porter*, I had been on a very "Atkins-like" diet for almost four months and had lost nearly forty pounds. I was down to 124 pounds, probably the thinnest I'd ever been, even when they pulled me out of my mother's womb. (No, come to think of it, I was at 115 when they yanked me out.) But then my heart started to beat erratically and my blood pressure rose dramatically, so one more diet went out the window! (Incidentally, that show was a "revuesical," put together by Ben Bagley. It starred many talented people, including Carmen Alvarez, Elmarie Wendell, Harold Lang, and William Hickey, a famous acting coach who later had roles in several films; he played Cher's grandfather in *Moonstruck*, for one.)

To show you how I hang onto things, one night during that diet, Arthur Siegel, Marilyn Cantor, and I were having dinner at the home of Marilyn's best friend, Charlotte Kent. A wonderfully funny writer, she wrote a song in which a prisoner sings, "It's appalling—my *New Yorker* was three weeks late!" She wrote another song for Sophie Tucker in which Sophie, playing a madam in a whorehouse, sings, "They all go upstairs but me." Anyway, Charlotte was also a fabulous cook. I sat there at the table watching Arthur and Marilyn eat everything: beef stroganoff, chocolate soufflé, you name it! And I said, "Charlotte, you have got to promise me, promise me, that after I am through dieting you will make this meal again." She said, "I promise, I will." Three weeks later she died, and I never, ever forgave myself for passing up that meal. I'm still upset about it!

ॐ

ON GRACE KELLY, SOPHIE TUCKER, AND ETHEL MERMAN *Decline and Fall* was not only a great show that ran for 273 performances, but it also allowed me to meet a lot of people I admired. In fact, I remember more famous people coming backstage after that show than during any other production I have ever been in. This was the show Maurice Chevalier had in mind when he referred to me as "the American Bea Lillie." He gave me an autographed photo of himself, signed "From your newest friend and lover." The Kennedys came to see our show five times! Grace Kelly spotted me at lunch at La Caravelle after seeing the show the night before, and the next thing I knew, I had Princess Grace stopping by my table to tell me how much she'd enjoyed it. I was so flattered, I barely knew what to say!

In that show I did an impression of Sophie Tucker, and one night Sophie called the box office and warned them, "Don't tell the little lady, Ballard, that I'm going to be there." Sophie was known for wearing corsages when she performed, so as part of my impression I wore a long corsage that went from my neck to my toes. Well, sure enough, Sophie came backstage and I timidly stammered, "Miss Tucker, I hope you don't mind my doing a satire on you." Sophie responded, "Well, little lady, you can put those flowers right up your ass!" Then she laughed, and said she had loved the show.

Ethel Merman also came backstage—as she usually did when she came to see me perform—and asked, in her booming voice, "Hey, Ballard, where's the john? I have to take a piss." Ethel was always very blunt, and never one to put on airs. She was also an impressive artist who should be given credit for almost single-handedly introducing the entire ASCAP catalogue of songs from 1930 to 1960.

While performing in *Decline and Fall* in New York, I became well acquainted with Fred Astaire's sister, Adele. She was Fred's first dancing partner. They became quite a famous team, first as child stars in vaudeville, and later in a string of hits on Broadway, including *Funny Face* and *The Band Wagon*. While they were together, Adele had been the star of the team and drew rave reviews for her comic brilliance. Then in 1932 she married a British lord and quit show business for good, leaving Fred to conquer Hollywood. Though they lived far apart, Adele told me that she spoke to her brother every day of her life. To my amazement, Adele once gave me her personal scrapbook as a gift. I quickly gave it back, telling her the book was much too valuable to give away.

Before she left New York, Adele invited me to visit her in Ireland. Six months later, I received a postcard from her that said, "Kaye, please come, we'll have such fun!" The problem was, there was no return address. I called Adele's husband at the time, a Mr. Douglass (she was no longer Lady Cavendish), who was still in New York, and explained that Adele had not given me an address. He said, "Kaye, what's on the front of the postcard?" I told him it was a picture of some castle called "Waterford." "Well," he said, "that's it." Adele's home was Waterford Castle in Ireland! Unfortunately, I was never able to take the time off from work to go and visit before she passed away in 1981.

ON MR. KENNETH AND JACKIE ONASSIS The classiest hair stylist in New York by far is Mr. Kenneth. He has been doing my hair since the 1950s. His clientele list reads like the New York social registry, and for good reason. Not only does he give the best cuts in New York, but he is an artist with integrity. Integrity, in a ladies hair salon? I can only imagine the amount of filth and dirt (and by that I mean really good, juicy gossip!) floating around his shop on any given afternoon. And I have yet to hear Mr. Kenneth utter a single unkind word about anyone or repeat a client's confidence. (He also tells the best jokes!)

I have met so many people in Mr. Kenneth's salon that it's hard to select just a few to mention. Gloria Vanderbilt comes to mind first. Gloria may have been "born to the purple," as they say, but she has endured a lot of sorrow and betrayal in spite of her fortune. One day she confided in me that she wanted to find a mate for her sweet little dog, Anna. "Kaye," she said, "I just cannot deny her anything, and I think she is lonely. The problem is, poor little Anna cannot accept anything new." Well, Gloria did eventually find another dog for her precious Anna and named her Desiree. However, after meeting Desiree, Gloria said, Anna became so agitated that she had to be put on intravenous feedings for several days! Gloria fell in love with my little puppy Emily and did a drawing of her. That wonderful sketch is one of my most cherished possessions.

I also met Bunny Mellon of the Washington, D.C., Mellon family. One afternoon she came into the salon wearing an incredible raincoat. It was very lightweight and yet very warm. When I complimented her on it, she asked, "Would you like me to order one for you, Kaye?" I said that I would, and Mrs. Mellon replied, "I'm calling Paris this afternoon and shall speak to Givenchy personally." "Uh-oh," I thought. "How much is this coat going to cost?" A few days later Bunny's butler delivered the coat to my apartment. When I peeked at the bill, I nearly fainted. It cost 18,500 francs, approximately $3,500! That was in 1961. I was working for David Merrick in *Carnival*, and I was certainly not able to pay that much for a coat. But I was saved. The coat was too large, so I sent it back with the butler. When Mrs. Mellon called to see if she could order another one in a smaller size, I thanked her but declined. It can be dangerous to hob-nob with the rich and famous!

One day at Mr. Kenneth's, I found myself running late for a matinee performance of *Carnival*. My hair was still in rollers and I was in a complete panic when Happy Rockefeller rushed to my side. "Here, Kaye, let me help," she said, while hastily pulling curlers from my head. I still cannot believe I had a Rockefeller play beautician for me in order to help get me to work on time!

Often I would see Jackie Onassis in the shop. One morning I discovered her sitting alone in a booth. Without giving it a thought, I stuck my head in the door to say hello. "Good morning, Mrs. Onassis!" I said cheerfully. Well, I must have been a bit overzealous, because she jumped straight up out of her chair. I felt terrible. I quickly apologized for startling her, and as I walked away I thought how awful it must be for this lovely woman to live daily with that kind of fear. (I did get an autograph, though!)

ON DAN BLOCKER FROM *BONANZA* In 1972, I did a *Flip Wilson Show* with Dan, the gentle giant of a guy who played Hoss Cartwright on *Bonanza* for all those years. He was a sweet guy, and so well known from that show that people recognized him wherever he went. We were sitting around talking and he said to me, "Ya know, I've got a place in Switzerland where I go on weekends—I need privacy. You can't git any privacy in this country." All the way to Switzerland for solitude? I thought, "Why doesn't he just go into his backyard? Why doesn't he just go into the other room and close the door?" He died five months after we did the show, after catching pneumonia on the plane. So there's your privacy.

ON MOTHER TERESA One day in 1992 I received a call from my friend Bradley James, in California. I was in New York, where for four months that year I did a show of Irving Berlin's music called *Say It with Music* at the Rainbow and Stars with Jason Graae, Liz Callaway, and Ron Raines. It was a wonderful experience. Bradley is a terrific performer with a beautiful voice who happened to be a good friend of Mother Teresa. He had met her by chance in a church in L.A. Bradley is a very spiritual man, and he happened to be sitting in the back of the church, all by himself, when Mother Teresa noticed him. They talked for a bit and continued to stay in touch with each other until the day she died. Bradley was calling to tell me that if I wanted to meet Mother Teresa, she would be at St. Rita's in the Bronx the following morning at six. The Bronx at that time was more frightening to me than Calcutta, but who could pass up a chance to meet Mother Teresa? When I arrived at the church early the next morning, there were several tiny women in long, white, flowing robes with blue striping, all milling about. Then an even tinier woman entered from another room and was suddenly surrounded by a flock of children. There was no doubt who had entered. Mother Teresa gave everyone there a religious medallion. I remember touching her hand as she gave me mine. I've met presidents, movie stars, and people who have more money than I could ever dream of having, but this woman had a presence that quite literally inspired awe. A short while later, I followed her into the rectory and watched quietly as she ate a breakfast consisting of a slice of cheese, a pear, a single piece of whole wheat bread, and Sanka. Never mind working in the slums of Calcutta—what discipline to only eat as much as she needed!

When Mother Teresa died, the sisters of her order made prayer cards with a few strands of her hair sealed in each. I am lucky enough to have one, and it is one of the few things I keep with me at all times. Thank you, Bradley. Mother Teresa will soon be an official saint. To me, she already is. It was a blessing to be in her presence.

ON COLLECTING AUTOGRAPHS When I did *Night of a Hundred Stars* I was in the dressing room with Lauren Bacall, Ann Miller, Ethel Merman, all these great, great stars. I said, "I want you all to sign my program." Lauren said, "Oh, Ballard, you are so corny!" (Skip a beat, and then . . .) "That's not a bad idea!" And pretty soon everyone in the dressing room was passing around programs in a signing frenzy. I remember yelling, "Imagine, Helen Hayes just asked for mine!"

ON YOUTHFUL PROMISE I've said there are certain people, like Barbra Streisand and Nathan Lane, whom you meet when they are young and you just know they will become stars. I've met and worked with hundreds of young performers, like the ladies in our *Funny Girl* concert, who have great careers in front of them—people you look back on and are so proud to say, "I knew them when." For instance, in 1966, soon after Judy Garland discovered Peter Allen and his partner, Chris, in Australia, the Allen Brothers were opening for me at the Diplomat Hotel in Florida. Peter was engaged to Liza Minnelli at the time, and she was busy paying her dues in a summer stock production of *The Pajama Game*. Almost forty years later, it was a very surreal experience to see the lives of Liza and Peter played out onstage in *The Boy from Oz*. When I did *Wonderful Town* at City Center in 1963, there were two unknown actors in the company, James Kirkwood (who would become a famous writer) and Reid Shelton (who went on to play the original Daddy Warbucks in *Annie*). If you have some talent and a lot of luck, and, most important, if you stick with this business long enough, it'll usually pay off sooner or later.

ON GAY MEN I have always enjoyed camp humor, and I have to say that, in general, gay men have that market cornered. People ask, "Why do all the gay men love Judy Garland, Barbra Streisand, Bette Midler, and Tracey Ullman?" Because they have taste, that's why! And great humor. I once knew a gay man who was with the infantry during the war and wore false eyelashes into battle!

There is a lot of talk about gay marriage these days, and I'm not sure how I feel about it. I do feel that all Americans should share the same legal rights. Religious questions aside, I believe that all people have the right to be happy. As far as commitment is concerned, no piece of paper is going to define one human being's relationship with another.

My dear, dear friend Cris Alexander and his partner, Shaun O'Brien, have been together for more than fifty years, and they are truly the most well-adjusted people I have ever met. Cris was a great friend and co-conspirator of Patrick Dennis (creator of *Auntie Mame*). He is an accomplished artist, actor, singer, and dancer who used me (and even my Nana) in several brilliantly funny pictures he staged and photographed for Patrick Dennis's *Little Me: The Intimate Memoirs of that Great Star of Stage, Screen and Television, Belle Poitrine*. Sid Caesar starred in a huge hit musical based on this book.

Another gay gentleman I absolutely adored was Michael Garrison. I had first met Mike in England. He and Robert Conrad produced the television show *The Wild Wild West*. Mike died after he bought a beautiful new home in Bel Air, California. He slipped on the marble staircase and hit his head on the way down. Oh, how I miss him and his unbelievable sense of humor.

Some time after Mike had returned to the United States, he and I were walking along Fifth Avenue. I was congratulating him on his recent marriage (to a woman). As we walked, he fondled his wedding ring and said, "Oh, Kaye, I am so happy. I should have done this a long time ago. It's the greatest thing I've ever done in my life." Just then a gorgeous man walked by and Mike instantly slipped the ring off his finger and tried to make it into an earring! This was hilarious to me, but probably wouldn't have been so funny to his new bride, had she been there. I hope that people today are finally discovering they can be who they are.

Mike told me about the time he and some of his friends were riding around New Jersey in search of a gay bar. They weren't having any luck, so he pulled up next to a police car, punched his fist into his hand, and in his manliest voice said, "Officer, you gotta help me. My brother is a fruit and we gotta find him because my mother is dying." "Well," the officer responded, "there's Oil Can Sally's just down this block, and The Connection is across the street, and over there is Little Pink Mamas." Mike started to pull off, and as he did one of his friends rolled down the window and yelled, "Thanks, Mary!"

You have to surround yourself with funny, good-hearted people whenever you find them, because they are precious, and when they are gone, they are impossible to replace.

⇝

ON ANDY WARHOL Andy loved a woman named Haila Stoddard, who was appearing on the soap opera *Secret Storm*. She was the producer of a show I did called *The Beast in Me*, and Andy said, "I'll do the costumes." Well, it was all very creative, but everything was attached with Velcro: there were little pieces of fabric everywhere. We ended up in Dr. Dentons! And the program listed the costume designer as "Leo Van Witsen." I have no idea how he came up with that name or what it meant.

It wasn't until I got to know Andy better that I realized how famous he was. I saw his painting of the Campbell's Soup can. I said, "Oh, that's a nice painting of a soup can." We'd go eat at the restaurant Serendipity, and when the waiter brought the check, Andy would wave it off, saying, "Don't bother me with that." He had a running tab there and he never looked at it. He could have been ripped off horribly.

Andy took me to his apartment, where everything was covered with Reynolds Wrap. I said, "What is this?" He said, "It's an *environment*." I said, "Interesting." That night, he asked me to go down to the Village, where there was going to be a "happening." It was nuts. I couldn't stand it. Funny, though. There were so many crazy people running amok. Of course, everybody there, including Holly Woodlawn, ended up becoming famous in Andy's movies.

Andy gave me a copy of his mother's book—which has since disappeared from my library—inscribed to "Kay-pie." It contained her drawings. Andy's mother was as "out there" as he was. The book would be worth a fortune today, because she had only twenty-six copies printed.

ॐ

ON THE U.S. MILITARY One time, Arthur Seigel and I were working in Omaha, and we were invited to tour the Strategic Air Command base, where they have the "red phone." We had to fill out all these papers and were carefully checked out . We waited three days for security clearance, and when we finally arrived, they gave us name tags with our names misspelled. I thought, "Oh, this place is *really* safe."

The military guides gave us a tour of the facility and showed us movies about "bomblettes," the weaponry they were using in Vietnam. I couldn't believe it. The army had tried to make killing "cute" by inventing bomblettes! Don't worry, they're just little bombs! A guide also told me that personnel there could reach anyone, anywhere in the world, on the phone in just four seconds. "You can get anybody in four seconds?" He said, "Yes, it costs us $35 million a year." Amazing! We were paying $35 million dollars a year so our government could talk to other countries in four seconds. I thought to myself, are we going crazy or what?

ॐ

ON FRANK SINATRA He had a house about a mile away from mine in Palm Springs, but it wasn't like he ever came over for lunch. Our relationship had gotten off to a bad start when I was still with Spike Jones. I was eighteen or nineteen at the time, and we were on a Freedom for America radio program together. I was so excited to meet Frank that I naively walked right up to him and shouted, "Paesan!" Hey, I thought it was the thing to do—we were both Italian, both there helping out the war effort. He looked at me and said, "I beg your pardon, I'm an *American.*" Well, I was devastated. But I chalked it up to the fact that I wasn't attractive enough.

Frank was a very complex man, and one of the greatest performers who ever lived. We ran into each other from time to time throughout our careers, and he even introduced me in the audience from the stage in Las Vegas. But I never got a chance to explain what I had meant the day of the radio show, and I felt funny around him from that moment on.

ॐ

ON JAMES LIPTON I really respect and appreciate those who enjoy success in show business but remain unchanged by the attention. I'd met James Lipton previously, but when I was staying at the Oakwood Apartments in Burbank in 1989, I'd go to the gym in the morning (believe it or not) and try to work out. James was there, too, and he told me about his plans to launch an Actors Studio interview project. I thought, "Oh, Actors Studio. Interview all those people you have to hug to hear!" But the more James talked about the idea, the more I thought it could really become something. The success of *Inside the Actors Studio* has brought him incredible fame; it's as if he's become a rock star. I ran into James recently at Sardi's, and you know something? He was just as gracious and charming as he'd been back in Burbank. I thought, "That's what really makes him special." Now, James, why don't you invite me to come on the show?

જી

ON YET ANOTHER FLOP Speaking of 1989, I was staying in Burbank because I'd finally gotten another series. I was cast as Mrs. Travalony on a syndicated show about a ventriloquist's mannequin who really talked. The title adequately describes that fact that I signed the contract: *What a Dummy*.

જી

ON ED SULLIVAN I appeared on *The Ed Sullivan Show* three times, and each time I marveled at the fact that this man had his own show. He was always very nice and pleasant, very likeable. But the only reason he was in show business was because nobody had *fired* him. He had begun as a columnist and was very lucky to be in the right place at the right time. When he started *Toast of the Town* (the original name for *The Ed Sullivan Show*) in 1948, the field of television variety was wide open, and Ed just went along for the ride. He would come up to you fifteen minutes before you were to go on and tell you to cut a five-minute bit that you had been performing for years down to three minutes—it was nuts. He had no understanding of performers, yet he hosted the most important and influential talent showcase in the nation for twenty-three years. I'll never forget some of his comments and introductions. After Edith Piaf sang, he said, "Let's have a big hand for the little lady." When Peggy Lee finished a song, he said, "Miss Peggy Lee . . . and now for a real star, Topo Gigio!"

જી

ON JOHNNY CARSON I remember that Johnny once said of Bette Midler, "You know, Kaye, she reminds me of you." Johnny was fabulous at what he did, but he ran warm and cold. He could be very complimentary, and he had me on his show many, many times. But then, if we met at a restaurant, he would act like he didn't know who I was. I think what a lot of people have said is true: He was a very shy, private man who came alive in front of the camera. That made him hard to get close to, and I think that's the way he wanted it. I do feel that he gave in to the "dumbing down" mentality toward the end of his long run. His strength was interviewing people in whom he was actually interested. Just as Steve Allen and Jack Parr had been before him, Johnny was always engaging, because (or at least you believed) that he was actually listening. Merv Griffin has the same quality. In later years, Johnny's *Tonight Show* guest roster seemed to be more about ratings and who was the "flavor of the minute" and had something to promote. But there'll never be another one like Johnny (or Jack or Steve or Merv), because the vast majority of the people watching don't have the patience or interest it takes to scratch the surface of anything or anyone. And . . . I'll say it one more time, the world today seems to have no appreciation for wit and class.

ON PERRY COMO I loved Perry, and I loved being a regular on his show. Everyone always had the impression that he was so low key and calm, and he was. But he also had a Moscow Mule (consommé and vodka) every night before he went on. He had every show blessed by Father Bob before we performed. Perry was so cute kneeling down to pray in his boxer sorts and tux shirt. He learned to knit to pass the time in rehearsal. I wish I had a picture of that. Perry also loved to golf. I remember (and this was after *West Side Story* had closed) he heard the song "Maria" and said, "Hey, that's a nice song. What's it from?" Paul Lynde said, "Do have a tunnel directly from the golf course to the studio? Who hasn't heard 'Maria'?" One of Perry's priests (he had several) drove me home one night. We were in the car and he said, "You know, there is something very comforting about driving a middle-aged woman home." I was still in my *thirties*!

ON BOB HOPE Bob was one of the first people to build a home in Palm Springs, and he loved it there as much as I do. The only time we worked together was in the early 1970s when he asked me to do a live show for his Bob Hope Desert Classic golf tournament. It was billed as a "Night of Comediennes," a theme he had also used for one of his annual television specials. Female comics are not generally as insecure as male comics, but they *do* tend to be jealous of each other—except for my darling Phyllis Diller and a lady who came up to me while we were doing that show. I had never met her, but I must have looked sad or pensive sitting in my chair, because Minnie Pearl came over, grabbed my hand, and said, "I hope you're happy." She was so gracious and sincere. I never saw her again, but I'll never forget her kindness.

You didn't get paid for working with Bob Hope, but you got to go over to his house for dinner, and that was enough. His wife, Dolores, was always exceptionally gracious, and they both loved puppies the way I do. They built a spectacular, round, glass-walled mansion up in the hills overlooking the valley, but they rarely used it. Their real home was down in the flats, the house they had built more than fifty years ago. Bob had been all around the world several times over but still loved coming back to his home in the desert.

ON YET ANOTHER FLOP In the mid-1980s I starred in an awful show opposite Eddie Bracken. *Barbary Coast* was supposedly headed for New York but never made it. A multimillionaire named Penzer, from San Francisco, wrote and produced the show, and we played it for a few weeks in Birmingham and a few weeks in Detroit. Marcia Rodd originally played my role, and I remember only two things about it. I had to sing the lyric "My teardrops marked time 'til dawn" and there was an earthquake onstage—part of the show, that is. However, a real earthquake would have been a blessing. We all had to fall from one side of the stage to the other like we were in a musical version of *Star Trek*!

ON IMOGENE COCA I did a play called *Beloved Enemies* with Imogene Coca. Her husband, King Donavan, was also in that production. Imogene and Sandy Dennis are the two most thrilling people with whom I have ever been onstage. They were immersed in the world of a play with you 100 percent, and once you stepped onstage with them, it was sheer, exhilarating excitement from the first line to the last. I loved Imogene so much that I still have a scarf she gave me; I have never worn it because I don't want anything to happen to it. *Beloved Enemies* was a very good comedy, which deserved to go on to success, but it never made it to New York. It started out as *Apartment 8 Strikes Back*. The writer, George Tibbles, was considered a television writer (he had done shows like *My Three Sons* and *The Betty White Show*), and that's why I think the play wasn't taken seriously. It was about two sisters who live together and don't speak. They live in a bad neighborhood, so anytime someone comes to the door, they play a record of dogs barking. My character used an umbrella as a sword. Anyway, one day two Puerto Rican street kids (a sister and brother) break into their apartment, and the sisters catch them. The play is sort of a Pygmalion story, because after the boy gets away, the sisters keep the girl and end up transforming her into a lady. I remember my favorite line to Imogene at the end of the show: "How come I eat the same thing you eat and I get fat and you stay thin?"

ON MIKE DOUGLAS AND HENRY MORGAN I was very hurt when Mike Douglas didn't mention me in his book. I guest-hosted his show seven times! I helped him out whenever he called and brought many of my friends on his show. *The Mike Douglas Show* was always interesting, because, unlike *The Phil Donahue Show*, which was mostly informative, it was always based on entertainment. When Mike's show was in Cleveland, my Nana came to the taping and we went out into the audience to talk to her. I even sang her a song in Italian. Comedian Henry Morgan was on that show. A couple of decades earlier I had done my first television appearance, in 1951, on *Henry Morgan's Great Talent Hunt*. I remember one of the lines he used on his show. He was giving the weather forecast, and said, "Today is going to be muggy, followed by Tuegy, Weggy, and Thurgy." Still makes me laugh. Henry and I also did a radio show with Art Carney. I borrowed lunch money from Art, and every time I saw him after that he'd say, "Kaye, you still owe me $1.99." The little things that stick in your head!

ON WORKING IN 1970s TELEVISION I want to say a word about my television appearances in the 1970s. People are always asking me about shows I did like *The Love Boat, Love, American Style*, and *The Match Game*. Thirty years later, the people who grew up watching these shows consider them to be iconic. *TV Land* and *Nick at Night* celebrate them. I suppose it is only natural to have a special place in your heart for what you knew as a child, but you have to remember, what I knew as a child was Spencer Tracy and Bette Davis movies. I guess I would equate seventies television to the serials that played before the main feature at the movie theater—pleasant diversions, but hardly great art. I had a good time doing these shows, though, and they paid well.

These shows were the television version of star dinner theater. People like Van Johnson, Martha Raye, Sid Caesar, and Pat O'Brien capitalized on the fame they had earned in movies and early television by working in the only places left to them to make a living. So, for me, the best thing about the shows was the chance they provided to work with people like

Jack Gilford, who sat around during breaks talking about show business. It's interesting that star dinner theater and shows like *The Love Boat* have died off with the legends.

ᔑᕤ

ON SURVIVING BREAST CANCER After all these years, I still don't know about the afterlife. Is there one? Who knows? As Katharine Hepburn said when someone asked her if she believed there was a heaven: "Well, I won't know, because I'll be dead, won't I?" Back in 1994, I was forced to think about the afterlife more than I ever wanted to.

I had gone for my yearly mammogram in Palm Springs, and the doctor found something. But, he said, I could wait six months to have it checked out further. So off I went to New York. But for some reason, in the back of my mind I knew I should have myself checked out right away. I went to a doctor in New York, and he said that it didn't look good and that I should go immediately to the hospital. The doctor told me they could do a lumpectomy or I could have a mastectomy. I asked him, "What would you do, if you were me?" and he said he would have the breast removed. So I did.

There are no words to express the rush of feelings that came over me upon hearing that I had cancer. It felt like an instant flush of fever and adrenaline. I guess that's what it's like when despair, anger, and fear hit you all at once, like a huge emotional train wreck. All I wanted to do was to get the surgery over and done with right away! Get the cancer out of my body! I recovered from the surgery very well. But even today, if I get the slightest little twinge of something, I think, "Uh-oh." I don't suppose that will ever go away, so I try not to think about it.

Two years after the first surgery, I was working with Phyllis Newman in Stephen Sondheim's *Follies* at the Paper Mill Playhouse. She said, "Kaye, why don't you have the other breast removed? That's what I did and it was the best decision I ever made." So when I came home I thought about it and decided to have another operation. The doctor asked if I wanted reconstructive surgery and I said, "Reconstruction? I'm seventy, where am I going?" Phyllis was right—it was the best decision I have ever made.

It may seem strange to put such a serious story in my "Afterthoughts." But that's exactly how I feel about it. My cancer is simply one of the stories of my life. I hope other women going through the same experience can take heart in the fact that I'm still here, going strong and enjoying my life (I'll always enjoy life as long as there are movies, and eating and gambling and puppies). But my experience doesn't qualify me to be any sort of champion for the cause. When something as traumatic as breast cancer comes your way, there is a rallying call from close friends and relatives. It's a wonderful feeling that fills you with strength and hope. But in the end, no one can really help you get you through it but yourself.

ON DISCOVERING NEW TALENT Performing in nightclubs and on television variety shows kept me constantly on the lookout for new material. I had to write my own or keep my eyes peeled for good writers. Sheldon Harnick (*Fiddler On the Roof, She Loves Me, Fiorello*) came to see me perform in Sag Harbor, New York recently and was surprised to learn that I remembered buying one of his first songs when he was fresh out of Northwestern University. I paid him a hundred and fifty dollars for a song that went something like, "My love gave me a pair of golden earrings but the romance is cold and my ears have turned green." I *love* talent. When a writer, director, painter, or performer is fresh and original, that talent grabs you with a thrill that makes you know that person has got it. I've experienced that feeling with songwriters—Sheldon and certainly Fred Ebb come to mind—and also with such performers as Joy Behar and Roseanne Barr. While I was on *The Steve Allen Comedy Hour* back in 1980, long before *The View,* Joy did a guest appearance and I knew that kid "had it." Roseanne is another true original. She has an innate intelligence that comes through in her material. I will always appreciate the kindness and sensitivity she showed to my friend Virginia Graham shortly before Virginia died. Both Joy and Roseanne had the guts and determination to stick with this business until people noticed them. Bravo ladies!

ON PERFORMING AT 80 I wanted to prove to myself I could do it. When they asked me to reprise my role in Ronald Harwood's *Quartet* in Sag Harbor, New York, I had to think about it. *Quartet* is a lovely show about four aging stars who end up in a home for retired opera singers. They are asked to sing together one more time at a celebration for Verdi's birthday. Doing the show meant I'd have to travel to New York, rehearse and relearn the part (once a show is closing the lines are out of my head by the curtain call), and schlep out to Long Island and perform a very difficult play for just a few performances. But I'm glad I did because, believe me, the experience was thrilling and the company was wonderful. We were directed by the brilliant Jack Hofsiss, who won a Tony Award for *The Elephant Man,* and I was privileged to perform with three marvelous actors. Paul Hecht, with whom I had done the play in 2002 at the Berkshire Theatre Festival; Simon Jones; and best of all, a magnificent actress, Siän Phillips, who came in from England to be with us. How lucky I was to have the opportunity to work with these accomplished artists.

ᴓ

ON RICHARD BURTON Even at 80, life has a way of bringing little coincidences together to let me know that I am still learning. The Bay Street Theatre, where we performed *Quartet*, was cofounded by Julie Andrews's daughter Emma Walton, along with Stephen Hamilton and Sybil Christopher. Sybil was the first Mrs. Richard Burton and mother of Kate Burton. Richard and Kate starred in the Great Performances version of *Alice in Wonderland*, which I did in 1983. Richard told me that I should attempt the classics. Sir Richard Burton told *me* that. I remembered what he'd said a year later when I was offered *She Stoops to Conquer* with E. G. Marshall, Nathan Lane, and Tovah Feldshuh. His advice gave me the courage to go through with the role and that show gave me the confidence to know I could tackle almost anything. I put these last two afterthoughts together because they show how people and events, no matter how many years apart, can relate to one another. You have to pay attention. The older I get, the more I believe that there are very few actual coincidences.

Chapter Twenty-One

Epilogue

I hate criticism. There, I've said it. I have never been good at taking it, and it puts me immediately on the defensive. Quite a career I chose if I didn't like people evaluating me, huh? I can get ten good reviews and one bad one, and I concentrate on the bad one. That somebody wouldn't like me—I can't bear the thought, on or offstage.

But you want to know what I really can't take? A compliment. At least if someone hates you or hates a performance you gave you can get angry, fight back. What do you do if someone loves you? I've always been at a loss over that one. Can you trust that person to keep loving you? Does he or she love you for you, or want something else? But this uncertainty keeps life interesting, doesn't it? If there weren't all this damn conflict and turmoil surrounding us how would we ever learn anything?

Unlike my mother and my sister Jean, I am not a good cook, but I know what I know, and I can make a pretty good beef stroganoff. So here's a recipe, from me to you. These ingredients were first mixed together in 1925 and the dish has been slowly baking for more than eighty years. It's definitely not low-fat and can be murder on your blood pressure. Some people can't stand it—and they're allowed. To some it is an acquired taste, even though at its base, it's a very plain, ordinary dish that wants nothing more than to please.

CATHERINE BALOTTA A LA MODE

    1 cup honesty
    1 cup insecurity
    ½ cup (maybe ¾) talent
    2 tablespoons of Catholic guilt
    1 teaspoon Italian spice
    Sometimes nuts, sometimes not

Mix all together and place in a very warm oven for eight decades. Add ice cream. (Always add ice cream.)

Not too long ago, I was with a friend and complaining, I guess, about the fact that I felt I had never really "made it" in my chosen profession. "Wait a minute," my friend interrupted. "Kaye, you have been in this business for more than sixty years. You have known everyone, worked with legends, been on a hit TV show, worked on Broadway and in the biggest nightclubs, you name it. I'm sorry, but to a lot of people, that looks like making it!"

"No," I replied, "not really."

"Then you tell me . . . ," my friend continued, ready to whop me upside the head, "you tell me what would constitute making it? Millions of dollars?"

"Yes," I said, "and I would have liked to have won a Tony Award. At least to have been nominated. You know, acceptance of my peers."

"Uh-huh. So," my friend continued, "if you had a million dollars in the bank and were surrounded by a bunch of trophies, you think you would be sitting here today telling me that you were satisfied with your life?"

"Yes! I mean, maybe. I mean, I don't know." I had been caught.

My career has been a cornucopia of triumphs and missteps. I suppose when you come to think of it, that is also pretty accurate as a description of most people's lives. But in show business, I wanted to be the *one*. The person at the top, the one who got the big break. You know what the pisser is? What if I had that but never realized it? Maybe I was too busy looking at where the other guy had gotten to appreciate where I was.

As Elaine Stritch asked at the end of her brilliant one-woman show, "Well, what has this all been about?" In her show, she said she was reclaiming a life she felt she had almost missed. I am "claiming" also. Claiming responsibility for a life filled with extraordinary experiences and marvelous people who I don't want to be forgotten. The whole thing is simple. I guess I have to learn to like me. I have to be able to give myself a compliment. All alone, in the dark, I have to be able to say, "You know what, Kaye? You didn't do so badly. In fact, you might even have *made* it. Congratulations." Maybe if I read this book a few more times, I'll really start believing it.

All right, so let's get on with it. I've been trying my best to sum it all up, put it in a nutshell, get to the point . . . maybe I just did.

By the way, did you know that famous people can actually go to the *New York Times* and read their obituaries? What a scary thought. Very efficient, in terms of ensuring accuracy, but rather pushy of them, if you ask me. Now here's an even scarier thought: What if I went down there and found out that I wasn't even on the list? So what?

Hey, Ma, what do you know? I did the best I knew how . . . just like you.

P.S. (My last one, I promise.) I know the minute this book is printed, I will remember twenty-seven more stories and 143 people I forgot to mention. Please don't call. I promise you'll be in volume two! By the way, I forgot to tell you how I lost 10 pounds in 53 years: One weekend I didn't eat any bread or pasta and took three water pills!

A Kaye Ballard
Show Business Timeline

1940s

1943
First club act, Chin's Chinese Restaurant
Singer, USO Stage Door Canteen
Singer/comedienne, burlesque tour

1944
Singer/comedienne, vaudeville, RKO circuit
Singer/comedienne, The Spike Jones Orchestra

1945
Singer/comedienne, The Spike Jones Orchestra

1946
Three to Make Ready (Broadway tour)

1947–49
Once in a Lifetime (stock and regional theater)
Look Ma, I'm Dancin' (stock and regional theater)
Annie Get Your Gun (stock and regional theater)

1950s

1950
Touch and Go (Prince of Wales Theatre, London)
Royal Command Performance (London Palladium)

1951
Two on the Aisle (pre-Broadway tryout)
Henry Morgan's Great Talent Hunt (television guest appearance)
The Mel Tormé Show (television guest appearance)

1952

Top Banana (Broadway tour)
Roberta (studio cast recording)
Oklahoma! (studio cast recording)

1953

The Gershwin Rarities, Vol. 1 (studio cast recording)

1954

The Golden Apple (off-Broadway and Broadway)
The Golden Apple (original Broadway cast recording)
In Other Words/Lazy Afternoon (45 rpm recording)
The Colgate Comedy Hour (television guest appearance)

1955

Lyrics by Lerner (studio cast recording)
Triumph of Love/Where Were You Last Night? (45 rpm recording)
Don't Tell Pa/In Love and Out Again (45 rpm recording)
Reuben, Reuben (pre-Broadway tryout)
Ed Sullivan's Toast of the Town (two television guest appearances)
Pleasure Dome (pre-Broadway tryout, Washington, D.C.)

1956

Kraft Television Theatre (television guest appearance)
Great to Be Alive (Las Palmas Theatre, Hollywood, California)

1957

The Girl Most Likely (feature film)
The Girl Most Likely (motion picture sound track)
Cinderella (television special)
Cinderella (television sound track)
Ed Sullivan's Toast of the Town (television guest appearance)
The Ziegfeld Follies (national tour)

1958

The Fanny Brice Story in Song (full-length LP recording)
The Parade Is Passing Me By/A Difference of Age (45 rpm recording)

1960s

1960

Kaye Ballard Swings (full-length LP recording)

1961

Carnival (Broadway)
Carnival (original Broadway cast recording)
The Perry Como Kraft Music Hall (television series regular)
Play of the Week (television guest appearance)
Kaye Ballard, Live? (full-length LP recording)

1962

Boo Hoo, Ha, Ha (full-length LP recording)
The Best of Irving Berlin's Songs from "Mr. President" (full-length
    LP recording)
Peanuts (full-length LP recording)
Gypsy (Dallas Summer Musicals)
The Perry Como Kraft Music Hall (television series regular)

1963

Wonderful Town (City Center, New York)
The Beast in Me (Broadway)
I'll Remember Him/Here and Now (45 rpm recording)
I Want You to Be the First to Know/Maybe This Time
    (45 rpm recording)
Nightclub act (Mr. Kelly's, Chicago)
Nightclub act (Plaza Hotel, New York)
The Perry Como Kraft Music Hall (television series regular)
The Merv Griffin Show (television guest appearance)
The Ed Sullivan Show (television guest appearance)

1964

Ben Bagley's Cole Porter Revisited (full-length LP recording)
A House Is Not a Home (feature film)

1965

The Decline and Fall of the Entire World as Seen through the Eyes of Cole Porter (off-Broadway, Square East Theatre, New York)
The Decline and Fall of the Entire World as Seen through the Eyes of Cole Porter (original cast recording)
My Dog Met Your Dog/An Onion and You (45 rpm recording)
The Tonight Show with Johnny Carson (television guest appearance)

1966

The Tonight Show with Johnny Carson (television guest appearance)
To Tell the Truth (television guest appearance)
Nightclub act (Diplomat Hotel, Hollywood, Florida)

1967

The Mothers-in-Law (television series regular)
The Hollywood Palace (television guest appearance)
The Tonight Show with Johnny Carson (three television guest appearances)

1968

The Mothers-in-Law (television series regular)
Rowan & Martin's Laugh-In (two television guest appearances)
The Tonight Show with Johnny Carson (five television guest appearances)

1969

The Leslie Uggams Show (two television guest appearances)
The Mike Douglas Show (television guest host, three weeks)
The Tonight Show with Johnny Carson (two television guest appearances)

1970s

1970

The Mike Douglas Show (television guest host, four weeks)
Which Way to the Front? (feature film)
The Doris Day Show (television series regular)
Love, American Style (television guest appearance)
The Tonight Show with Johnny Carson (four television guest appearances)

1971
The Doris Day Show (television series regular)
The Tonight Show with Johnny Carson (four television guest
  appearances)
Here's Lucy (television guest appearance)
Love, American Style (television guest appearance)

1972
The Tonight Show with Johnny Carson (five television guest
  appearances)
The Flip Wilson Show (television guest appearance)

1973
Molly (Broadway)
The Carol Burnett Show (two television guest appearances)
Match Game (television guest appearance)
Love American Style (television guest appearance)
The Tonight Show with Johnny Carson (three television guest
  appearances)

1974
Sheba (pre-Broadway tryout)
Match Game (television guest appearance)
Celebrity Sweepstakes (television guest appearance)

1975
Nightclub act (Persian Room, Plaza Hotel, New York)

1976
Nightclub act (Persian Room, Plaza Hotel, New York)
The Ritz (feature film)
Freaky Friday (feature film)
The Muppet Show (television guest appearance)
Police Story (television guest appearance)

1977
Alice (television guest appearance)

1978
The Love Boat (television guest appearance)

1979
The Love Boat (television guest appearance)
Fantasy Island (television guest appearance)

1980s

1980
Falling in Love Again (feature film)
The Dream Merchant (television movie)
Boomer (television guest appearance)
The Steve Allen Comedy Hour (television series regular)
Trapper John, M.D. (television guest appearance)

1981
The Pirates of Penzance (Broadway)
The Love Boat (television guest appearance)
Broadway Salutes NYC Opera (concert, New York State Theater, New York)
So Long, 174th Street (original cast recording)
Trapper John, M.D. (television guest appearance)

1982
Night of 100 Stars (television special)
Pandemonium (feature film)

1983
Alice in Wonderland (television special)
4 Girls 4 (national tour)

1984
"Hey, Ma!" . . . Kaye Ballard (Kennedy Center, Washington, D.C.)
"Hey, Ma!" . . . Kaye Ballard (Promenade Theatre, New York)
She Stoops to Conquer (off-Broadway, Triplex Theatre, New York)
Snow White (Beverly Theatre, Los Angeles)

1985
The Ladies Who Wrote the Lyrics (full-length LP recording)

1986
Nunsense (Coconut Grove Playhouse, Florida)
The Perils of P.K. (feature film)

1987
"Hey, Ma!" . . . Kaye Ballard (New Wharf Theatre, Monterey,
    California)
The Law and Harry McGraw (television guest appearance)
"Hello, Kaye" (TV special, not aired)
In Performance at the White House (PBS, Washington, D.C.)

1988
Tiger Warsaw (feature film)
Working 42nd Street at Last (Martin R. Kaufman Theatre, New York)
The Female Odd Couple (Poconos and Bucks County, Pennsylvania)

1989
Eternity (feature film)
Monsters (television guest appearance)
The Super Mario Bros. Super Show (television guest appearance)

1990s

1990
What a Dummy (television series regular)
Fate (feature film)
Modern Love (feature film)

1991
Hey, Ma! (CD)

1992
Say It with Music (Rainbow and Stars, New York)

1993

All My Children (television guest appearance)
Then and Again (CD)
There Is Nothing like a Dame: Broadway Broads (CD)

1994

Due South (television movie)
Ava's Magical Adventure (feature film)

1995

Jaye & Kaye, Long Time Friends (CD)

1996

The Rosie O'Donnell Show (television guest appearance)

1997

No, No, Nanette (Paper Mill Playhouse, New Jersey)
The Rosie O'Donnell Show (television guest appearance)
Funny Girl (Long Beach Civic Light Opera, California)

1998

Follies (Paper Mill Playhouse, New Jersey)
The Modern Adventures of Tom Sawyer (feature film)

1999

Baby Geniuses (feature film)
The Rosie O'Donnell Show (television guest appearance)
Over the River and Through the Woods (off-Broadway,
    John Houseman Theatre, New York)

2000s

2000

The Million Dollar Kid (feature film)
Little Insects (feature film)
Another Final Farewell Appearance (club date and CD)

2001

The Full Monty (Broadway tour)

2002

Quartet (Berkshire Theatre Festival, Massachusetts)
Funny Girl (Actors' Fund concert, New York)
A&E Biography: Doris Day (television interview)

2003

Nunsense 20th Anniversary All-Star Tour (national tour)
Broadway: The Golden Age (feature film documentary)

2004

The Pool of Desire (feature film)

2005

Palm Springs Follies (Palm Springs, California)
Kaye Ballard Sings Her Favorite Songs (CD)

2006

Quartet (Bay Street Theatre, Sag Harbor, New York))

Can you believe it? Sixty-three years! In all that time I played more nightclubs than I can count and, sadly, I can't recall all the dates. Likewise, I couldn't find dates for a few shows like *Girl Crazy, Red Hot and Cole, The Robber Bridegroom, Pippin,* and *Li'l Abner,* or television shows like *The Jack Paar Program* and *Girl Talk.* If some of you saw any of those and can remember *when,* drop me a line!

By the way, not only am I still here . . . I'm still *available.*

Kaye Ballard's
Acknowledgments

Aside from the people I've already mentioned in the book, I've appreciated so many other people being in my life . . .

My doctors: Dr. Lawrence and Mary Cone, Dr. David and Janice Kaminski, Dr. Karl and Laura Schulz, Dr. Gary Annunzata, Dr. Irwin and Lucia Smigel, Dr. Joseph Cleary, Dr. Bednar, Dr. Manuel Jefferson, Dr. Cory Horshinski, Dr. Wendy Roberts, Dr. Barry and Brina Kohn, Dr. Peter Schulz, Dr. Sumner Freeman, and Dr. Jonathan Braslow, all for keeping me alive long enough to write this book!

Muriel Nellis for not giving up on the book. And to Mark Glubke, Allison Devlin, and all the people at Back Stage Books for having the interest and faith to publish it.

Don Kane for keeping me working and "visible" on *The Merv Griffin Show* through the lean times.

Monty Morgan for booking me many times on *The Jack Paar Show, Girl Talk*, and Robert Morley's cooking show.

Michael Orland, my new Arthur Siegel.

Ralph Young, Ronnie Schell and Shecky Greene, Tracey Ullman, and Steve Lawrence and Eydie Gormé, because they truly make me laugh!

Michael Masters, who takes care of my puppies, a dog's best friend and mine!

Former Rancho Mirage mayor Dana Hobart, who was kind enough to have a street named after me before I died.

Riff Markowitz, thank you, and congratulations for revitalizing Palm Springs with your fabulous *Palm Springs Follies*!

A special thank-you to a real friend who was there at the beginning of this book, Pat Gandolph.

And, of course, these very special friends in my life—you were always there for me: Father Dominic Riccio (thank you for all your prayers), Beau James, Myvanwy Jenn, Robert Ratigan, Phyllis Rowan, Arthur Novell and Eddy Lamkay, Gavin and Patti MacLeod, Margo Manfredi, Jack "Bye Bye" Molthen, Billy Braendel, Marilyn Cantor, Liliane Montevecchi, Tom Tomc, Michael Kerker and Bob Lees (a brilliant writer and a true-blue friend), Mike Costly, and Betty Ann Grove.

One night, after I had appeared on *The Tonight Show with Johnny Carson* many, many times, Robert Dolce, the show's talent coordinator, took me aside and said, "Johnny doesn't want you on the show anymore because you're too nice to people and you seem to like everyone." Well, Robert, Johnny was wrong . . . I don't like you! But here are some more of the people I really *do* like: Manuel Carbonnell, Jack Caputo, David Kaufman, Ted Chapin, Patsy Englund, Ron and Jane Harris, Louise Lasser, Mitzi Mayer, Sylvia Silver, Gloria Greer, Jim Jenkins, Doug and Kathy Hepler, Sandy Stewart, Mike Baker, Jim Lowe, Steve Rutberg, Rex Reed, Shirley Scully, Tony Lang, Jon Voight, Jan Forbes, Cary Wiger, Bill and Susan Seaforth Hayes, Jean Mendolia, Janice Morgan, Diane Judge, Jaye P. Morgan, Wayne and Dana Abravanelle, Arlene Ott, Ric and Rozene Supple, John and Susie Edwards, Bob LaChance, Gordon Hecht, James Hecht, Paul Hecht, Rick McKay, Joan Fontaine, Bruce and Jane Fessier, Loren Freeman, Mark and Holly McNeil, Maurice Bratt, Robert Garrison, Vicki Hobart, David Levy, Armand Assante, Sheila Smith, Peter and Laurie Marshall, Val Andrew, Barbara and Bob Crommelin, Phyllis Rowan, Robert Ratigan, Philip Owen, Joe Pennario, Peg Hadley, the Chiari family, Dom and Carol DeLuise, Loren Freeman, Peggy Eisenhauer, Shelley Goldstein, Marc Breaux, Kay and Stan Stanton, Don Thomas, Frankie Ray, Suzzane Buhrer, Mike and Stephanie Costley, Kenneth Battelle, Jim Bailey, Carl Ballantine, Kelley Bishop, Lee Leonard, Pedro Almadovar, Shelley Berman, John Bohab, Billy Charlap, Pat Carroll, Curtis Roberts, Liz Callaway, Carleton Carpenter, Clairborne Cary, Cloris Leachman, Keely Smith, Everette DeSanchez, Marge Durante, Paul Goldenberg, Helen Gallagher, John Kirby, Hillary Knight, Peter Gallagher, Bill Gillespie, Kenny Gibson, Lainie Kazan, Paul Lisnek, Brian Lozell, Jean Carroll, Nathan Martin, Timothy Grey, Hugh Martin, Michael O'Hugley, Nadine and Bob Quinn, Tommy Tune, June Wilson, Gore Vidal, Joey English, V. S. Hume, Amanda and Burt Able, Eve Southwood, Lee Roy Reams, Craig Prater, Steven Paul, Pam Pauley, Rita Moreno, Ron McDougall, Mirian Lederer, Tim Luke, Piper Laurie, Carol Lawrence, Marcia Lewis, Nathan Lane, Lewis Stadlin, Julie Wilson, Fagle Liebman, Flo Dryer, Betty White, Shirley MacLaine, Billy Tallon, Jason Graae, Lou and Harv Sarner, Judy Brubaker, Terry Comeaux, Billy and Adrienne Van

Zandt, Breck Wall, Bill Witte, John Alsop, Pam Chandler, Gary Chandler, Shelley and Kay Brodsky, Andrea Burns, Billy Charlop, Elizabeth Wilson, Lenny and Debbie Green, Michael Childers, Bill and Meredith Asher, Marian Seldes, Estelle Parsons, Chris Morlot, Raquel Rettberg, Peter Huzyk, "Cleopatra," Lucille Maher (one of my favorite artists), Rosemary and Newell Alexander, Pat and Joe Manhart, Clark Bason, Ella Brennan, Mr. and Mrs. Tom Troupe, Sara Ballantine, Charles Durning, Dorothy Kloss, Ken Prescott, Paul Krassner, Nancy Cain, Tracy and Ray Rodriguez, Cris Alexander, Sean O'Brien, Jane Withers, Gordon Moller, Charles Townsend, Stuart Ackley, Michael O'Haughey, Darren Zentena, Julie Harris, Linda Lavin, Sheila Cooper, Lucy and Bruno Gaspari, Philip Owen and Tracy O'Dwyer, and a *lot* of other people—forgive me, I'm having a "senior moment," but you know who you are!!

Thank you for reading, and be sure and look for my sequel: *How I Found 10 Pounds in 53 Minutes!*

Jim Hesselman's Acknowledgments

Dear Kaye,

You are a consummate performer who has been working at your craft for more than sixty years. There is no one in twentieth-century show business whom you have not known, worked with, or met. You are a legendary (sorry for that word) singer/comedienne who has conquered burlesque, vaudeville, big bands, nightclubs, movies, and television. Yet after all your incredible accomplishments you still feel as though you never quite "made it." I think there is a lesson there—all of us have the potential to lead extraordinary lives. And yet, no matter how much hard work, how much laughter, or how many tears we pack into the time we have on this earth, none of it matters if we don't take a step outside ourselves in order to appreciate it—to say, "I did all right." Well, Kaye, you did more than all right. I love you, Miss Balotta.

P.S. A group of aliens land on earth and gather up hundreds of human specimens to take back to their planet. As their spaceship flies off, one lone human being runs after it, crying out, "Take me! Take *me!*" The aliens yell back, *"No, you're ugly!"* (I love to hear you laugh.)

Index

About the Co-author

JIM HESSELMAN is a free-lance actor, director, and playwright from Milwaukee, Wisconsin, who met Miss Ballard when he served as assistant stage manager for the *Nunsense 20th Anniversary All-Star Tour*. For nearly twenty years, he and his partner, Cary, have made their home in Louisville, Kentucky, where they have a production company, Theatre Island Productions. Jim is very grateful to Dan Goggin and Scott Robbins for introducing him to Kaye, to J. R. Stuart and Aleene Pfaffinger for their support during this process, and most of all, to Cary Wiger. Currently, Jim is working with actress Lee Meriwether and television pioneer William Asher on their memoirs.